# Force and Diplomacy

RAYMOND G. O'CONNOR

# FORCE & DIPLOMACY

*Essays Military and Diplomatic*

## UNIVERSITY OF MIAMI PRESS
*Coral Gables, Florida*

For Thomas A. Bailey

# Contents

*1* Force and Diplomacy in American History    1

*2* Naval Strategy in the Twentieth Century    11

*3* Disarmament Between World Wars    22

*4* The Negotiation and Enforcement of
Multilateral Agreements    36

*5* The Application or Threat of Sanctions
Under the League Covenant    47

*6* Attempts to Modify or Implement the
Sanctioning Provisions of the League Covenant    63

*7* Agreements Embodying Sanctions Outside the
League Covenant: Violations and Responses    68

*8* United States Responses to Treaty Violations
by the Use of Sanctions, 1931–1941    81

*9* The Sanction of Nonrecognition as Practiced
by the United States    97

*10* Roosevelt and Churchill: A Reinterpretation
of the Diplomacy of World War II    118

*11* President Truman's Control of
National Security Policy    126

*12* Victory in Modern War    142

Index    163

# Acknowledgments

"Force and Diplomacy in American History" was published in *Military Review* in March 1963 and is reprinted by permission of the Department of the Army.

"Naval Strategy in the Twentieth Century" was published in the *Naval War College Review* of February 1969 and is reprinted by permission of the U.S. Naval War College.

The studies comprising chapters 3 through 9 inclusive were prepared in their original form as part of a contract with the United States Arms Control and Disarmament Agency. The judgments are those of the author and do not necessarily reflect the views of the United States Arms Control and Disarmament Agency or any other department or agency of the United States government. Chapter 9 was presented as a paper at the American Historical Association meeting, December 1969.

The thesis of chapter 10 is developed in a larger context and in greater detail in Raymond G. O'Connor, *Diplomacy for Victory: FDR and Unconditional Surrender* (New York: W. W. Norton & Co., 1971).

Chapter 11 draws on material and ideas in Raymond G. O'Connor, "Harry S. Truman: New Dimensions of Power," in Edgar E. Robinson, ed., *Powers of the President in Foreign Affairs, 1945–1965* (San Francisco: Commonwealth Club of California, 1966). This chapter was presented as a paper at the Organization of American Historians meeting, April 1965.

"Victory in Modern War" was published in the *Journal of Peace Research*, 1969, no. 4, and is reprinted by permission of the International Peace Research Institute, Oslo, Norway.

# Force and Diplomacy

# CHAPTER ONE

# Force and Diplomacy in American History

THIS GENERATION OF AMERICANS FACES A NEW CHALLENGE IN NATIONAL security. Vulnerable to the most devastating weapons of destruction ever devised by man and left with the leadership of the "Free World's" struggle against communism, Americans have developed a greater appreciation of military power. But even with the bulk of the federal tax income going for defense and the future of mankind in the balance, the correlation between military power and successful foreign policy is not generally understood.

Much of the confusion in the United States over military affairs is due to a fortuitous geographical isolation from other powerful nations and an alleged antimilitarist tradition. For more than 150 years the United States sat smugly behind its ocean moat and usually fought wars only when it chose. Furthermore, most Americans, unaware of the decisive role played by the armed forces in the development of the nation, think of themselves as peace-loving people in contrast to the warlike populations of other countries. Yet it was through the force of arms that the United States won and maintained its independence, displaced the Indians, and rounded out its territory. Even in times of peace the mere presence of sufficient armed strength often enabled the nation to preserve its integrity and protect and promote its interests.

The failure to realize that military institutions and their consequences are essential elements of the nation's history has created a tendency to regard the armed forces as an alien element in society, a necessary evil in time of peace and of some value only during periods of war. Knowing how military power determined the course of events at crucial periods in the past might eliminate much of the present confusion.

## AVAILABLE FORCE

The first task of government is to provide for the safety and security of the people. The government must have force at its disposal to protect men from each other and from both internal and external threats. The armed forces, distinct from local police, are designed primarily to function as an arm of foreign policy. Thus their objective is to protect and promote the interests of the nation at home and abroad.

There are many ways of using military power to implement policies, the most dramatic and extreme use being war. In a more moderate sense, however, a country's mere possession of adequate military force often discourages or deters other nations from molesting that country's interests. In regard to the more extreme use, the Prussian strategist Karl von Clausewitz said: "The most important single judgment a political or military leader can make is to forecast correctly the nature of the war upon which the nation is to embark. On this everything depends."

If a nation is defeated in war the government has failed to fulfill its primary function, so the first consideration must be "to provide for the common defense."

The value of armed strength was demonstrated in the United States before it became a nation. In 1775 a number of the British colonists began fighting against the mother country in order to obtain a modification of objectionable policies. During the course of this conflict the colonists declared their independence, partly because it enabled them to conclude a military alliance with France and thereby secure the assistance necessary to defeat Great Britain. In this case the very nature of the struggle modified the original objective for which the war was fought. It should also be pointed out that though the American nation was created in the crucible of war, a military "victory" was not attained. At the conclusion of the Revolution, not only were there more British than American troops in the colonies, but the British still occupied strategic positions. Yet fighting was brought to an end when the political objective of independence was achieved.

## ENTANGLING ALLIANCES

A second early instance of limited war was the quasi-naval conflict with France from 1798 to 1800. President John Adams secured congressional authorization to conduct hostilities at sea in retaliation for French attacks on American shipping, but he resisted heavy pressure to broaden the conflict. The president was determined to use only those means necessary to attain the desired end, and he was successful through the use of sea power alone in persuading the French government to accede to many American demands.

Adams' successor, the pacifically inclined Thomas Jefferson, began his administration with an exhortation against "entangling alliances," though when Napoleon's activities in the Western Hemisphere appeared to threaten American safety, Jefferson thought it might be necessary to "marry ourselves to the British fleet." His subsequent exasperation over Britain's highhanded violation of American neutral rights provoked an embargo designed to coerce England into complying with the rules of international law. But as Rear Admiral Alfred Thayer Mahan, the American exponent of sea power, observed, this self-imposed blockade of the United States had all the inconvenience of a blockade by an enemy and none of the advantages of actual war—that is, the opportunity to capture adjoining British territory or British ships.

By 1812 the failure of all other measures led to war, but inadequate preparation and an inept military policy brought a peace that achieved none of the diplomatic objectives of the conflict. It is interesting to note that negotiations for a settlement were underway while the war was being waged, and that the demands made by each nation fluctuated with the course of battle.

During this early period of the nation's history many of the political leaders wanted to acquire Spanish Florida for its strategic and economic value. Spain relinquished this territory to the United States in 1819, largely because an indiscreet invasion by General Andrew Jackson convinced the Spanish authorities that they were incapable of defending the area. Jackson, also one of the more successful Indian fighters, made a significant contribution to the winning of the West. This greatest of all United States territorial acquisitions, which involved wresting the land from the natives, was accomplished through the use of force.

## WILLING TO FIGHT

When James K. Polk became president in 1845 he was faced with two major problems in foreign affairs: a dispute with Great Britain over the northern boundary of the Oregon Territory and an altercation with Mexico over the southwestern limits of the recently annexed Texas. The British government relinquished its former position and compromised largely because the United States appeared willing to fight over the issue.

The Texas affair was more critical, especially in view of the president's desire to acquire California. The matter was finally settled by a war brought to a successful conclusion by a two-pronged invasion of Mexico. The United States obtained more land than had been originally contemplated, though a sum of money was paid in order to make the settlement more palatable to the Mexican government.

With the purchase of a strip of territory along the border in 1853, the United States, with the Mexican cession and a clear title to Oregon and Texas, had increased its original holdings by two-thirds and had completed its continental expansion. Nearly all of this territory had been acquired through military force.

## BRINK OF WAR

The issues that brought about the Civil War had little to do with foreign policy. During the course of the conflict, however, the French emperor, Louis Napoleon, took advantage of America's domestic troubles and established a puppet regime in Mexico. This clear violation of the Monroe Doctrine initially was not resisted by the United States. With Lee's surrender though, a force of 50,000 seasoned Union veterans under the command of General Philip Sheridan moved into Texas, and Secretary of State William Seward began to pressure the French government to remove its troops from Mexico. Louis Napoleon reluctantly yielded under the implied threat of war and withdrew his army, marking the end of his dream for conquest in the Western Hemisphere. A firm demand by the United States, supported by adequate available force, had maintained the principles of the Monroe Doctrine and preserved the integrity of the American nations.

The three decades that followed the Civil War were distinguished by at least two occasions in which the United States was brought to the brink of war over disputes with European nations.

The first occurred in 1887 when Germany sought to establish herself as the predominant power in the Samoan archipelago. The United States and Germany had secured coaling and commercial rights in the islands, but Germany sought to exercise political control of the government. The United States, deeply concerned over the implicit economic and strategic threat, appeared willing to fight over the issue. This determined stand induced German Chancellor Bismarck to convoke a conference that resulted in a joint protectorate which endured until the archipelago was divided between the two nations in 1899.

A second altercation with a European power took place in 1895 when Great Britain became involved in a border dispute with Venezuela. President Grover Cleveland and Secretary of State Richard Olney accused

England of violating the Monroe Doctrine and made it clear that the United States would not tolerate any coercion of Venezuela. The president's announced resolve to use force to prevent this interference in the affairs of a Latin American state was largely responsible for a compromise solution to the problem.

The war with Spain in 1898 was notable in several respects. It was the first conflict with a European country since the War of 1812, and it was waged ostensibly to free the Cuban people from oppression. The original objective, however, was considerably modified due to the way in which the the war was conducted.

The startling victory of Dewey at Manila Bay and the subsequent military efforts to maintain this strategic advantage were largely responsible for the U.S. decision to retain the Philippines. Thus, as a result of the war, the United States eliminated Spain as a power in the Western Hemisphere, consolidated the defense of the Caribbean and the approaches to the contemplated isthmus canal, and dramatically announced to the world that a new *great* power had appeared to challenge the nations of Europe. The implications of this challenge were most apparent in the Far East, where competition for markets and influence had intensified.

Furthermore, the Spanish-American War took place at a critical period in American development, when the nation was, as Mahan put it, looking outward. Continental expansion had been completed, the industrial complex was producing more goods than could be consumed at home, and competition for world markets had increased as latecomers sought to follow the imperialist pattern to greatness established by England. The modern United States Navy, begun in the 1880s, had proved itself; many regarded it as the means to further prosperity.

## INTERNATIONALISM

In 1901 the most ardent proponent of internationalism succeeded to the presidency as the result of an assassin's bullet. Theodore Roosevelt believed in wielding the "big stick," and one of the more successful examples of U.S. gunboat diplomacy was his military interference in the Panamanian revolution of 1903 to gain the favorable canal treaty. The president announced: "I never take a step in foreign policy unless I am assured that I shall be able eventually to carry out my will by force," and he adjusted his diplomatic objectives to the means available for their implementation. His caution was revealed in the Far East when he refused to oppose certain Japanese moves because they did not threaten American interests sufficiently to justify war. Theodore Roosevelt, in spite of his occasional belligerent utterances and avowed faith in the role of force, was careful to avoid any rash challenges to a major power.

Even Woodrow Wilson, one of the least warlike of presidents, discovered that his foreign aims required frequent use of the armed forces. His refusal to accept the Huerta government in Mexico eventually led to his authorizing the invasion and occupation of Veracruz. The raids of the bandit Pancho Villa provoked him to direct General Pershing to undertake the fruitless expedition across the border. The president sent troops to Haiti in 1915 and to the Dominican Republic in 1916 to preserve order and prevent possible occupation by European nations.

The First World War and Germany's violation of America's neutral rights by indiscriminate submarine warfare led to a series of diplomatic crises and an appeal by Wilson to Congress for the recognition of a state of war. Germany might have been more inclined to respect the precepts of international law if the United States had possessed a powerful army and navy, for the leaders in Berlin were convinced that a resumption of unrestricted submarine warfare would end the war before the militarily weak United States could influence the outcome. In any event, the allies were able to prevail with the assistance of American men and material, though Wilson was not successful in his effort to bring the country into the newly created League of Nations.


## DISILLUSIONMENT


The 1920s and 1930s were characterized by a general disillusionment toward war, military power, and involvement in foreign disputes. The army and navy decayed as economy, disarmament, and isolation became the national watchwords and the Kellogg-Briand Peace Pact of 1928 gave the impression that war had been outlawed.

Moderately successful attempts at disarmament added to the illusion that military force as an instrument of national policy was obsolete. Conferences at Washington in 1921–1922 and London in 1930 limited the size and composition of fleets, but the equilibrium of naval power that had been established by treaties was deceptive. Based on prestige and mathematical factors, the ratios that established relative fleet strength bore little relationship to the policy commitments, binding or assumed, or the vital interests of all the signatories. When Japan, Germany, and Italy began to alter the existing order through the use of force, no single nation was ready to provide opposition and the device of collective security broke down. The moral suasion and economic sanctions of the League of Nations proved impotent when confronted with armed aggression in

Manchuria and Ethiopia, as well as in Europe. The final humiliation occurred at Munich in 1938 when a British prime minister surrendered to the arrogant Hitler after having been told by his military advisors that England was not prepared to wage war against Germany.

The United States made no significant efforts to restrain these threats to world order. The Japanese invasion of China in 1931 was met by protests and the Stimson doctrine of not recognizing territorial adjustments made by force. The outbreak of the Italo-Ethiopian War provoked the first of a series of neutrality acts designed to prevent the nation from being drawn into a foreign war, but with the Japanese invasion of China in 1937, President Franklin D. Roosevelt publicly advocated a "quarantine" of aggressors by peaceful nations. Stunned by public disapproval of such an interventionist proposal, the president did nothing until the ruthless bombing of the U.S. gunboat *Panay* in December of 1937 shocked the administration into action.

## REARMAMENT

Advised that the United States was militarily incapable of conducting a war against Japan in the Far East, the president in January of 1938 asked Congress for a huge increase in naval appropriations. As Hitler demonstrated the insatiability of his ambition by the occupation of Austria and the remainder of Czechoslovakia, and Japan continued her military operations in China, the nations of Europe and the United States frantically began to rearm in an effort to cope with the situation. When the invasion of Poland in September of 1939 brought a declaration of war by England and France, it appeared as though German aggression would be halted, but the swift and unpredicted collapse of France in the spring of 1940 sent a shock of fear through the United States.

President Roosevelt realized that the Atlantic Ocean was no adequate barrier against attack. Meeting with the Senate Military Affairs Committee in January 1939, he warned that America's first line of defense was those buffer states between Hitler and the Atlantic. The French army and the British navy preserved the balance of power in Europe and permitted the United States the luxury of a one-ocean fleet. With the crushing defeat of France in the spring of 1940, the land barrier that protected the Western Hemisphere was eliminated, and the American military buildup shifted from the Pacific to the Atlantic as the president redoubled his efforts to support America's last line of defense in Europe. Military appropriations skyrocketed and the first peacetime draft in history was instituted. The Lend-Lease bill provided for material assistance to embattled Britain and later to the USSR, but ships had to be withdrawn from the Pacific to counter Nazi naval harassment of convoys.

## INSUFFICIENT POWER

The president was impaled on the horns of a dilemma due to his lack of military power. Hitler was the head and Germany the heart of this force of evil which threatened free institutions and the safety of the United States, and Roosevelt was anxious to avoid a conflict in the Pacific because it would impede the war effort in Europe. On the other hand, he had to keep enough pressure on Japan to prevent the collapse of China, the severance of the British lifeline, or an attack on the Soviet Union. Roosevelt simply did not have enough military power to meet the demands, and it was always the case of robbing Peter to pay Paul.

The most satisfactory solution to the dilemma was war with Germany. In that way the president could get the authority to implement his program and the war spirit to provide the necessary sacrifices. Only the mobilization of the industrial might and military manpower of the United States could do what Roosevelt considered essential for the safety of the Western Hemisphere and the Free World.

## COMPLEX DIPLOMACY

The diplomacy of World War II is extremely complex, but Franklin Roosevelt has been severely criticized on the grounds that he, unlike Winston Churchill, did not recognize the correlation between military strategy and diplomatic objectives. Actually, a Joint Chiefs of Staff directive approved by the chiefs of state specified, "The principal Allied objective [in Europe] is to prevent Germany from ever again becoming a threat to the peace of the world." This aim envisioned a fight to the finish and fairly severe peace terms, and it involved concessions to the USSR, which had suffered most from German aggression and appeared to offer the only hope for the future containment of German ambitions.

Among the more controversial aspects of the war was General Dwight D. Eisenhower's decision to halt the American advance at the Elbe River instead of pushing on with the prospect of capturing Berlin before the Russians did so. Actually, the military situation dictated this action and it had no bearing on the postwar settlement because occupation areas had been established earlier. Roosevelt, too, had compelling reasons for making concessions to the Soviets, for his military advisors insisted that their aid was essential in the war against Japan in order to avoid a longer and bloodier struggle.

The president's decision to guarantee Russian demands in the Far East as a concession for this participation has been criticized in light of subsequent events, especially the development and use of the atomic bomb and Japan's early surrender. But one principle of law is that actions should be assessed on the basis of what a reasonable man would do under the circumstances. Too, the president was anxious to see that an organization of nations was formed, among other things, to prevent future wars. Compromise and cooperation were necessary to achieve this most important of objectives, and the truly unfortunate aspect of the wartime agreements was that the USSR did not keep its commitments.

Another unhappy result of the war was that the balances of power in Europe and the Far East were destroyed, and the USSR moved immediately to fill the vacuum that was created. The events of the late 1940s revealed the Soviet Union's aggressive intentions, and the untried President Harry Truman determined to resist either unilaterally or through the United Nations.

The Truman Doctrine in 1947 provided weapons and economic assistance for Greece and Turkey; the Marshall Plan of 1948 helped in the economic reconstruction of Europe and lessened the appeal of communism; and the Point Four Program of 1950 furnished technological aid to other nations. The NATO Treaty in 1949 offered military guarantees against aggression in Europe, and the Rio Pact of 1947 provided similar assurance against an armed attack on any American republic.

Thwarted by these efforts at containment, the Communists tested Western determination by a resort to war in Korea in 1950. This appeal to the final arbiter in disputes between nations was probably due to frustration in other dimensions of conflict, but it was met by President Truman without hesitation, through the instrumentality of the United Nations. His decision reflected a familiarity with the sad fate of the League of Nations which had failed to act decisively when confronted with similar aggressions in the 1930s, although it revealed a distressing weakness in the military posture of the United States. This "police action" was not carried through to military victory, but it demonstrated the validity of limited warfare designed to achieve a diplomatic objective.

The administration's policy of containment was challenged during the presidential campaign of 1952, and a "liberation" of captive nations was demanded. Yet a negotiated settlement was accepted in Korea in 1953, and the following year the partition of Indochina was effected, partly because it was impossible to commit sufficient American troops without weakening the defense perimeters in the rest of the world. The new administration adopted a military policy based not on victory but on deterrence, using the threat of "massive retaliation" to discourage aggression. This put the United States in the position of having to choose between nuclear war and retreat, and ignored the prospect of localized or brush-fire wars. In effect, there was no graduated deterrent to different degrees or types of aggression.

In the past fifteen years the United States has erected a series of military alliances and guarantees outside the framework of the United Nations, all directed toward the containment of "international communism." Yet our military policy has fluctuated in response to unforeseen aggressive moves of varying degrees of magnitude. The threat of military force, plus its availability and the clear willingness to use it, has accomplished the objective of containment, notably in the cases of Taiwan, the Middle East, and Cuba. But the amount of force that could or should be committed to resist the various dimensions of aggression has not been defined.

The United States is in a somewhat paradoxical position. The nation wants peace, but not at any price; it is dedicated to resistance to Communist aggression by whatever means necessary, yet it has been spoiled by having enjoyed a relatively free security by virtue of geographical position, the nature of weapons, and an avoidance of alliances.

The United States no longer has the time to create the necessary forces after hostilities begin. Finding herself in the same position that European countries have occupied for many centuries—immediate danger—the nation has been having trouble adjusting its thinking to encompass this new vulnerability. The United States cherishes a long and proud heritage of antimilitarism, a tradition that is at odds with the primacy of military power. But the nation was conceived and developed by people who believed that death was preferable to the extermination of liberty and who made it possible for others to enjoy the benefits of a free society.

Perhaps world war is now worse for both sides than any possible alternative, and perhaps war has outlived its social usefulness. It should be realized, however, that military power is never created and never exists in a political vacuum. Military power is an instrument of policy and should be used as such. A nation must decide what it wants to accomplish and then make the necessary sacrifices to furnish the means. If the sacrifice is too great and alternatives are more desirable, then the sights must be readjusted. And one might reflect on the fact that war is merely the ultimate form of competition, the final arbiter in conflicts between men and nations. Perhaps more attention should be directed to the elimination of the cause, not the symptom, of this problem.

# CHAPTER TWO

# Naval Strategy
# in the Twentieth Century

WHEN FLEET ADMIRAL CHESTER W. NIMITZ RETIRED AS CHIEF OF NAVAL
Operations he submitted to the secretary of the navy a paper entitled "The
Future Employment of Naval Forces," which he began by quoting the
following words of Sir Walter Raleigh: "Whosoever commands the sea,
commands the trade; whosoever commands the trade of the world, commands the riches of the world, and consequently the world itself." Admiral
Nimitz then added, "This principle is as true today as when uttered, and
its effect will continue as long as ships traverse the seas." In the fifth
century B.C., Pericles said, "A great thing in truth is control of the sea,"
and Themistocles stated, "He who commands the sea has command of
everything." We are also told by Thucydides that "Minos [of Crete] is
the first to whom tradition ascribes the possession of a navy." The purpose
of these initial quotes is to point out that sea power has been considered
by historians and statesmen, as well as military authorities, to have been
an essential element of national greatness throughout recorded history.

Of course it would not be entirely fair to present only one position
on the matter, so at this point, and here only, I shall quote from Sir
Halford Mackinder who promoted a land power thesis:

> Who rules East Europe
> Commands the Heartland;
> Who rules the Heartland
> Commands the World Island;
> Who rules the World Island
> Commands the World.

I hope to trace the development of naval strategic thought in the
twentieth century and the naval policies followed by the major nations
during the same period. Thus I intend to combine both theory and practice,

for ideas, consciously or unconsciously, motivate the actions of men and nations.

The conditions prevailing in the world as the nineteenth century neared its end were most suitable for a resurgent interest in naval power. Among the Western nations there emerged a "new" imperialism directed toward an exploitation of the vast resources of Asia and Africa. The United States, having occupied all available contiguous territory and producing more industrial and agricultural products than it could consume, justified its overseas venture under various guises such as duty, destiny, dollars, and divinity. Japan, forced from its isolation and feudal structure, adopted Western techniques to develop her economy, her armed forces, and her foreign policies. Moreover, technological advances in ship construction and ordnance had rendered obsolete the older navies. The steel, steam, and rifled gun vessel marked the modern navy and enhanced its value as an instrument of expansion.

At just this time, within the framework of this remarkable juxtaposition of circumstances, an obscure American naval captain began publishing a series of lectures that he had delivered at the Naval War College. Alfred Thayer Mahan was a historian, a geopolitician, and a military analyst. He was steeped in the doctrines of the Swiss strategist Jomini, whose ideas had been taught to future Civil War generals by the elder Mahan, a professor at West Point. Mahan sought insights and lessons in history, including evidence of the crucial role played by sea power—or the lack of it—in deciding the fate of nations.

Strategy, according to Mahan, is all that pertains *before* the contact of the fleets, and, in strategy, unlike tactics which changed, certain virtually constant principles could be deduced. The sea, politically and socially, could be regarded as a great highway, and the key to much of the history and policy of nations bordering the sea could be found in three factors: production, shipping, and colonies. He enumerated the "principal conditions affecting the sea power of nations," namely, (1) geographical position; (2) physical conformation, including natural products and climate; (3) extent of territory; (4) number of population; (5) character of the people; and (6) character of the government, including therein the national institutions. Contending that the rise and fall of modern nations rested upon command of the sea, he believed that ultimately such control rested in a powerful navy, although the components previously mentioned were vital. Mahan took issue with a popular French school of naval strategists known as the *jeune école* which advocated the *guerre de course*—commerce raiding—as a decisive method of waging war. This school understandably had been stimulated by the development of the motor torpedo boat. But Mahan insisted that the primary function of a navy in time of war was the destruction of the enemy forces, which could be accomplished only by a major fleet action. Concentration of force was mandatory, and his admonition to "never divide the fleet" permeated his writings.

It is easy to see in the context of the times why Mahan's message was welcomed by many governments, and why his doctrines were eagerly embraced by the newly arrived "have-not" nations as well as the great powers. "Sea power," he wrote, "is but the handmaid of expansion, its begetter and preserver; it is not itself expansion." Thus he sought to disarm the anti-imperialists. "The surest way to maintain peace," he said, "is to occupy a position of menace." So he sought to avoid the "warmonger" label and disarm the pacifists. As for the necessary defense posture, Mahan wrote, "It is not the most probable of dangers but the most formidable that must be selected as measuring the degree of military precaution to be embodied in the military preparations henceforth to be maintained." His primary concern was capability rather than intentions. Mahan also had something to say for the lesser powers. He saw a need for the buildup of the German fleet around the turn of the century because of its use as a deterrent to Great Britain. Germany, he said, "needs a navy of such strength that the greatest naval power will not lightly incur hostilities." If Germany wished to pursue a "point of foreign policy to which Great Britain objects" the latter would "be especially cautious in determining the extent to which this policy should be opposed."

The exact amount of influence exerted by Mahan is impossible to determine, but many national policies came to reflect his doctrines, and his works were read and quoted by the leading statesmen of the day. Building programs were tailored to conform with his fleet action concept, and competition in naval construction among the powers kept pace with their competition for influence and empire on the international scene.

Meanwhile, the United States seemed to validate the Mahan thesis when in 1898 its "new navy" defeated Spain by maritime actions as far afield as the Southwest Pacific and furnished the means of acquiring an island empire. While some authorities believed the Philippines to be an asset both as a colony to be exploited and as an outpost to enhance American influence in the Far East, some felt, as did Theodore Roosevelt later, that these islands were "our heel of Achilles." The Philippines extended the defense perimeter some 7,000 miles, necessitating a change in ship design to provide a greater cruising radius. The naval base acquired in Cuba provided for American dominance in the Caribbean and over approaches to the contemplated isthmian canal, which Mahan deemed essential.

As for other nations, England emerged from her "splendid isolation" in response to threats to her interests and found her first ally in Japan.

At this time there were two schools of naval strategy in Great Britain. The "Blue Water" school was represented by Admiral Lord Fisher's statement in 1904:

> The Navy is the 1st, 2nd, 3rd, 4th, 5th . . . ad infinitum Line of Defence! If the Navy is not supreme, no army, however large, is of the slightest use. It is not *invasion* we have to fear if our Navy is beaten, it's STARVATION!

General Wolseley represented the "Bolt from the Blue" school when in 1896 he declared:

> I know nothing that is more liable to disaster and danger than something which floats in the water. We often find in peace and in the calmest weather our best ironclads running into each other. We find great storms dispersing and almost destroying some of the finest fleets that ever sailed. Therefore, it is essentially necessary for this country that it should always have a powerful army, at least sufficiently strong to defend our own shores.

The Anglo-Japanese Alliance of 1902 enabled Britain to withdraw part of her Asiatic forces and deploy them in European waters to counter German and Russian moves. Japan was given a free hand to halt Russian penetration in China, and the decisive victory at Tsushimo offered further evidence of Mahan's dictum.

At this point the United States was building against Germany, considered the most likely threat to the Monroe Doctrine. Britain, which in 1889 had adopted the "two-power" standard, in 1909 was forced to settle for a program that called for a sixty percent superiority over the German navy. Japan was continuing along conventional lines when she began to have problems with the United States, and each nation became concerned over the other. In the meantime the all-big-gun *Dreadnaught* vessel came to be universally accepted as the "backbone of the fleet" and made other battleships obsolete. Mahan's "capital ship theory" prevailed among the major naval powers.

Another vessel appearing at this time was the submarine. Since it was still in its early stages of development and propelled by gasoline engines, most strategists, including Mahan, saw its function primarily for coastal defense or as a part of the fleet. But in 1912 the first American diesel submarine, the U.S.S. *E-1*, was commissioned with Lt. Chester W. Nimitz as commanding officer, and a year later the German navy had its first diesel boat. As Philip Lundeberg has noted, "It was the adoption of the Diesel engine for surfaced submarine propulsion that transformed the submarine from an accident-prone, short-range, coastal defense auxiliary into an economical highseas raider." Yet the enormous potential of the submarine for commerce destruction, a vessel that would vindicate the *guerre de course* school, was not apparent when the First World War erupted. The danger of submarine torpedo attack made close blockade of ports impracticable and made more difficult invasion or raids on enemy seacoasts. Fleets were compelled to strengthen their destroyer escort and on occasion to change their anchorage to less desirable but better protected locations. In the Dardanelles campaign, submarines and mines were significant factors in thwarting naval efforts to provide support. And in spite of Britain's surface naval superiority, German submarines brought England to the verge of paralysis by destroying commerce. Only the belated introduction of the convoy-escort system, aided by American vessels, saved the day.

As for surface action, by 1916 the British fleet was so weakened by submarine and mine attrition that Jellico and Fisher felt that the outcome of an engagement with the German fleet would be "doubtful." The basic strategy was stated in a memorandum from Admiral Jellico to the Admiralty dated April 12, 1916, just six weeks before the action at Jutland:

> The first axiom appears to me to be that it is the business of the Grand Fleet to nullify any hostile action on the part of the High Sea Fleet; secondly, to cover all surface vessels that are employed, either in protecting our own trade, or in stopping trade with the enemy; thirdly, to stop invasion, or landing raids. . . .

The Battle of Jutland was the major naval encounter of the war, and it has been considered a strategic victory because Britain maintained its control over the main approaches to the North Sea. Arthur Marder has pointed out, however, that "a decisive victory would have opened the way into the Baltic for a British squadron." The options then available would have provided for "the opening up of a supply route to the hard-pressed Russians, and so prevented the Revolution of March 1917; the tightening of the blockade by preventing iron ore and other essential war materials from reaching Germany from Sweden; and an amphibious attack on the Pomeranian coast *a la* Lord Fisher." In a brilliant study of submarine warfare during the First World War, Philip Lundeberg has concluded, "It is clear, in any event, that undersea warfare contributed powerfully to the repeated frustration of Britain's peripheral strategy, most precisely in her inability to establish a common maritime front— either in the Baltic or in the Black Sea—with her Eastern ally against Germany." The submarine not only came close to starving England into submission, but it nullified much of the Allied surface superiority and significantly altered the course of the war.

Aircraft development introduced another factor into naval warfare. Employed in antisubmarine efforts, the airplane was also used as a commerce destroyer and as an adjunct to the fighting fleets. The development of the aircraft carrier increased its potentiality in the aforementioned activities and assured the future role of the airplane as a component of the battle fleet. In spite of these innovations, and regardless of a new school of thought that believed in the primacy of the submarine and the airplane, predominant opinion clung to the battleship as the basic element of naval power. Submarines and aircraft, it was contended, had not prevented the British fleet from performing its primary mission of containing the German fleet, protecting the British Isles from invasion, blockading Germany, destroying German merchant vessels, and permitting the American army to reach France.

The armistice and peace that followed the First World War found the victorious nations confronted with an entirely new set of power relationships. The United States, with the Naval Construction Bill of 1916 directed toward the creation of a navy "second to none," had rejected membership in the League of Nations and was groping for a role in world affairs. Japan had improved her position in the Far East considerably, both militarily and commercially, while Germany and Russia had been eliminated as factors in the power balance in that area. Great Britain regarded both the United States and Japan as rivals for naval supremacy and world trade.

The outcome of this confused state of affairs was the Washington Conference of 1921–1922. Convened for the purpose of settling the Far Eastern situation and halting an expensive and alarming naval race, this conference revealed the basic maritime strategies of the major powers. In this and subsequent conferences that took place until 1936, each nation followed conventional doctrine for the most part. The battleship was accepted as the "index of naval power," and ratios were established that limited tonnage for "capital ships," i.e., ships displacing more than 10,000 tons and mounting guns over 8 inches. In addition, limitations were placed on the construction of aircraft carriers. England, understandably, attempted to have the submarine outlawed, but France led in defeating the move largely on the grounds that it constituted the "poor man's navy." Of course, as a result of the Naval Limitation agreement reached at Washington, building spurted in the unrestricted categories of cruisers, destroyers, and submarines. A conference at Geneva in 1927 failed in large part because the British wanted a great many cruisers, contending that their farflung empire warranted a greater number of these vessels in order to patrol the lengthy sea-lanes. The United States insisted on parity or equality with Great Britain, and Japan would not accept the same ratio for smaller vessels that she had for capital ships and carriers. In 1930 the London Conference did succeed in establishing agreement among the three major naval powers on the limitation of all classes of warships. Great Britain accepted parity with the United States and reduced the number of cruisers from seventy, as at Geneva, to fifty. Japan secured parity in submarines and an improved ratio for cruisers and destroyers. France and Italy refused to join in this new agreement for various reasons.

In the meantime, controversy over the role of air power raged in military and political circles. The airplane was universally accepted as a scout, as an eye of the fleet, and for spotting and reporting the results of gun salvos. The great argument was over its efficacy as a weapon. During the 1920s and 1930s it could be said that air power was accorded a greater role in the American navy than it was in the British, more in the Japanese navy than the American, and more in the Italian navy than in any other. The annual American fleet exercise that first saw the use of the two carriers *Lexington* and *Saratoga* took place in 1929, and this and subsequent war games clearly demonstrated the value of carrier-based planes in launching surprise attacks on land targets, notably Panama, Hawaii, and the West Coast. At the time of the attack on Pearl Harbor though, both the United States and Great Britain were committed to the primacy of the big gun ship, were woefully lacking in carriers, and were pitifully inadequate in antisubmarine vessels.

France and Italy concentrated their efforts on preparing for war in the Mediterranean with shore-based aircraft, heavily gunned high-speed cruisers and destroyers, submarines, and virtually unsinkable battleships. Neither expected to establish control of the area, and Italy's primary objective was to prevent a superior sea power from exercising maximum command of the Mediterranean.

When the European war broke out in 1939, Great Britain expected to employ its overwhelming naval superiority to contain and strangle Germany while keeping open communications with the Continent and overseas sources of men and materiel. The German navy employed the defensive-offensive strategy urged by Mahan for an inferior force, and the brilliant Norwegian operation was only one of many embarrassing episodes for the British. During 1940 and 1941 the American navy was being deployed in a manner designed to aid England and later Russia in the struggle. The fleet remained at Pearl Harbor following the exercises in early 1940 in order to pressure the Japanese government to refrain from aggression in the Far East and affect the situation in Europe. American ships in Atlantic waters patrolled and escorted convoys, and in May 1941 the president sent major units from the Pacific to bolster British efforts in the Atlantic.

The Japanese attack at Pearl Harbor was an essential element in a grand design. With the American fleet incapable of contesting Japanese moves, territory would be occupied, bases would be established, and a veritable "fortress area" would be created in the Southwest Pacific. The

United States, faced with a huge and time-consuming effort, would eventually agree to a peace settlement giving Japan much of what she wanted. But the Japanese, afflicted with the "victory disease," decided to move into the Central Pacific where their forces received their major rebuff at Midway. The decision to attack the American fleet at Pearl Harbor was reached after a good deal of debate, and some authorities believe it was not such a stupid move. Some Japanese leaders, however, felt that the American fleet should have been induced to enter the Western Pacific and engage the Japanese fleet under the shelter of its land-based planes, with total destruction virtually assured. When, or whether, the United States would have recovered from such a disaster in order to wage war effectively against Japan, while at the same time providing the effort necessary against Germany, is impossible to determine. Actually, Fleet Admiral Nimitz later noted that it was fortunate the United States did not know of the approach of the Japanese task force toward Hawaii, for Admiral Kimmel would have steamed forth to meet it, and, in Admiral Nimitz's words, "the Japanese would have sunk every one of our ships in deep water," primarily because of superior air power.

The best brief recapitulation of the naval strategy of World War II is to be found in Samuel Eliot Morison's use of the strategic concept of the "three C's," convoy, contain, and conjunct, which he borrowed from Sir Julian Corbett's work on *England in the Seven Years War*, and which Admiral Morison insists prevails to this day. The convoy and escort of merchant vessels was brought to a high art, although Germany sank over five and a half million tons of Allied shipping. As Stephen Roskill says, "at two periods (at the beginning of 1941, and in the early spring of 1943), the enemy's efforts brought him within what now seems to have been measurable distance of success—as indeed they had in 1917." Methods used to "contain" included bottling up the enemy warships or destroying them at their bases. Amphibious or combined operations are defined by the old term "conjunct." The effective coordination of these dimensions of naval warfare constituted the overall strategy for victory. Fleet Admiral Halsey has given his assessment of the technological contributions. "If I had to give credit to the instruments and machines that won us the war in the Pacific," he wrote, "I would rank them in this order: submarines first, radar second, planes third, bulldozers fourth." Of course it is men as well as machines that participate in war and influence their outcome, and decisions, judgments—correct or incorrect, chance, luck, the breaks, all had a role ranging from insignificant to decisive in determining the course of the conflict. "The personal equation," Mahan concluded, "though uncertain . . . , is sure always to be found."

To summarize the role of sea power in this gigantic struggle: control of the Pacific was essential in order to defeat Japan, and control of the Atlantic and the Mediterranean was necessary to defeat Germany and Italy. So without arguing which was the predominant factor in each case, there is no question that without a victory at sea there would have been no victory on land or in the air.

The postwar situation found the United States and Great Britain with huge navies, but the old antagonists against which they had been built were eliminated. Russia, predominantly a land power, posed little perceptive maritime threat even if the euphoria of victory and peace through the United Nations had not existed. The rush to demobilize, the international atmosphere, and fiscal compulsions led to drastic cutbacks in the military programs of the major nations. Two factors soon compelled the United States to modify its leisurely approach to defense: first, drastic changes in weapon technology and delivery systems made the nation immediately vulnerable to attack from overseas; second, the United States assumed vastly increased political commitments abroad in facing the challenge of Communist aggression. But many felt that air power had replaced sea power as America's first line of defense, and one air force general expressed a widespread feeling. "To maintain a five-ocean navy to fight a no-ocean opponent," he said, "is a foolish waste of time, men and resources." So the navy, to avoid being written off as obsolete and in order to compete for a share of the defense budget, emphasized the role of carrier aviation in attacking land targets rather than ships. During the Korean war the navy "mobile airfields" made a notable contribution and they were accorded "sanctuary" status by the enemy. Also, the navy revitalized the significance of sea power by instituting a blockade, bombarding land installations from warships, mounting amphibious operations, and providing essential logistics support. The Korean experience demonstrated that control of the sea could be vital in waging limited wars, even against nonnaval powers.

During the Korean conflict Admiral Radford, chairman of the Joint Chiefs of Staff, urged a blockade of China but was unable to secure permission. Whether such action would have had the effect that he and General MacArthur anticipated is an open question, although the navy was prepared to implement the proposal. In 1954, when the French position at Dien Bien Phu was in jeopardy, Admiral Radford advocated an air attack by American carrier-based planes to relieve the garrison, but again he was overruled.

The American navy played a significant part during the cold war, although its actual impact as a deterrent to Communist aggression will not be known until Soviet records become available or Kremlin leaders publish their unexpurgated memoirs. When in 1946 Russian ambitions threatened

Iran and the Dardanelles, President Truman sent the battleship *Missouri* with escorts to Istanbul. As subsequent crises occurred in the Mediterranean the United States revealed its interest through the presence of naval units at critical points, and by 1948 the Sixth Fleet had been formed to stabilize the situation in that area. In the Far East the Seventh Fleet displayed the flag and brought its influence to bear in peace and war. The experience of limited war and the advent of the nuclear-powered submarine restored the navy to its previous major role in American defense policy, and when guided missiles appeared the Polaris nuclear submarine provided a movable and virtually invulnerable launching platform. Great Britain, beset by financial problems and a rapidly shrinking empire, abdicated her position as mistress of the seas. She plans to have no aircraft carrier, no battleship, or even a large cruiser. Her navy will consist of a few dozen frigates, destroyers and escort craft, four Polaris-type submarines, eight nuclear-powered fleet submarines, and about forty conventional submarines.

Russia, not surprisingly, has emerged as a rival to American naval dominance, and her efforts should be viewed in light of the competition on the international scene and the virtual equilibrium prevailing in other dimensions of military activity. The Soviet surface navy is formidable and relatively modern. The huge submarine fleet is being rapidly augmented by faster and quieter nuclear-propelled vessels designed as hunter-killers and missile launchers. The naval air arm is developed and adept at patrolling and antisubmarine work, while mine laying and mine-sweeping capability far exceeds that of the United States. She has constructed two aircraft carriers for helicopter operations. Her merchant fleet is expanding rapidly, her fishing fleet will soon be the largest in the world, and her oceanographic research activity is extensive.

Certainly the Russians realize that the sea is probably the most "exploitable" area of the globe, exploitable in a diplomatic as well as a material sense. The Soviets can counter the American presence, which has been predominant, without provoking a drastic reaction. They can demonstrate their sympathy and support for governments by placing their units at the scene in the traditional manner. They have demonstrated most dramatically their ability to pose a challenge to American domination of the sea and influence the behavior of nations. Their peacetime strategy is offensive, probing more vulnerable areas by astute deployments. In the event of war their strategy would doubtless be defensive-offensive as befits a nation with specialized rather than totally balanced forces.

So where does this find naval strategy today? Stephen Roskill emphasizes three elements of sea power. First, what he calls the "strength element," composed of those instruments that operate on, under, and above the sea. These are fundamental and ultimate. Next is the "security element," the bases from which the strength element operates. Finally, the "transport element"—the merchant navy, the ships, the crews, and the yards to build and repair the vessels. In regard to the final element, an article in the *United States Naval Institute Proceedings* concluded that "The threat of the Soviet merchant ship as an instrument of decisive military, political, and economic importance is very real and lethal."

One cannot help but be struck by what seems awfully familiar in Roskill's analysis, and it may be worthwhile to revert to the past for a moment. Professor Gerald S. Graham, in his book, *The Politics of Naval Supremacy*, has observed that "In the eighteenth and nineteenth centuries sea power was probably most influential when it was least conspicuous. Even in time of peace it functioned as a powerful instrument of diplomatic action and compulsion." Today sea power is conspicuous without hostilities, and prestige is more important in a shrinking world with mass population involvement, though the principle remains the same. Professor Graham goes on to refer to the "so-called age of Pax Britannica." "It would be wrong," he contends, "to suggest that the Royal Navy imposed a British peace on the world," for "Britain was in no position to seek or to ensure the peace of mankind by means of her fleet." In 1871 the head of the British government stated that the Royal Navy was almost valueless for any purpose other than the defense of home shores. If capability were not enough, Lord Rosebery told Queen Victoria, "We cannot afford to be the Knight Errant of the World, careering about to redress grievances and help the weak." This, too, sounds familiar, and the limitations of power should be even more apparent in light of present-day consequences.

Yet it is difficult to avoid concluding that the strategic significance of sea power has increased, most notably in its impact on land warfare. It is now capable of operating inland, with an even greater potential for what is called "blackmail" and for affecting the outcome of wars, either unconventional, limited, or general. In fact, it is likely that sea power is destined to become a more potent force on the international scene as the two major powers compete in various dimensions of activity for what they deem to be their essential interests. Moreover, the versatility of sea power will appeal more to smaller nations as they pursue their objectives in an increasingly volatile world. But naval strategy is a component of military strategy, which is an element of national strategy. The parts are not disparate for they form a continuum, which, if properly designed and manipulated, can provide the maximum security as long as international anarchy prevails.

# CHAPTER THREE

# Disarmament
# Between World Wars

DURING THE PERIOD BETWEEN THE TWO GREAT WARS DISARMAMENT NEGO-
tiations played a significant role in international affairs, both within and
outside the framework of the League of Nations.[1] Disarmament became
extremely popular after World War I. In the minds of a large part of the
public, as well as of many writers and theorists on the subject, disarmament meant literally, if only as a distant prospect, the complete elimination
of armaments and the wars that were believed to flow from their very
existence. For practical statesmen, and as an object of practical negotiations, the term meant some sort of reduction of existing armaments and
limitations on their future proliferation. Many authorities blamed the
outbreak of hostilities in 1914 on the arms race that had begun near the
end of the preceding century and continued at an accelerated pace until
war began. Wilson had embodied the principle of disarmament in his
Fourteen Points and the League Covenant, and he believed it essential
to the maintenance of world peace. The huge cost of armaments and the
continuation of naval competition after the armistice produced a clamor
for economy, and vivid memories of the recent horrors of war added
to the pressure for a reduction or elimination of the means by which it
might be waged. In the immediate postwar years, moreover, the temporary
absence of serious causes of friction among the victorious powers and the
helplessness of those regarded as the would-be aggressors seemed to
create an opportunity for real progress toward disarmament.

Seven major problems dominated the disarmament negotiations of the
interwar period:

1. Security—a government is established to provide for the safety and
security of the people, and no responsible statesman is likely to agree to
a position of relative military power that will place his nation at the mercy
of a potential or extant foe. This security is not confined within national

boundaries but extends to the protection and promotion of the national interests both at home and abroad.

2. The differing needs of nations in terms of responsibilities and types of armaments.

3. National pride, which concerns the domestic impact of numerical ratios that establish a "status" relationship with other countries.

4. Differing weapons and their equivalents—the yardstick or formula controversy.

5. Proper division of policy-making responsibilities between civilian and military authorities.

6. Public opinion, i.e., the extent and nature of the popular will as it exerts pressure on those entrusted with the power of decision.

7. Inspection or controls designed to insure that agreements are not violated.

One issue that posed a potential threat to peace was the situation in the Far East. Japan had taken advantage of the conflict in Europe to extend and consolidate her influence in Asia. This development, combined with a popular demand for a reduction in governmental expenditures, encouraged the United States to call a conference in Washington, the Washington Conference on Limitation of Armaments, to discuss Far Eastern affairs and strive to reduce armaments. Delegates from Great Britain, Japan, France, Italy, China, the Netherlands, Belgium, and Portugal met in November 1921; only the first five of these nations participated in negotiations on disarmament.

A consideration of the conference from the viewpoint of the United States illustrates the complexity of the situation and the way in which the seven problems enumerated earlier made themselves manifest. It should be pointed out that agreement was reached only on naval armament, and then on only two categories of warships, namely, capital ships and aircraft carriers.

The yardstick used by the American delegates in determining the nation's needs was the assemblage of basic principles of national policy which the navy had to be prepared to uphold even in the absence of formal treaty commitments. Among these were the tradition of no entangling alliances, i.e., no allies could be counted on for assistance in any conflict; the Monroe Doctrine, or the right to act against aggression from abroad in the Western Hemisphere; the Open Door policy in China; the defense of possessions in the Caribbean and the Central and Western Pacific; and the protection of trade routes and access to raw materials. In addition to these "principles," the existing power structure in the world was pertinent insofar as it affected the United States. While the League provided machinery for the amicable settlement of disputes, Japan's consolidation of her position in Asia posed a great threat to American interests. With the temporary removal of the menace of aggression by Germany and Russia, the Anglo-Japanese Alliance appeared to be directed against the United States. American naval experts believed that even if the Anglo-Japanese Alliance were dissolved, the United States would need equality in naval strength with Great Britain and (because of distance and bases) a two-to-one superiority over Japan in order to be able to deal with a threat from either nation.

Faced with these basic security problems the American delegation set about formulating a specific program. Three plans emerged. The first, based on tonnage of ships afloat, would have given Britain considerable superiority. The second, based on tonnage of ships built, building, and projected, would have granted Japan virtual parity with the United States. The third, based on tonnage of ships built and building, gave America equality with Britain and a sizable advantage over Japan. The third plan was adopted, and, using battleships as "an index to naval power," the relative strength of the British, American, and Japanese fleets was determined to be approximately in the ratio of 5:5:3. It was further agreed—and was an inducement to Japan to accept this ratio—that except for the Japanese home islands no further fortification would be done of the islands in the Western Pacific. Since this meant maintaining the status quo in the Philippines and Guam, this agreement was made at the expense of the effectiveness of American fleet operations in that area. Limitations were placed only on capital ships and aircraft carriers; cruisers, destroyers, and submarines were not included. The report of the American delegation concluded that "the limitation of capital ships, in itself, substantially meets the existing need, and its indirect effect will be to stop the inordinate production of any sort of naval craft."[2]

The Washington conference, which ended February 6, 1922, also witnessed the conclusion of two other agreements which bore a direct relationship to the Naval Limitation Treaty. The Four Power Treaty (signed by the United States, Britain, Japan, and France) was designed to supplant the Anglo-Japanese Alliance and neutralize the threat of Japanese expansion in the Far East by nonaggression pledges and a provision for consultation in the event of disputes between the contracting parties. The Nine Power Treaty affirmed the territorial integrity of China and the principle of the Open Door.

An analysis of the results of this conference from the American point of view and in terms of the seven problems enumerated earlier leads to the following conclusions. Public opinion was satisfied, for the treaties appeared to ensure peace and economy. Inspection provisions were ignored, for their inclusion was considered unnecessary and a reflection on the honor of sovereign nations. America's national pride was satisfied by achieving parity with Great Britain, hitherto the acknowledged mistress of the seas, and by gaining superiority over Japan. The question of differing weapons and their equivalents was not involved since only capital ships and aircraft carriers were limited. Yet, with respect to the problems of security and the interplay of civilian and military policy views, the implications of the conference were more complicated. Applying the "index of naval power" employed by the delegation, namely, capital ships, the United States would now be well prepared to protect the Western Hemisphere against the theoretical possibility of an attack by Great Britain, the only nation capable of launching one. Moreover, American naval strength was sufficient to protect possessions in the Caribbean and in the Central Pacific, and most trade routes. But the Naval Limitation Treaty deprived the United States of the capability of enforcing unilaterally her policies in the Far East. The great threat to American interests in that area was not to the Philippines but to China, and for the first time the United States formally adhered to the Open Door policy by a duly approved and ratified treaty. Japan accepted naval limitation because she believed it provided her the security she needed in home waters, a view echoed by the American naval planners themselves. On this point, indeed, professional military views were clearly overridden by the civilian policymakers, for the naval experts failed to secure the two-to-one superiority over the Japanese that they deemed essential, and they had to abandon the prospect of island bases in the Western Pacific. As Elihu Root, one of the delegates, observed, the outcome of the conference was "the complete negation of naval policy."[3] In effect, military advantage was sacrificed to the broader gains which, at the time, seemed a real prospect.

The civilian statesmen viewed security not merely in terms of armaments but in the broader context of goodwill and international agreement. Furthermore, the treaties appeared to halt naval competition, stabilize the Far Eastern situation, and contain Japan. But the United States found itself a party to treaties designed to maintain the status quo at a time when the nation, in rejecting League membership, seemed to have renounced the principle of collective security. The pledge in the Four Power Treaty to "consult" was vague enough to satisfy the most ardent opponent of League membership, and there was no shadow of a commitment to apply sanctions against a violator. Yet the treaties clearly deepened American involvement in Asia, for they placed an obligation on the United States to make a concerted effort to maintain the territorial integrity of China, and this obligation was formalized by a duly ratified agreement.

The American delegation seemed, on the whole, not to understand the relationship between military power and national objectives. The ratio it advocated was not based on obligations and responsibilities but on the numbers of capital ships that each nation possessed or was in the act of building. The delegates were anxious to reach an agreement and they did, but the equilibrium of naval power that had been established was deceptive. Based on prestige and mathematical factors, the ratio bore no relationship to the nation's policy undertakings, formal or implied. The agreement at Washington provided America with the naval power to wage a successful war against her least likely antagonist, Great Britain, and deprived her of the ability to check her most probable foe, Japan. The failure to gear American capabilities to American responsibilities was most apparent.[4]

The optimistic expectations of the American delegation concerning the end of the naval race were not realized, for the years following the conference were studded with generally vain efforts to stop the unbridled production of auxiliary vessels. These efforts were complicated by the activities of France in the League Preparatory Commission for a Disarmament Conference. In the first place, France, being a continental power, wanted a "total" disarmament conference that would place restrictions on land and air weapons. This, to France, was more important than naval craft. Secondly, France insisted on security before disarmament. The League Covenant and the Locarno treaties of 1925 did not provide her with satisfactory assurances against aggression, but as the conversations continued within the League Commission, President Coolidge invited the signatories to the Naval Limitation Treaty to a conference at Geneva in an effort to limit the building of auxiliary craft. France refused the invitation on the grounds that the conference was not designed to deal with the issues she thought most pertinent. Italy refused because of the French refusal, since Mussolini's weapons had to be geared to those of his neighbor.

The failure of the Geneva Naval Conference of 1927 has often been blamed on the appointment of naval officers as delegates, whose inflexibility and myopic outlook on international affairs prevented any sort of compromise. Actually, the naval delegates had little to do with the outcome. Lack of adequate preliminary discussions was partly responsible, but the conference failed primarily because Great Britain demanded a good many more cruisers than she was willing to allow the United States. Even if this obstacle had been overcome, the conference would probably have foundered on Japan's demands, for she was not willing to extend the 5:5:3 ratio to auxiliary vessels. At the heart of much of the difficulty was the fact that the United States had no bargaining power. Unlike the conditions prevailing in 1921, the United States was far behind the other nations in cruiser construction and the delegation was forbidden to discuss the nonfortification of naval bases.

Great Britain and Japan, unlike the United States, were not committed to the numerical ratio of 5:5:3 in their demands, but viewed the situation in terms of their commitments and responsibilities. For Britain, adequate sea power meant a fleet equal in combat strength to any in the world, plus sufficient cruisers to patrol and maintain the lines of communication linking the segments of its empire. Japan's concept of sea power envisioned a fleet capable of defeating whatever force might threaten its command of the Western Pacific. Also, in Japan's case national prestige was involved, and the country's pride had been wounded by a ratio which a Japanese diplomat wryly expressed as "Rolls Royce, Rolls Royce, Ford." U.S. policy was based on a "navy second to none," and parity meant at least equality in naval combat strength with Britain, whose bases and armed merchant ships made equality in total sea power a myth. The naval officer delegates may have helped to hold the line, but the areas of disagreement were so vast that compromises of sufficient magnitude to arrive at a treaty were out of the question.[5]

The failure of this conference damaged Anglo-American relations, as did the Anglo-French Naval Compromise of 1928. A bilateral agreement obviously directed against American cruiser policy, the compromise was canceled on receipt of strong protests from Washington and Rome. A year later, however, a new American president and a new British prime minister entered office dedicated to mending the breach between the two countries and to implementation of disarmament. Both leaders believed that the Kellogg-Briand Pact provided sufficient security to enable nations to agree on reduction and limitation of armaments. President Hoover's ambition in foreign policy was to "lead the United States in full cooperation with world moral forces to preserve peace," and he believed that this purpose was embodied in the Kellogg-Briand Pact.[6] Of course "world moral forces" were always present in securing adherence to treaty provisions or discouraging aggression, but the incorporation in a solemn pact of the renunciation of force as an instrument of national policy, except in the case of attack, held greater promise than heretofore for the effectiveness of moral force as a deterrent.

The problem of disarmament cannot be divorced from developments in international affairs and national aspirations. Since the end of the war France had been obsessed with the desire to provide guarantees against aggression in Europe, primarily against a resurgent Germany. Consequently her attitudes toward the League and toward disarmament were dominated by a concern for security. Great Britain, on the other hand, believed that a restoration of European prosperity was dependent on an economically sound Germany. To aggravate the situation, Great Britain was reluctant to accept military commitments to aid France in the event of aggression, and efforts to make the League Covenant more binding in terms of sanctions and military assistance were often thwarted by British statesmen. France viewed Britain's retreat from continental responsibilities and from the idea of collective security with misgivings. The improvement in Anglo-American relations that began in 1929 with preliminary conversations on a naval disarmament conference further deepened French suspicions.[7]

The conversations designed to bring about a disarmament conference began between U.S. and British representatives in the spring of 1929. Conducted at first through normal diplomatic channels, the exchanges soon took the form of cables between Secretary of State Stimson and Prime Minister Ramsay MacDonald. It was early agreed that naval personnel would be employed solely as advisors, not as delegates, in keeping with one of the accepted reasons for the failure of the Geneva conference. Confusion over the problem of equating different types of ships, such as the respective values of cruisers mounting eight-inch and six-inch guns, was apparently eliminated by an American suggestion of a formula that would evaluate ships in terms of total combat effectiveness rather than relying on displacement and gun caliber. This suggestion was made formally by Hugh Gibson, chairman of the American delegation to the League Preparatory Commission, in April 1929, and it was greeted with a burst of enthusiasm in the United States, Great Britain, France, and Japan. The psychological impact of this "yardstick," as it became known, helped establish a satisfactory atmosphere for disarmament negotiations.[8]

Negotiations designed to reach a preliminary agreement before a formal conference (another "lesson" of the abortive Geneva meeting) continued unabated between British and American representatives. Only lip service was given to Japanese and French requests to participate. Each of these nations feared that they would be presented with an Anglo-American *fait accompli*, and the statesmen in Washington and London were hard put to dispel these suspicions. The cordial exchange of notes between the two nations, an acceptance of parity with the United States in auxiliary vessels, and a reduction in British cruiser requirements from seventy to fifty, created so high a degree of rapport that in October 1929 Ramsay MacDonald visited the United States. The discussions between the prime minister and the president covered a multitude of subjects, but no formal agreement was reached on disarmament or any of the other topics, such as freedom of the seas and an amendment to the Kellogg-Briand Pact to provide for consultation. Nevertheless, the visit markedly improved Anglo-American relations.

The London Naval Conference of 1930 lasted from January to April. Despite the months of preliminary negotiation there was much work to be done, for although the outstanding issues remaining were few, they were formidable. In the cruiser category Britain and the United States were 30,000 tons apart, and the comparative value of six-inch and eight-inch gun cruisers was still not defined. Japan steadfastly refused to accede to the American proposal to apply the ratio established at the Washington conference to all types of vessels. Italy's demand for parity with France was rejected, as was the latter's plea for a security treaty and League of Nations sponsorship of any disarmament agreement. Unless concessions were forthcoming the conference would fail, and neither the delegates nor their advisors gave evidence of compromise. The rapport which had begun in Washington between Secretary of State Stimson, who headed the American delegation, and Ramsay MacDonald continued in London, where the two statesmen worked closely to resist Japanese demands and secure agreement between France and Italy. Except in the case of the Japanese and Italian delegations, naval officers acted only as advisors, but they did serve on the committees established to handle technical problems. Many of the world's leading statesmen participated, and one diplomat later observed that it was "the last of the great conferences done in the tradition of the Congress of Vienna."[9] Also, most of the basic problems were worked out by delegates in private discussions that circumvented the open plenary sessions and even the committee meetings.[10]

The negotiations were extremely complex. For example, Great Britain was willing to accept parity with the United States in auxiliary vessels, but she was committed to demand a fleet equal to the combined strength of the two most powerful Continental navies, those of France and Italy. France was unwilling to reduce her demands unless England provided her with military guarantees against aggression, and the British government refused to provide these guarantees without some support from the United States. The suggestion from France of a consultative pact including the United States was rejected by President Hoover on the grounds that linking it with disarmament would carry an implication of military assistance. France accordingly rejected a limitation on auxiliary vessels, though her failure to adhere to the pact was in part due to her refusal to accept parity with Italy.

The three-power treaty that emerged revealed that the United States had made the greater concessions. The British concept of equality in naval strength was generally accepted over the objections of most American experts and in spite of the fact that it had been previously rejected by the U.S. government. Japan received a sixty percent ratio in eight-inch gun cruisers, seventy percent in six-inch gun cruisers, seventy percent in destroyers, and parity in submarines. The American *sine qua non* had been abandoned in the face of Japanese recalcitrance.

On the other hand, the treaty marked the first general limitation on the size, characteristics, and numbers of all naval vessels for the world's three major naval powers. Yet Hoover's aim of reducing armaments had not been achieved, for the United States had to build nearly a billion dollars worth of ships in order to meet the established ratios. Japan improved her relative power position considerably, thereby placing the United States in an even weaker position for supporting its policies in the Far East. This change was accomplished by formal agreement, not by what might be called "free competition." The American statesmen were basing their approach to disarmament and world order on the moral force of the Kellogg-Briand Pact, not on the imperatives of national objectives and their implementation. Japan's exploitation of this approach began the following year in Manchuria.

It is difficult to avoid the conclusion that Hoover and his colleagues were determined to produce a treaty and were willing to make the necessary compromises. The president had spoken so long and so often of the need for disarmament in terms of economy and peace that failure would have been a great disappointment to him and to the public. His concept of public opinion, gained largely through comprehensive press analyses that he had specially prepared, convinced him that the people shared his convictions and wanted an arms agreement. Moreover, there is evidence to indicate that he regarded Japan as a bulwark against communism in the Far East, a view that may have influenced his reaction to Japanese demands. In any event the criteria used by the American statesmen were highly suspect, and the equilibrium of naval power established by the London Naval Treaty of 1930 was perilous in the extreme.[11]

The treaty, nevertheless, was hailed by many as a notable step toward the limitation of all armaments, and the League Preparatory Commission for a Disarmament Conference accelerated its efforts after the London conference. A significant departure from previous agreements was included by the commission in a draft treaty proposing creation of a disarmament commission that "not only would superintend the carrying out of the treaty terms, but would deal with infringements of the conventions."[12] The inclusion in the draft of a provision for inspection and control by an international body marked a further departure from the concepts of sovereignty and honor among nations in observing agreements. It was also an acknowledgment of the difficulties inherent in the implementation of a total limitation of weapons as compared with the relatively simple dimension of warships.

The Conference for the Reduction and Limitation of Armaments (known as the World Disarmament Conference) met at Geneva on February 2, 1932, with fifty-nine nations, including the United States, in attendance. The international situation, with the persistent worldwide economic crisis, the German-Polish dispute, the Chaco War, and the Japanese invasion of Manchuria, scarcely provided a setting conducive to agreement. France began by introducing the "Tardieu Plan," which urged that nations place their more powerful weapons "in escrow" to be used only when directed by the League or in the event of invasion; that an international police force be established under the orders of the League of Nations Council; and that the security provisions of the League Covenant be strengthened and applied to violations of the Disarmament Convention. Two major objections were made to this plan. First, there was little likelihood that the major powers, including Russia and the United States, would accept commitments that actually exceeded those in effect under the covenant. Second, the proposal made no provision for modifying the German situation, and circumstances were such that a drastic modification of the Versailles settlement seemed imperative. Only France was really committed to the Versailles settlement. Not only was Germany unwilling to accept a permanently inferior position, but she had the support of Great Britain and Italy in her aspirations for rearmament and for reestablishment of her position as a major power on the Continent. The British countered with a plan that avoided the issue of collective security and advocated proportionate reductions of arms and a "qualitative" approach whereby weapons of a more aggressive nature would be prohibited. The distinction between aggressive and defensive weapons was more apparent than real, and no agreement on such a classification could be reached. When the U.S. proposal for abolition of all offensive armaments failed of adoption, President Hoover countered with a proposal for a three percent overall reduction of armaments.

As the negotiations dragged on, a new administration took office in Washington. Both the new president and his secretary of state "knew there could be no peace without suitable reduction and limitation of armament,"[13] and a new American approach was contained in a message from Roosevelt and a speech by Norman Davis, head of the American delegation, in May 1933. In terms of previous American policy, the offers were revolutionary. A nonaggression pact would commit all nations to retain their armed forces within their own borders and to agree to consult with other countries in the event of a threat to the peace. The United States would not interfere with any sanctions imposed on an aggressor nation if in the view of the United States the aggressor had been correctly designated. In addition, the principle of supervision of armaments was approved. Of greatest importance to the advocates of collective security was America's departure from her traditional insistence on the principles of neutrality and freedom of the seas, principles which many insisted rendered ineffectual the application of economic sanctions under the League Covenant.[14]

Roosevelt's gesture, however, failed to provide the impetus for a general agreement. As one British diplomat put it, "the Americans talk very big when there is nothing doing, but old Norman Davis is the direct spiritual descendant of the Duke of Plaza Toro."[15] The president was unable to secure congressional authorization to implement his proposals, and he was reluctant to jeopardize urgent domestic legislation by waging too vigorous a campaign over the issue.[16] Moreover, Hitler had come to power in Germany and his demands further weakened the spirit of compromise needed for agreement. The international situation had changed drastically from the tranquil atmosphere of 1930 that had made the London Naval Treaty possible. Japan's successful venture in Manchuria had revealed the failure of collective security under the League in the covenant's first challenge from a major power, and the prospect of a resurgent Germany presaged a threat to the peace of Europe. When Germany announced in October 1933 that it was withdrawing from the conference and from the League, prospects for agreement virtually disappeared. In May 1934, Norman Davis removed any hope that the New World would come to the aid of the Old by declaring that the United States "would not participate in European political negotiations and settlements and would not make any commitment whatever to use its armed forces for the settlement of any dispute anywhere."[17]

The World Disarmament Conference thus foundered on a number of shoals. The divergent policies of Great Britain and France on the issues of collective security and rehabilitation of Germany were directly in conflict. Japan's successful venture into Manchuria and her departure from the League shortly after agreeing to a comprehensive limitation of naval weapons brought disillusion to those who believed in the efficacy of disarmament, and it promised further turmoil in the Far East. The belligerent utterances and arbitrary actions of the new German government heralded trouble in Europe. And the early indication of further American involvement in world affairs had not only failed to materialize but had been replaced by what appeared to be a reactionary isolationism. Each nation viewed the situation in the light of its own immediate interests and its own problems, both in terms of security and aspirations. The armaments that the conference had been designed to control were merely means, not ends, and it was the inability to agree on ends that defeated this most elaborate attempt at disarmament.

Meanwhile, in the summer of 1934, American, Japanese, and British authorities began preliminary conversations in preparation for the naval disarmament conference scheduled for the following year under the London Naval Treaty of 1930. The United States hoped to maintain the existing ratios, but Great Britain demanded additional cruisers and Japan demanded parity with the United States and Great Britain, a move which these nations were determined to resist.[18] France and Italy rejected outright the principle of ratios. An attempt by Prime Minister Ramsay MacDonald to have the United States take the initiative in thwarting Japan so Britain could concentrate on European affairs was rejected.[19] On December 29, 1934, Japan gave the requisite two-year notice of her intention to withdraw from the Naval Limitation Treaty of 1922. The fact that the London Treaty of 1930 was due to expire December 31, 1936, meant that the forthcoming conference would have to produce an agreement to replace the others.

In view of the position taken in preliminary negotiations, the five nations that met in London in December 1935 had little expectation of success. Japan's claim for a "common upper limit" was so strongly resisted that her delegates left the conference. Eventually, the United States, Great Britain, and France reached an agreement that called for "qualitative" rather than "quantitative" limitation, and restrictions were placed on the size of certain types of vessels and the caliber of guns. The treaty also provided for advance notification of construction programs, and an "escalator clause" allowed signatories to exceed the restrictions in the event of competitive building by another nation. Though Norman Davis testified that the new treaty might be more enduring than the Washington and London agreements because of its "flexibility," it lasted only two years.[20] In 1938, the United States and Great Britain announced that they were resuming competitive building due to the accelerated naval construction of Japan. Each nation resolved to rely henceforth on its own resources for the security which a multitude of negotiations and treaties had failed to provide.

## NOTES

1. There is an enormous amount of literature on disarmament between the two world wars, and this resume is not intended to be encyclopedic or authoritative. For a good survey see Merze Tate, *The United States and Armaments* (Cambridge, Mass., 1948). More recent material may be found in the works cited in the following notes and in External Research Staff, State Department, *Studies in Progress or Recently Completed, Arms Control and Disarmament* (Washington, 1963).

2. Conference on the Limitation of Armament, *Senate Document*, Congress, second session, no. 126, p. 812. Secretary of State Charles Evans Hughes, who headed the delegation, solemnly declared: "This treaty ends, absolutely ends, the race in competition of naval armaments." Quoted in Harold and Margaret Sprout, *Toward a New*

*Order of Sea Power; American Naval Policy and the World Scene, 1918–1922* (second ed., Princeton, 1943), p. 256.

3. Quoted in Philip C. Jessup, *Elihu Root* (New York, 1938), vol. 2, p. 452.

4. There are numerous accounts of the Washington Conference. Among the better treatments are Raymond Leslie Buell, *The Washington Conference* (New York, 1922); Harold and Margaret Sprout, *Toward a New Order of Sea Power;* Yamato Ichihashi, *The Washington Conference and After* (Stanford, 1928); John Chalmers Vinson, *The Parchment Peace: The United States Senate and the Washington Conference, 1921–1922* (Athens, Ga., 1955). Recent studies are Thomas H. Buckley, *The United States and the Washington Conference, 1921–1922* (Knoxville, Tenn., 1970); and William Reynolds Braisted, *The United States Navy in the Pacific, 1909–1922* (Austin, Texas, 1971). Also see Charles Leonard Hoag, *Preface to Preparedness: The Washington Conference and Public Opinion* (Washington, D.C., 1941).

5. For recent treatments of the Geneva Naval Conference, see L. Ethan Ellis, *Frank B. Kellogg and American Foreign Relations, 1925–1929* (New Brunswick, N.J., 1961), pp. 157–192; Raymond G. O'Connor, *Perilous Equilibrium: The United States and the London Naval Conference of 1930* (Lawrence, Kansas, 1962), chap. 2; Gerald E. Wheeler, *Prelude to Pearl Harbor: The United States Navy and the Far East, 1921–1931* (Columbia, Mo., 1963), chap. 6.

6. Herbert Hoover, *The Memoirs of Herbert Hoover: The Cabinet and the Presidency, 1920–1933* (New York, 1952), p. 330.

7. See W. M. Jordan, *Great Britain, France, and the German Problem, 1918–1939* (London, 1943); and Arnold Wolfers, *Britain and France between Two Wars: Conflicting Strategies of Peace since Versailles* (New York, 1940).

8. For an account of the yardstick, its reception, and its role in the subsequent negotiations, see Raymond G. O'Connor, "The 'Yardstick' and Naval Disarmament in the 1920s," *Mississippi Valley Historical Review,* 45(1958):441–463.

9. Hugh R. Wilson, *Diplomat Between Wars* (New York, 1941), p. 236.

10. The following note, while not strictly correct, indicates the attitude of at least one delegate. "My dear Tardieu, The whole purpose of the appointment of Committees is to gain time so that the *real issues* may be settled by *informal* discussion *outside.* I just said the same to Briand." Henry L. Stimson to André Tardieu, January 27, 1930, Stimson Papers, Yale University Library, no. 3F–0417.

11. The most recent detailed account of the London Naval Conference is my previously mentioned book, *Perilous Equilibrium.* The negotiations are treated in detail, and press opinion in the various nations is analyzed after each major development, beginning with the Washington treaties of 1922.

12. Draft Convention of the Preparatory Commission for the Disarmament Conference, Office Document C687, M 288, 1930, ix, articles 40–52, cited in Payson S. Wild, Jr., *Sanctions and Treaty Enforcement* (Cambridge, Mass., 1934), p. 8.

13. Cordell Hull, *The Memoirs of Cordell Hull* (New York, 1948), vol. 1, p. 222.

14. The president's message to chiefs of state of all countries participating in the General Disarmament or International Monetary and Economic Conferences, May 16, 1933, is printed in *Papers Relating to the Foreign Relations of the United States, 1933,* vol. 1, pp. 143–145. Norman Davis' address of May 22 is on pp. 154–158. For correspondence relating to the conference, see pp. 1–355.

15. Sir Alexander Cadogan (chief advisor to the United Kingdom delegation at Geneva) to Anthony Eden, "in the early days of 1933," quoted in Eden, *The Memoirs of Anthony Eden: Facing the Dictators* (Boston, 1962), pp. 31–32.

16. See Robert A. Divine, "Franklin D. Roosevelt and Collective Security, 1933," *Mississippi Valley Historical Review,* 48(1961):42–59, though I don't agree with Divine's conclusion. See also, Wayne S. Cole, "Senator Key Pittman and American Neutrality Policies, 1933–1940," *Mississippi Valley Historical Review,* 46(1960):644–662.

17. *Foreign Relations, 1934,* vol. 1, p. 81 (May 29, 1934).

18. Norman Davis to Franklin Roosevelt, London, March 6, 1934, President's Secretary's File, London Naval Conference, 1934–1936 folder, FDR Papers, Hyde Park.

19. Ibid., Davis to Roosevelt, November 6, 1934.

20. *Senate Hearings*, Committee on Foreign Relations, London Naval Treaty, 1936, p. 33. For an account of the London Naval Conference of 1935–1936, see Arnold J. Toynbee, *Survey of International Affairs, 1936* (London, 1937), pp. 49–116. The administration version is found in *The Memoirs of Cordell Hull*, vol. 1 pp. 444–459.

# CHAPTER FOUR

# The Negotiation and Enforcement of Multilateral Agreements

THE NEGOTIATION OF MULTILATERAL AGREEMENTS AMONG NATIONS PREDATES written history, and efforts to insure the enforcement of such agreements have varied throughout the centuries. An obligation is inherent in any treaty—there are rights but there are also duties, and each party, in enjoying advantages that previously did not exist, also acquires commitments which restrict its freedom of action. During the later Middle Ages treaties "were solemnized with the utmost gravity, and a breach of their letter involved the spiritual crime of perjury and brought dishonor as well as the more impersonal penalties of excommunication and interdict."[1] Moreover, a violation of a treaty by one party could, at the very least, release the other from his obligations, and this loss of treaty "rights" is virtually an automatic "penalty" assessed against the transgressor.[2] The eighteenth century Swiss jurist Emer de Vattel, whose writings on international law were so attractive to the political leaders of the new United States, maintained that fidelity to treaties was a sacred obligation, but he wrote, "Taught by sad experience that the sacred and inviolable duty of fidelity to treaties is not always a safe assurance that they will be observed, men have sought to obtain securities against perfidy, means for enforcing observance independently of the good faith of the contracting parties."[3] One method of securing adherence to the terms of a treaty which Vattel suggested was by guarantee, whereby a third party, usually a powerful nation, agreed to insure that the parties to a treaty abide by its terms.

The modern landmark of this type of agreement is the Treaty of Blois (1505) between France and Aragon, with England assuming the obligation to see that both parties observed its terms. More sophisticated treaties of guarantee later emerged, especially in the nineteenth century.[4] Usually these treaties either specifically authorized or implied that the guarantor could utilize whatever method was necessary to secure observance of the treaty, including force. Yet there was no provision for compelling the guarantor to meet his commitment, and the means for evading this responsibility could usually be found.[5]

The quest for peace among nations has provoked a number of plans and a few experiments in what has come to be called "collective security."[6] The Greek city states and the universal state of Rome attacked the problem with varying degrees of success. The Italian city states, in what today's social scientists would term a microcosmic effort, formed the Second Holy League in 1495 in an unsuccessful attempt to preserve peace. Wars often appear to have a sobering effect on nations and stimulate a desire to prevent their recurrence. The example most often cited as the precursor of modern security treaties is the Treaty of Munster (1648). As part of the peace settlement which brought to an end the Thirty Years' War, the treaty was concluded by the Congress of Munster which had convened four years earlier. The negotiations were lengthy and tortuous, for "It was one thing to get the representatives to meet, it was quite another to get them to set to work."[7] Rejecting an armistice, the claims of the delegates fluctuated with the course of the campaigns, but exhaustion and stalemate finally brought an end to the longest period of war and peace deliberations in history. Article 123 of this pact obligated "all parties . . . to defend and protect all and every article of the peace against any one . . . ," and in the event negotiation failed, article 124 committed "all and every one of those concerned in this transaction . . . to join the injured party, and assist him with counsel and force to repel the injury. . . ."[8] Herein were embodied the concepts of a collective guarantee of the treaty to which all members subscribed, the element of security, machinery for settling disputes by negotiation, and the prescription for sanctions up to and including war against the offending party.

The long, bloody, and disrupting conflicts of the French Revolution and empire were responsible for the next notable development in collective guarantees for the observance of treaties and the maintenance of peace. The victorious allies joined in a series of agreements designed to eliminate the Napoleonic dynasty, stabilize the territorial settlements made at the end of the war, and generally maintain the status quo in Europe. The Treaty of Chaumont (1814), the Quadruple Alliance (1815), and the Treaty of the Holy Alliance (1815), with subsequent modifications, were the formal agreements by which the Great Powers committed themselves to the preservation of peace through collective action by commitments to punish by force any transgressor.[9] This loose and not always effective association, which worked through alliances and periodic conferences of the Great Powers, was succeeded by or developed into the Concert of Europe which emerged in the second quarter of the nineteenth century.

Though authorities disagree on the question of separation, it is clear that many of the principles embodied in the treaties following the Napoleonic wars prevailed. The Concert of Europe succeeded where the Holy Alliance had failed, primarily by providing for change where circumstances demanded and establishing a system of procedure. The first step in the procedure was discussion. The state or states involved might or might not be present. The second step was diplomatic intervention with specific recommendations. If this failed the Concert might intervene by force of arms, though this step was seldom necessary. After the dispute was resolved the Concert took steps to preserve the settlement, usually in the form of treaties of guarantee either separate from or embodied in the treaties of settlement. Examples may be found in the treaties of 1831 and 1839 which guaranteed the neutrality of Belgium, and in the Treaty of Paris (1856) and the Treaty of Berlin (1878) which guaranteed the territorial integrity of Turkey.

While the Concert of Europe was not institutionalized, had no formal membership, charter, or scheduled meetings, it functioned by the common consent of the major powers when a situation arose that seriously threatened the peace of Europe. Based on the old alliances, the principle of legitimacy, and the balance of power, the Concert of Europe was generally successful in preserving the peace. Other reasons for its success may be found in the fact that few of the disputes it handled were sufficiently vital to the state or states involved to warrant war, the fact that the Great Powers believed the principles espoused by the Concert to be most consistent with their own interests, and the methods utilized in resolving conflict. As one authority has observed, ". . . the treaty of guarantee, as used by the Concert, and embodying as it does a clear right to intervene for its execution in the future, is very nearly the last word in the creation of international control."[10] The major nations assumed this responsibility because their position and resources gave them the authority, they had more experience in diplomacy, and their stakes were greater than those of smaller countries. Few nations were willing to challenge the collective might of the Great Powers, which included the British navy. While there may not have been a Pax Britannica in a literal sense in the nineteenth century there is little doubt that the existence of the British fleet and England's support of the Concert helped preserve peace in Europe.

Efforts to halt the slave trade produced controversy, modifications in international law, and some effort to impose sanctions. A British proposal that the goods of nations that refused to take appropriate steps to prevent the trade in slaves should be boycotted was unsuccessful, but a series of agreements providing for penalties against the crew or owner of a vessel was forthcoming.[11]

The later decades of the nineteenth century witnessed an increase in competition among nations. This international rivalry was in large part a manifestation of the "New Imperialism" arising from a greater concern for prestige, trade, and the exploitation of unclaimed areas of Africa and the Far East. The unification of Germany in 1871, accelerated industrialization, and the imperial ambitions of Germany and Russia produced strains on the Concert of Europe and moved England to abandon her "splendid isolation" and seek allies. In 1899 the czar of Russia called an international congress to meet at the Hague to discuss the problems of disarmament and peace. Though twenty-six nations attended and high hopes were raised, success could only be claimed if the conference were regarded as an excessively modest beginning. No measure of disarmament was achieved though resolutions were adopted for the humanization of war. The establishment of a Permanent Court of Arbitration was deceptive, for none of the nations committed themselves to use the court.

A second Hague conference in 1907, attended by forty-four nations, was no more successful than the first in providing for a reduction or limitation of weapons, though it did adopt conventions regulating certain aspects of warfare. Most significant for this study was a provision that "The state of war should be notified to the neutral powers without delay and shall not take effect in regard to them until after the receipt of a notification . . ."[12] Herein a sanction was involved, for unless a nation at war officially notified a neutral, the latter was under no obligation to observe the duties of a neutral under international law. The failure of the Hague conferences to deal effectively with the problems before them was probably a reflection of the unwillingness of nations to accept limitations on their freedom of action. Under the Concert of Europe the nations concerned were, in each case, dealing with a specific situation where the advantages and disadvantages of various courses of action could be weighed. The rejection of compulsory arbitration at the Hague conference or a commitment to accept the decision of others for the settlement of future disputes was consistent with the desire to retain control over issues affecting the national interest. Though the intensified international rivalry helped bring about the Hague conferences, it also rendered impossible the conclusion of effective agreements for disarmament and peace.[13]

In spite of the understandable reluctance of statesmen to turn over their country's fate to some type of international tribunal, the search for peace continued. Even in the United States, which had long enjoyed a "free security" from the quarrels of Europe, there was considerable agitation for a reduction of arms and collective measures to prevent aggression. In 1910 Congress authorized the appointment of a commission to study the questions of disarmament and "of constituting the combined navies of the world an international force for the preservation of universal peace."¹⁴ Consistent with the American tradition of faith in the arbitration of disputes that began with the provision for arbitration contained in the Jay Treaty of 1795, was borne out so convincingly in the settlement of the *Alabama* claims controversy in 1872, and was affirmed by the first Hague conference, the United States began to negotiate arbitration treaties. In 1904 Secretary of State John Hay negotiated ten bilateral arbitration agreements that committed the nations in advance to arbitrate specific types of disputes through the Hague Court. Even though the terms excluded matters that might result in war, the Senate inserted a proviso that required its approval of each question at issue in every instance of arbitration. President Roosevelt withdrew the treaties, claiming that under such restrictions they made no new contribution to international peace. Elihu Root, who succeeded Hay as secretary of state, managed to change Roosevelt's opinion, and in 1908 he negotiated bilateral arbitration treaties with twenty-four countries, including all of the major powers except Germany. Each arbitration required the approval of the Senate, and the majority were for a period of five years with provision for renewal. Under Taft, pacts were concluded with Great Britain and France in 1911 providing for the arbitration of all "justiciable" questions by the Hague Court or a mutually acceptable separate tribunal. When the Senate approved the treaties with a reservation allowing it to determine which matters were "justiciable," Taft refused ratification.¹⁵

When Woodrow Wilson became president his secretary of state, William Jennings Bryan, negotiated conciliation pacts with thirty nations. Designed to supplement the Root treaties, these pacts committed signatories to submit all disputes not settled through the regular channels of diplomacy to permanent investigatory commissions. During the period of investigation the nations were required to avoid hostilities, but there was no compulsion to accept the recommendation of the commission.¹⁶ Opinions differ on the efficacy of these treaties, though both Bryan and Wilson took pride in their acceptance and the former considered them the major achievement of his life. One authority has regarded them as "most nearly the forerunners of the movement to outlaw war."¹⁷ Certainly the arbitration and conciliation pacts revealed that the United States, in marked contrast to its traditional noninvolvement in European political affairs, was leading a movement for the preservation of peace on an international scale. The lack of specific penalties in the event of noncompliance was overlooked by many in the popular belief that tangible agreements had been made that were designed to avoid war. Furthermore, any country failing to observe a treaty for the peaceful settlement of disputes was exposing itself to the censure of world opinion, an automatic sanction that appeared to possess some validity in an age of enlightened, rational statesmen. The morality that some believed would prevail among nations was probably best expressed in the Award of Tribunal in the North Atlantic Coast Fisheries Arbitration, September 7, 1910:

> Every State has to execute the obligations incurred by treaty *bona fide*, and is urged thereto by the ordinary sanctions of international law in regard to observance of treaty obligations. Such sanctions are, for instance, appeal to public opinion, publication of correspondence, censure by parliamentary vote, demand for arbitration with the odium attendant on a refusal to arbitrate, rupture of relations, reprisal, etc.[18]

Under the circumstances, lacking an international jurisdictional body with the authority and power to enforce its decisions, an obvious impossibility at the time, the Hague conventions, the arbitration treaties of Root, and the conciliation conventions of Bryan all pointed to a new era in international relations and a minimization of the likelihood of war. In retrospect, with the advantage of knowing what happened, there is a tendency to belittle these pre-World War I efforts to insure peace. But these efforts prevailed in the past, and their example was not lost on subsequent generations.

One authority has observed that "The process by which international law has developed has not at the same time constituted a process whereby a public opinion has been created to give its institutions political power."[19] These pacts helped stir a public interest in the peaceful settlement of disputes and they placed the behavior of nations before the bar of world opinion. This development coincided with the development of representative government in the major countries of the world which allowed the people to have a greater voice in their government's affairs and compelled the leaders to justify their conduct to the electorate. Paradoxically, when war came in 1914, large segments of the population which had clamored for peace suddenly became equally enthusiastic for war.

The breakdown of the rudimentary peace machinery in 1914 was both disheartening and stimulating to those who wished to eliminate war. On the one hand it appeared to demonstrate that all the efforts of the previous fifteen years had been wasted, for not only had they failed to prevent a conflict but their efforts had culminated in the most devastating debacle of all times. On the other hand, the outbreak of war provoked some to point out that it revealed the inherent weakness of previous plans for peace, and that only drastic methods of controlling intercourse between and among nations would suffice. The horrors of World War I and the obvious incongruity of such a holocaust with the material, political, and intellectual advances of Western civilization spawned a host of groups dedicated to the elimination of war through some form of international organization.[20] Many agreed that something should be done, but there was considerable disagreement over the method. Arbitration and conciliation had not been completely discredited, and the American League to Enforce Peace believed that nations should be compelled, by force if necessary, to consent to conciliation before resorting to hostilities. It added, however, that nations should be "free to go to war if their interests demand that they should do so," which seemed to leave the matter where it had been for centuries. Further study revealed an attempt to distinguish between just and unjust wars, and some urged that the mere threat of force or the use of economic pressures would deter war.[21]

Basic to most of the plans put forward was the belief that peace must be maintained by collective action, i.e., that a number of nations must bear the responsibility "collectively" for the prevention of war. Most plans also contained provision for some method of coercion to induce nations to refrain from actions that would jeopardize the peace. The onus of world opinion, some felt, had been tried and found wanting. Others believed that it had not been given a fair chance, for the rapidity of events that led to the outbreak of hostilities in 1914 had prevented both the use of existing machinery for settling disputes and the development of the "moral force" of world opinion. The use of more stringent forms of coercion, including economic reprisals and military force, was not as popular with responsible world leaders as with the sideline critics. There was little responsible reaction when Pope Benedict XV sent a message to the belligerents in the summer of 1917 urging agreement on a reduction of armaments, compulsory arbitration of disputes, and the imposition of sanctions against a nation that rejected arbitration or failed to carry out a tribunal decision. But the continuation of the war, its ruthless character, growing public disillusionment over its validity, the entrance of the United States, and the idealistic utterances of Woodrow Wilson combined to produce an atmosphere in which some form of collective security appeared both possible and desirable. The inclusion in Wilson's widely heralded Fourteen Points of an appeal for "a general association of nations" and the popular reception of the idea forced responsible statesmen to give it serious attention. And when the president dramatically appeared in Europe to lead in peacemaking with an insistence on the inclusion of a society of nations in the final treaty, opponents of an international organization were doomed to disappointment.

Just what sort of machinery this organization would contain for the elimination of war was another matter, though it was generally agreed by proponents of a league that measures must be devised to discourage nations from using force in settling disputes. The use of joint coercive measures in the event of aggression was contemplated in the proposals submitted by Wilson, Lord Robert Cecil, and General Jan Smuts, and most of the drafts for a league submitted at the Paris conference contained some provision for sanctions. Yet there was considerable disagreement about their nature, when they should be employed, and how they should be implemented. The British urged more stringent guarantees, the French advocated an international military force and a virtual military alliance. Wilson appeared to vacillate on the issue, in part because of the restrictions imposed by the Constitution on the executive conduct of foreign affairs.[22]

The negotiations revealed that "political speeches necessarily possess a vagueness and a generalized aspect which unfit them for diplomatic interpretation."[23] The effort to translate Wilson's idealistic pronouncements into tangible treaty terms produced constant friction, expecially when confronted with the aspirations of national leaders. Another factor affecting the negotiations was the fact that "Popular passions here as elsewhere complicated the task of the democratic peacemakers who, unlike their predecessors at Vienna, worked under the direct pressure of powerful criticism in press and parliament."[24] The leisurely days when sovereigns determined the fate of Europe were gone, and the diplomats were obliged to function under constant harrassment. The dualistic function of the conference further added to the difficulties, for the delegates were striving to achieve a settlement along nationalistic lines in an international framework. The presence of "heads of state" was not all to the good, for the decision-makers were faced with the immediate solution of complex problems that often required greater deliberation than was possible under the circumstances. Adding to the confusion was the lack of advance preparation, for the vague and general agreements between the Allied and associated powers proved inadequate in light of the problems that had to be solved.[25]

The League Covenant did succeed in combining the various methods for the solution of disputes—peacefully through arbitration and conciliation and coercively through the use of sanctions. The most revolutionary doctrine embodied in the covenant in terms of departing from conventional international law was the classification of war as a crime except when authorized by the League.[26] Not only did the Preamble contain the obligation of member nations to refrain from war but Article 17 provided that sanctions could be imposed on a nonmember nation that resorted to war, whether the hostilities were a breach of a treaty or not.

Under the League Covenant sanctions could be applied in the following instances:

1. Under Article 10 to preserve the territorial and political independence of League members. No specific action was prescribed other than what the council might "advise." The word "guarantee" is not contained in this article, stricken at Wilson's insistence because it smacked of too firm a commitment.

2. Under Article 11 in case of "Any war or threat of war . . . the League shall take any action that may be deemed wise and effectual to safeguard the peace of nations."

3. Under Articles 12, 13, and 15 if a member resorted to war without submitting a dispute for arbitration to an appropriate tribunal and accepting the award.

4. Under Article 16 if a member resorted to war in violation of its agreements under Articles 12, 13, or 15, in which case "it shall *ipso facto* be deemed to have committed an act of war against all other Members of the League," who were obligated to institute an economic and personal boycott of the offending nation. Moreover, the council could "recommend" military action.

The complications and shortcomings of the covenant were to become more apparent later, but immediately differences of interpretation over the duties of member nations contributed to American rejection of the agreement. In spite of its imperfection, the covenant, which was made possible only by the aftermath of a great war, was a significant achievement in the development of international organization.

## NOTES

1. G. R. Potter, ed., *The Rennaissance, 1493–1520* (Cambridge, 1957), p. 263.

2. Hugo Grotius, *The Rights of War and Peace* (New York, 1901), chap. 15, sec. 12, and chap. 20, sec. 36.

3. E. de Vattel, *The Law of Nations*, trans. C. G. Fenwick (Washington, 1916), book 2, sec. 235. Vattel also contended (secs. 163 and 170) that a state could ignore the duties of a treaty if it conflicted with the state's obligation toward itself.

4. See D. J. Hill, *A History of Diplomacy in the International Development of Europe*, 3 vols. (New York, 1905–1906).

5. L. Oppenheim, *International Law*, Lauterpacht ed. (sixth ed., London, 1947), vol. 1, pp. 870–871.

6. See J. A. O. Larsen, "Federations for Peace in Ancient Greece," *Classical Philology*, vol. 36, pp. 145–162; Stanley Pargellis, ed., *The Quest for Political Unity in World History*. American Historical Association *Annual Report for 1942*, vol. 3 (Washington, 1944); Laszlo Ledermann, *Les précurseurs de l'organisation internationale* (Neuchatel, Switzerland, 1945); Elizabeth Souleyman, *The Vision of World Peace in Seventeenth and Eighteenth Century France* (New York, 1941); J. A. R. Marriott, *Commonwealth or Anarchy: A Survey of Projects of Peace from the Sixteenth to the Twentieth Century* (New York, 1939).

7. Henry Offley Wakeman, *Europe, 1598–1715* (New York, 1895), p. 121.

8. The text is printed in F. B. Sayre, *Experiments in International Administration* (New York, 1919), p. 173. See Andrea Rapisardi-Mirabelli, *Le Congres de Westphalie, ses négociations et ses résultats au point de vue de l'histoire du droit des gens* (Paris, 1929).

9. See Harold Nicholson, *The Congress of Vienna: A Study in Allied Unity, 1812–1822* (New York, 1946); H. G. Schenk, *The Aftermath of the Napoleonic Years: The Concert of Europe—an Experiment* (New York, 1948); Henry A. Kissinger, *A World Restored: Metternich, Castlereagh, and the Problem of Peace* (Boston, 1957); Walter A. Phillips, *The Confederation of Europe: A Study of the European Alliance, 1813–1923 as an Experiment in the International Organization of Peace* (London and New York, 1920).

10. Pitman B. Potter, *An Introduction to the Study of International Organization* (New York, 1922), p. 429. For the text of two treaties under the Concert of Europe see pp. 583–589. One historian, referring to the relative peace that prevailed in the nineteenth century, has written, "as a whole the political edifice was maintained in stability by the Concert of Europe, which was based, partly at least, on the mutual understanding of sovereigns." R. B. Mowat, *A History of European Diplomacy, 1914–1925* (London, 1927), p. vi.

11. See H. H. Wilson, "British Efforts to Crush the African Slave Trade, 1807–1927," *American Journal of International Law* 54(1950):505–526; Hugh G. Soulsby, *The Right of Search and the Slave Trade in Anglo-American Relations, 1814–1862* (Baltimore, 1933). For international law aspects of the efforts to halt the slave trade see C. John Colombos, *The International Law of the Sea* (fourth ed., London, 1959), pp. 395–400.

12. Hague Convention, 1907, No. III. Quoted in Payson S. Wild, Jr., *Sanctions and Treaty Enforcement* (Cambridge, Mass., 1934), p. 61, note 3.

13. For the Hague conferences see Frederick W. Holls, *The Peace Conference at the Hague, and Its Bearings on International Law and Policy* (New York, 1900); Calvin D. Davis, *The United States and the First Hague Conference* (Ithaca, N.Y., 1962); James B. Scott, *The Hague Peace Conferences of 1899 and 1907*, 2 vols. (Baltimore, 1909); Merze Tate, *The Disarmament Illusion: The Movement for a Limitation of Armaments to 1907* (New York, 1942).

14. United States, *Statutes at Large*, vol. 36, resolution 43, June 25, 1910, p. 885.

15. See Tyler Dennett, *John Hay* (New York, 1933); Henry F. Pringle, *The Life and Times of William Howard Taft*, 2 vols., (New York, 1939); William Stull Holt, *Treaties Defeated by the Senate* (Baltimore, 1933).

16. See Merle E. Curti, "Bryan and World Peace," *Smith College Studies in History*, vol. 16, nos. 3–4 (April, July 1931), pp. 143–164.

17. Hans Wehberg, *The Outlawry of War* (Washington, 1931), p. 7.

18. James Brown Scott, ed., *The Hague Court Reports* (New York, 1916), p. 167. "The question of the punitive war (Sanktionskrieges) was taken up at a late date in peace circles, namely at the World Peace Conference at The Hague in 1913. The ideas concerning the legitimacy of the military application of sanctions were so divergent in each congress that no definite resolution was passed on this subject. . . . " Wehberg, *The Outlawry of War*, p. 7, citing *Bulletin officiel du XX Congres universel de la Paix* (La Haye, 1913), p. 110.

19. Quincy Wright, *A Study of War* (Chicago, 1942), vol. 2, p. 937. This follows Root, who observed that "Laws passed, as they sometimes are, in advance of public opinion ordinarily wait for their enforcement until the progress of opinion has reached recognition of their value. The force of law is in the public opinion which prescribes it." Elihu Root, "The Sanction of International Law," *Proceedings of the American Society of International Law* (1908), p. 17.

20. See Henry R. Winkler, *The League of Nations Movement in Great Britain, 1914–1919* (New Brunswick, N.J., 1952); Randolph Bourne, ed., *Towards an Enduring Peace: A Symposium of Peace Proposals and Programs* (New York, 1916); James Bryce, et. al., *Proposals for the Prevention of Future Wars* (London, 1917); Theodore Paullin, *Comparative Peace Plans* (Philadelphia, 1943); John H. Latane, *The Development of the League of Nations Idea: Documents and Correspondence of Theodore Marburg*, 2 vols. (New York, 1932).

21. See Ruhl J. Bartlett, *The League to Enforce Peace* (Chapel Hill, N.C., 1944); and Roland N. Stromberg, "The Riddle of Collective Security, 1916–1920," in George

L. Anderson, ed., *Issues and Conflicts: Studies in Twentieth Century American Diplomacy* (Lawrence, Kansas, 1959), pp. 147–170.

22. See D. Mitrany, *The Problem of International Sanctions* (New York, 1925); Jan Christian Smuts, *The League of Nations: a Practical Suggestion* (New York, 1919); Edward H. Buehrig, "Woodrow Wilson and Collective Security," in Edward H. Buehrig, ed., *Wilson's Foreign Policy in Perspective* (Bloomington, Ind., 1957), pp. 34–60; Richard N. Current, "The United States and 'Collective Security' Notes on the History of an Idea," in Alexander DeConde, ed., *Isolation and Security* (Durham, N.C., 1957), pp. 33–55; Robert E. Osgood, "Woodrow Wilson, Collective Security, and the Lessons of History," *Confluence*, vol. 5 (Winter 1957), pp. 341–354; George Curry, "Woodrow Wilson, Jan Smuts, and the Versailles Settlement," *The American Historical Review* 46(July 1961):968–986; Seth P. Tillman, *Anglo-American Relations at the Paris Peace Conference of 1919* (Princeton, 1961).

23. H. W. V. Temperley, *A History of the Peace Conference of Paris*, 6 vols. (Washington, 1920–1924), vol. 6, p. 540.

24. David Thomson, ed., *The Era of Violence, 1898–1945* (Cambridge, 1960), p. 451.

25. Standard sources for the Peace Conference are Temperley, *History of the Peace Conference of Paris; Papers Relating to the Foreign Relations of the United States, the Peace Conference, 1919*, 13 vols. (Washington, 1942–1947); D. Hunter Miller, *The Drafting of the Covenant*, 2 vols. (New York, 1928); D. Hunter Miller, *My Diary at the Conference of Paris with Documents*, 21 vols. (New York, 1928); Edward M. House and Charles Seymour, eds., *What Really Happened at Paris: The Story of the Peace Conference, 1918–1919, by American Delegates* (New York, 1921); Charles Seymour, ed., *The Intimate Papers of Colonel House*, 4 vols. (Boston, 1926–1928); Ray Stannard Baker, *Woodrow Wilson and World Settlement*, 3 vols. (Garden City, New York, 1923–1927).

26. "The Covenant of the League of Nations represented the first significant break with the theory of traditional international law." Myres S. McDougal and Florentino P. Feliciano, *Law and Minimum World Public Order: The Legal Regulation of International Coercion* (New Haven, Conn., 1961), p. 138. Also see Royal Institute of International Affairs, *International Sanctions* (London, 1938), pp. 9–12.

# CHAPTER FIVE

# The Application
# or Threat of Sanctions
# Under the League Covenant

SIXTY-SIX POLITICAL DISPUTES WERE BROUGHT BEFORE THE LEAGUE OF Nations. Twenty of these were referred to other agencies, thirty-five were resolved by the League, and in eleven cases the League failed to settle the issues.[1] This survey is confined to a study of those disputes in which the threat or application of sanctions appeared to influence the outcome or those in which the failure to apply sanctions or the ineffectiveness of the sanctions applied revealed defects in the method of handling disputes.

The first such incident concerned the alleged violation of the frontiers of Albania, an issue which that nation brought before the League in April 1921. Albania had been granted autonomy from Turkey in 1912 and her independence had been reaffirmed by the Conference of Ambassadors in London in 1913. By the Treaty of London in 1915, however, the Allied powers provided for the partition of Albania between Italy, Montenegro, Serbia, and Greece, but in 1920 the proposal that Albania be placed under Italy as a mandate was canceled by an agreement between these two nations that Albania should be free. Yugoslavia and Greece demanded a revision of the frontiers in their favor, and Albania appealed to the League for assistance under Article 11 of the covenant. In September 1921 the League of Nations assembly appointed an impartial commission to investigate. In the meantime the Conference of Ambassadors, which had been seeking a solution, reaffirmed the frontiers of 1913 with a few minor revisions in favor of Yugoslavia. This decision was announced on November 9, 1921, at the same time that a declaration was signed in Paris by representatives of the British, French, Italian, and Japanese governments affirming Italy's primary interest in Albania and announcing that if the latter appealed to the League for protection these nations would recommend that Italy should be entrusted with the responsibility for the maintenance of Albania's frontiers.

At just this time the situation was drastically modified by a telegram from British Prime Minister Lloyd George to the League's secretary-general on November 8. The message asked that the council be assembled to assert that if Yugoslavia, which had troops in northern Albania, did not immediately observe her obligations under the covenant she would be compelled to do so under the threat of economic sanctions. When the council met on November 18, the Yugoslav government agreed to accept the decision of the Conference of Ambassadors concerning the frontiers of Albania and withdrew its troops "to avoid the dangers threatened by Lloyd George's telegram." According to one authority, "There can be little doubt that Albania owed her survival as an independent State to the action of the League—first and foremost, to her admission as a Member by the First Assembly, but also to the support given by the Second Assembly and to the threat of sanctions so unexpectedly sounded forth from London. This last was, indeed, of doubtful legality; but it was completely effective in preventing any attempt by the Yugoslav government to emulate the adventures of d'Annunzio in Fiume or of Zeligowski in Vilna."[2] Despite the fact that many of the decisions on which the settlement was based were effected by agencies outside the League, the final agreement was made under League auspices and under the threat of the institution of sanctions within the framework of the covenant. The League had demonstrated its effectiveness in providing additional machinery for the resolution of disputes from both a procedural and jurisdictional point of view.

The next major political dispute in which the League became involved was the Corfu incident of 1923. A commission had been appointed by the Conference of Ambassadors to implement the decision on Albanian borders. While engaged in this work an Italian general and his four aides were murdered in a Greek village on August 27, 1923. The Greek government immediately offered regrets and promised to punish the criminals, but Italy responded by presenting a drastic ultimatum. The Greek reply was conciliatory, though it rejected certain demands. Italy retaliated on August 31 by shelling and occupying the strategic island of Corfu. The Greek government then appealed to the League council under Articles 12 and 15 and offered to accept the council's recommendations or a decision by the Conference of Ambassadors. The element of dual jurisdiction was thus introduced to confuse the issue, and the Italian government contended that the matter was outside the province of the League because it was being handled by the ambassador's conference, and that the provisions of Article 16 were not pertinent because Italy had not committed an act of war. Yet pressure for an amicable settlement built up within the council and throughout the civilized world, and at an informal meeting of the council a settlement was drafted and forwarded to the Conference of Ambassadors, which adopted it with a few minor changes. Both parties agreed to accept the terms, which were favorable to Italy and required Greece to deposit a sum of money pending adjudication by the permanent court. Alleging a violation of the agreement, the council of Ambassadors withdrew its consent and ordered the immediate payment of the deposit as an indemnity to Italy.

This sudden about-face made what had seemed to be a League victory turn out to be a victory for the unilateral application of force. The first instance of a dispute between a minor and a major power had been decided in favor of the latter in apparent disregard of the League machinery. On the other hand, the council had acted promptly and an opportunity was provided for an airing of the controversy before the bar of world opinion. The entire matter was complicated by the question of jurisdiction, and the council addressed to a special Commission of Jurists a series of related legal queries. The resultant opinion in effect supported the Italian view that the League had no jurisdiction in the Corfu affair. One authority then commented, "If this interpretation is correct, it indicates a serious defect in the Covenant which demands amendment."[3] The application of sanctions under the covenant then became academic, but this opinion was delivered after the fact. In any event, the sanction of world opinion and the possibility of collective action under the League probably deterred further Italian aggression and prevented more extreme demands. This incident, however, plus the Franco-Belgian invasion of the Ruhr, provoked the aging Woodrow Wilson to declare that "France and Italy between them have made waste paper of the Treaty of Versailles."[4]

The next major challenge to League responsibility came in 1925 over a dispute between Greece and Bulgaria. A border incident, in which two Greek soldiers were killed, led to an invasion of Bulgaria by Greek troops. The Bulgarian government appealed to the League under Articles 10 and 11 of the covenant, and the president of the council, Aristide Briand, immediately informed both governments of their duties under Article 12 and asked that troops be withdrawn. The nations complied, and the council approved Briand's action and appointed a military commission to supervise the withdrawal. While the application of sanctions was not officially mentioned, there can be little doubt that this "big stick" lurked in the background and influenced the attitude of the disputants. "Briand and Chamberlain, fresh from their great days at Locarno, were in no mood to be defied by a small and shaky dictator. There were no public threats; but behind the scenes there was talk of a naval demonstration and even the sanctions of Article 16 of the Covenant."⁵ A Commission of Inquiry found Greece at fault and the council decided that she should pay an indemnity since her occupation had violated the covenant. This, in effect, was a punitive sanction.

Though hailed at the time as a victory for the League, which it was, circumstances were such that the outcome could scarcely warrant enthusiasm for the future of international organization as a peacekeeper. The decisive action was more reminiscent of the Concert of Europe, for the Great Powers were united, none of their interests were at stake, and the disputants were small nations. Greece may have felt that for the second time she had been exploited in the name of the League.⁶

The first determined attempt of the League to check a major power occurred in connection with the Manchurian Incident of 1931. The Chinese had resented the Japanese presence in Manchuria and a series of clashes finally resulted in the Japanese army taking matters into its own hands and launching an attack on September 18, 1931. The Chinese government appealed to the League under Article 11 and to the United States (as a sponsor of the Kellogg-Briand Pact) to restore peace. An order by the council to halt the fighting on September 21 was ignored, and on September 30 the council asked both nations to resume normal relations. Opposition from the United States and Great Britain prevented the appointment of a commission of investigation at this time. The former wanted to give the civilian authorities in Japan an opportunity to "get control of the situation."⁷ British inaction was due to several factors, among them the reluctance to rashly antagonize a nation that had been a leader in League cooperation. But as hostilities continued and it became apparent that Japan was not going to cease her operations, opinion among members of the League and in the United States began to harden. On October 17 the council invoked the Pact of Paris and on October 20 the United States followed suit. A second resolution by the council on October 24 asking Japan to withdraw its troops was nullified by the opposing vote of the Japanese delegate, for under Article 11 a unanimous decision was required. Finally, acting on a proposal made by Japan on November 21, the council voted on December 10 to send a commission of inquiry. Appointed in January 1932, it reached the Far East the following month.

In the meantime, on January 7, 1932, the American Secretary of State Henry L. Stimson sent identical notes to China and Japan asserting that the government "cannot admit the legality of any situation *de facto* nor does it intend to recognize any treaty or agreement which may impair the treaty rights of the United States . . . and that it does not intend to recognize any situation, treaty, or agreement which may be brought about by means contrary to the covenants and obligations of the Pact of Paris."⁸

This departure from the previous policy of conciliation was prompted by the failure of Japanese statesmen to halt aggression, a consolidating of press and public opinion against Japan, and the occupation of Chinchow. "The weapons of this new phase were, however, those of nonrecognition and publicity which in November had been decided upon as the strongest sanctions the American government would use."[9] Evidently Stimson urged then or later that the United States use at least the threat of economic sanctions but President Hoover refused to bluff, and he believed that economic sanctions were a first step toward war.[10]

When on January 29 Japan attacked Shanghai, China immediately appealed to the League under Articles 10 and 15, and later introduced Article 16. A special session of the assembly met on March 3 and the following day called on Japan to withdraw its forces from Shanghai. A week later the assembly adopted the Hoover-Stimson doctrine of non-recognition and efforts continued to bring an end to hostilities, which were finally terminated by an armistice on May 5. By November 1932 the council was ready to consider the report of the commission of inquiry (the Lytton Report), which it in turn referred to the assembly. While in general critical of Japan's actions, the report did not find Japan guilty of military aggression within the terms of the League Covenant, and it recommended the establishment of an autonomous Manchuria under League auspices. When the report was accepted by the assembly, Japan announced its withdrawal from the League.

In retrospect it appears strange that the League invoked no sanction other than the diplomatic and moral force of nonrecognition. On closer examination, however, the factors that militated against such action are evident and understandable. Why "the chief Members of the League had never seriously contemplated the use of sanctions"[11] during this incident can only be explained by an assessment of the national and international scene. Basically, the League had been moving gradually away from the idea of collective security in terms of coercion and had emphasized the methods of conciliation and arbitration. It was asking too much to expect that the members would reverse a trend that had proved so acceptable and moderately successful in dealing with disputes between small powers. This trend had been strengthened by the Pact of Paris and the disarmament negotiations, especially the London Naval Treaty of 1930 which offered hope for an end to competitive building and the elimination of arms races as a cause of war. The worldwide economic depression forced statesmen to concentrate on domestic recovery and diverted the public attention to problems at home. Moreover, the situation in China was so complex and the internal conditions had been so chaotic that it was impossible to draw a hard and fast line as to which of the disputants was at fault. By the time the situation had clarified to some extent the League was presented with a *fait accompli*. The use of economic sanctions was virtually out of the question. Their enforcement would have depended on the British fleet, which as a result of the naval limitation treaties would have been hard put to maintain a blockade against Japan. And without American cooperation economic sanctions probably would have been ineffectual. Also, as Stimson later observed, "none of the nations in Europe and America, even if able, had the slightest desire to go to war in such a controversy."[12] The major powers did not feel that their interests were sufficiently infringed upon to warrant military action, and the logistics problems involved in mobilizing and moving adequate forces to the other side of the world were overwhelming.[13] Added to the foregoing considerations was the fear that the expulsion of Japan from Manchuria would result in its being taken over by Russia. China and the Soviet Union had fought a minor war over the region in 1929 and the weakness of the Peking regime left a virtual vacuum that seemed destined to attract one of the neighbors. Finally, the intrinsic weakness of the League machinery in regard to the implementation of collective security measures ruled out any rapid and effective intervention. Even if France and Great Britain had been willing to take the necessary action the lack of planning and previous agreement on method would have rendered the operation impractical.[14]

Latin America provided the next occasion for League intervention. The Chaco War, arising out of a dispute between Bolivia and Paraguay over a desolate area known as the Gran Chaco, began December 5, 1928. Six days later the president of the League council, acting on its recommendation, advised both nations of their responsibilities under Article 4 of the covenant. Bolivia then invoked Articles 10 and 12, but the League took no action because an inter-American Commission of Investigation and Conciliation undertook to settle the dispute. On June 15, 1932, the fighting resumed, and on August 1 Paraguay appealed to the League under Articles 10 and 11. The council still hoped that the Committee of Neutrals in Washington, which had been working with the two parties, would be able to handle the issue, but on May 10 Paraguay declared war on Bolivia, which in turn invoked Article 16. Efforts by commissions and committees proved unavailing, and in November 1934 an arms embargo was imposed on the recommendation of the League Commission.[15] The removal of the embargo, in which the United States and many League members participated, from Bolivia was recommended by the assembly when Paraguay refused to accept the report of the Chaco committee. Paraguay withdrew from the League on February 23, 1935, and the dispute was finally settled in 1938 without further League action.

The sanction in this case was, of course, the imposition of the arms embargo. Its adoption was based largely on the fact that most of the weapons with which the war was being waged came from abroad, and this method of coercion appeared feasible. Though Paraguay agreed to peace talks within four months after the lifting of the embargo against Bolivia, there appears to be no evidence that the two actions were related. "Nor is it possible to pronounce dogmatically upon the effectiveness of the embargo."[16] In spite of government efforts a number of firms evaded restrictions on the export of arms and many shipments arrived via other Latin American countries. The situation, however, was ideal for the exercise of coercive measures through the use of an embargo since neither nation was capable of producing sufficient weapons to maintain its forces and wage war.[17]

The crucial test of the League as an agency of collective security came with the Italo-Ethiopian War. The incident began with an armed clash between Italian and Ethiopian soldiers on December 5, 1934, at Wal Wal, near the disputed border between Ethiopia and Italian Somaliland. Though Italy initially refused arbitration under a treaty of 1928, Ethiopian appeals to the League brought only an injunction to settle the dispute amicably under an arbitration commission, which after many delays found neither side at fault. On March 17, 1935, Ethiopia asked for council action under Article 15, but at just this time Germany announced her decision to rearm in violation of the Treaty of Versailles. At this point the British and French authorities were faced with a problem that was to color their approach to the Ethiopian affair throughout its course. France, more than Great Britain, regarded the potential threat of German aggression as the greatest menace to her security. In her opinion, Italian support against Germany, as incorporated in the Locarno pact and recent understandings between Mussolini and the French Premier Pierre Laval, was of supreme importance in the absence of firm military commitments from Great Britain. The prospect of a resurgent Germany unilaterally flaunting agreements under the fanatical nationalistic fervor of Hitler was to hamper effective League action throughout the crisis.

Initially, this conflict was to prevent the taking of immediate steps in response to the Ethiopian request under Article 15, and the council was engaged in the preparation of a report when, on October 4, Italy invaded Ethiopia in force. The inefficacy of a "cooling off" period was demonstrated, for ten months had elapsed since the Wal Wal clash. It was later revealed that Italy had been preparing for this campaign for at least two years, and conciliation could serve little purpose in the face of such long-range planning and determination.

Within a week the council and the assembly passed resolutions declaring that Italy had "resorted to war in disregard of her covenants," with only the labeled aggressor dissenting in the former and three of her neighbors, Austria, Hungary, and Albania, in the latter. In light of these resolutions the economic sanctions of Article 15 became applicable, but the Coordination Committee, established to determine future action, decided against complete nonintercourse with Italy and advocated a selective embargo on imports, exports, and loans. The imposition of these sanctions failed to deter Italy or slow up its military advance in Ethiopia, which was conquered by the spring of 1936. Germany's remilitarization of the Rhineland on March 7, 1936, ended any hope of further pressure on Italy, and in June the assembly voted to end the sanctions.

A detailed account of this episode which marked the demise of the League as an instrument of collective security is beyond the scope of this study. But a consideration of some of the factors that contributed to the failure of the League's only major effort to implement the sanctioning provisions of Article 16 is appropriate. Basically, it was evident that Great Britain and France would have to assume leadership in the situation. Only they had the military and financial power to insure the implementation of any League decisions, and certainly the smaller nations had neither the resources to put the necessary pressure on Italy nor the strength to risk antagonizing Mussolini. Thus, the burden of responsibility was placed on two powers whose European policies had been at odds since the end of the great war.

At the heart of their differences was the German problem. France wanted to maintain the status quo in regard to the Versailles settlement or at most allow Germany to pursue economic expansion to the East. Britain believed that a revived Germany was essential to the economic well-being of Europe and she was unwilling to commit herself to the military guarantee sought by France. Concerning the Treaty of Versailles, in Britain "it became a platitude to regard it as conceived in iniquity or wrought in folly."[18] Constant friction over this issue rendered impossible an effective collaboration on security matters, and in the Ethiopian crisis the French government neither completely fulfilled its League obligations nor avoided offending Italy, whose assistance was desperately wanted in containing Germany.

The British approach was also confused and contradictory, and the factors responsible are numerous and complex. Domestically, a strong aversion toward war had developed with resultant pleas for peace through League cooperation, disarmament, and noninvolvement in military alliances. The contradictory aspects of these positions were not always apparent, as the results of a "Peace Ballot" in 1934 indicated. The popular revulsion to the Hoare-Laval compromise plan of 1935, which offered

Italy generous concessions in Ethiopia but was rejected by both disputants, forced the resignation of the foreign secretary and revealed a desire
to support the League efforts against Italy. There was, however, little
inclination on the part of either the British or the French governments, or
the people, to risk war in the implementation of sanctions. The issue did
not sufficiently jeopardize the interests of the two nations, the British
fleet had been weakened by disarmament agreements, and it was feared
that Hitler would take advantage of any conflict to continue his unilateral
revision of the Versailles treaty.

   Another source of confusion was the difficulty of making economic
sanctions effective. Looming large in this context was the United States,
which enjoyed a considerable trade with Italy. Though Secretary of State
Hull announced a "moral embargo" that involved the maintenance of
trade with Italy at its pre–1935 level, no legislation was forthcoming to
implement this request and it was violated with impunity.[19] The decision
to institute selective sanctions deprived the action of much of its coercive
effect, for trade in many essential supplies continued. The decision to
exclude oil from the embargo may have been made because of the belief
that it would provoke Mussolini to war, but in any event it eliminated
what might have been the most effective commodity.[20] A continually
vexing issue was the inequality of sacrifice made by the various nations
in carrying out the sanctioning decrees. The economy of smaller nations,
especially, was severely damaged by the ban on certain exports to Italy
and efforts were made to alleviate the situation with a resultant weakening
of pressure. Another factor that lessened the impact of sanctions was the
organization of the Italian economy under Fascism. Highly centralized
control with an emphasis on self-sufficiency had prepared the nation for
at least a short-time war in the face of a curtailment of foreign trade. This
fact, added to the relatively minor demands made on the military machine
by an almost primitive foe, combined with the inadequacy of the League
actions, rendered ineffectual the attempt to influence the outcome in
Ethiopia.

   An assessment of this experience is both tempting and rewarding, for
there has been a tendency among historians and others to view the incident
as a clear-cut lack of nerve on the part of Great Britain and France.
From the foregoing account of the reasons for the failure of collective
action when confronted by an obvious violation of at least three treaties
(the treaty of 1906 between Italy, France, and Great Britain; Article 10
of the covenant; and the Kellogg-Briand Pact) it is apparent that the
decisions that faced the statesmen of these two nations were neither simple
nor easy. Among the "lessons" that emerge, however, are the following.
Primarily, a government and its people must place at the forefront of

their interests a wholehearted commitment to resist aggression by whatever is necessary. This commitment must transcend any other "interest,"
for only then can compelling decisions be made in sufficient time to
influence the course of events. Moreover, an awareness of this attitude
could serve to deter all but the most foolhardy potential aggressor. In the
implementation of collective efforts, speed is a primary consideration, not
only in terms of the willingness of nations to take the necessary steps but
in regard to the institution of coercive measures. In 1935 no machinery
had been established to deal with the nature, extent, or operation of
economic sanctions. While it might not be practicable to prepare a detailed plan for every specific possible violator, a permanent organization
with adequate policy directives and the proper information could implement any collective decision with a minimum of delay. Moreover, unity
of purpose and effort is essential. As was pointed out by the Russian
Foreign Minister Maxim Litvinov at the time, "If sanctions were to be
applied, not, as the Covenant prescribed, to every case of aggression and
by every Member of the League, but only by those Members who chose
to do so and in such cases as they might select, the whole system of collective security would be gone."[21] Part of this lack of solidarity was due not
merely to the weighing of interests, as mentioned above, but to the failure
to realize that a successful violation of one pact placed in jeopardy all
pacts. The danger of allowing policy to be determined by the axiom of
whose ox was being gored revealed a curiously shortsighted approach,
as Albania was one of the first to discover.

In certain respects the League experience with Japan during the Manchurian Incident was repeated. Labeling Italy an aggressor had brought
down on her the moral force of world opinion, but this external condemnation served to unite the Italian people more firmly behind their
government's policy. Also, the withdrawal of sanctions after victory in
Ethiopia seemed to demonstrate the League's impotence when faced with
a *fait accompli* and its virtual loss of interest in the matter. Moral condemnation then, appeared to lose momentum as the issue slipped into
the background, and its actual effect had been the opposite of what was
intended. When not followed up by more effective measures it aided the
transgressor.

One authority concludes that sanctions, to be effective, "must be directed against psychological rather than jural entities. . . . In the Ethiopian
case sanctions should have been directed against Mussolini and his
supporters in Italy and not against the Italian state as such."[22] The suggestion might be more pertinent today than it was then, and the experi-
ences of the war crimes trials would lend weight to the argument.

While the League was in the midst of deliberations on the Italo-

Ethiopian conflict, Germany announced on March 7, 1936, that she no longer considered herself bound by the terms of the Locarno agreements and reoccupied the Rhineland. Alleging that French negotiation of an alliance with Russia had nullified the Treaty of Mutual Guarantee, Hitler's move caught the other European statesmen by surprise at a time when their attention was directed toward Africa. France, as the nation most directly concerned, considered military action but desisted because of the expense of mobilization, the tense situation with Italy, and a general reluctance to risk war. The British government urged negotiations, aware of public sentiment in favor of a revision of the Versailles treaty, the peaceful temper of the people which Hitler catered to by offering a series of "peace" pacts, and the possibility of hostilities with Italy. The French government then did not ask for support from the other Locarno signatories or treat the case as a "flagrant breach" of the treaty. Instead, France brought the question before the council as provided for in Article 6, section 1, of the Locarno Rhineland Pact. France urged that sanctions be imposed on Germany but on March 12 Great Britain and Italy refused to support this step. The council met in London on March 14 and Germany sent a representative (von Ribbentrop) by invitation. Finally, on March 19, the council (with Chile abstaining) voted to censure Germany for violating Article 43 of the Versailles treaty and Article 1 of the Locarno pact. Subsequent discussions were unavailing, for Germany adopted a rigid attitude from which she would not budge. Hitler's bold stroke had succeeded.

Though many factors were responsible for the failure to check this flagrant violation of two obligations, some are more significant than others. Outstanding was the element of surprise, for unlike the action of Italy in Ethiopia there was no advance warning that the operation was going to take place. The Locarno signatories were completely unprepared to counter such an act, and although German military strength was only a fraction of that of France alone, no plans had been prepared to deal with violations of the Locarno agreement. Moreover, Hitler's timing was perfect, for he took advantage of the chaotic international and domestic situations. Great Britain and France were deeply involved in the Ethiopian affair and concerned over Japanese activities in the Far East. Political developments on both home fronts diverted the attention of the statesmen and weakened the unity of the governments. The Soviet Union, which adopted the most intransigent position against the remilitarization of the Rhineland, was suspect, and both France and Britain wanted her to contain Germany in the East but remain out of Western European affairs. Though Hitler at that time had no allies, the possibility of hostilities with Italy over the imposition of sanctions threatened to involve France and

Britain in a war against both nations. While the League Covenant and the treaties of Locarno and Versailles provided the juridical authority for coercive measures, the circumstances were such that negotiations seemed preferable to force.

No doubt France should have taken the lead in instituting drastic measures to remove the German troops, and one writer accuses the French statesmen of "cowardice."[23] Perhaps bold, aggressive leadership was lacking, leadership that might have been able to exploit the "lag" in public opinion which often occurs in the face of an unexpected development. Yet effective decisions are less likely when made under the stress of unforeseen contingencies. Germany had begun a unilateral revision of her unpalatable treaties at an earlier date, and the other nations should have been prepared for further such eventualities. The signatory powers had the military means and the desire to compel an observance of the treaties, and it is not completely accurate to accuse them of lacking the will to resist the German action. The missing ingredient was the procedure, and proper advance planning would have provided for prompt action and prepared the people for an acceptance of the necessary measures.

Though not strictly within the framework of a study of sanctions under the League of Nations, the Spanish Civil War which erupted on July 17, 1936, played a significant role in the breakdown of collective security. An early effort to insulate the conflict was made by the French premier, Leon Blum, on August 1, and by the end of the month the major European nations had signed a nonintervention pledge. France, Great Britain, Germany, Belgium, and Portugal had placed an embargo on arms to Spain, and on September 9 a nonintervention committee was established in London. When it became evident that all nations were not complying with the agreement, Spain appealed to the League, and on December 12, 1936, the council passed a resolution declaring that "every State is under an obligation to refrain from intervening in the internal affairs of another state." Yet violations of the League resolution and the nonintervention agreement were legion, initially on the part of Germany and Italy and later by Russia. The nonintervention committee was able to investigate and protest, but no provision had been made for any coercive measures to compel compliance with the pact.

During the conflict many other issues arose that concerned the relations among nations as well as the course of hostilities within Spain. During the Spanish Civil War, which lasted from 1936 to 1939,

> the League was called upon for eight purposes: (1) To be a medium for the circulation of documents and the broadcasting of grievances; (2) To consider and to condemn foreign intervention in the internal affairs of

member states; (3) To facilitate agreement upon the right of asylum in embassies and legations, and the right of removing persons given such asylum to places of safety out of the country disturbed; (4) To condemn war practices not in accord with international law or humanitarian rights; (5) To procure security for merchant shipping in the Mediterranean; (6) To prevent a rupture of international peace; (7) To oversee and report upon the withdrawal of foreigners from Loyalist Spain; (8) To report on aerial bombardment of open towns and cities, and of civilian population.[24]

In no case were sanctions contemplated, though they could have been invoked under Article 16 against acts of piracy or possibly aggression. An attempt to introduce coercive methods probably would have resulted in a flaunting of League authority and further weakening of the covenant.

In sum, the League did make a number of contributions and its activities may well have helped to prevent the conflict from spreading to other nations. Hampering further League involvement was the fact that the covenant had not been designed to cope with a domestic conflagration, especially one in which other nations participated unofficially. But in regard to collective action, "More clearly than ever, the League revealed its utter dependence upon the states composing it, and its inseparability from the policies and motives of state action."[25] England and France were concerned primarily with isolating the struggle and their policy of strict nonintervention was followed by the United States, which enacted special neutrality legislation to deny arms to both sides in conformance with the embargo instituted by European powers. In urging the passage of the Spanish Embargo Act "it was not the isolationists but Roosevelt, Hull, and the State Department who led the way."[26] The "neutrality" of the Spanish civil strife as practiced by the "democracies" was a desperate attempt to avoid involvement and it required a departure from traditional international law. The "neutrality" of Germany, Italy, and later Russia was intervention in support of political and ideological objectives.

Attention was abruptly focused on the Far East when, on July 7, 1937, fighting broke out between Chinese and Japanese troops in Lukouchiao. After fruitless negotiations, Japan invaded China, which on September 12, 1937, appealed to the League under Articles 10, 11, and 17 of the covenant. The appeal was referred by the council to the Far Eastern Committee of the assembly, which later reported that Japan had violated the Kellogg-Briand Pact and the Nine Power Treaty. This finding, which may have been encouraged by President Roosevelt's "Quarantine" speech of October 5, 1937, recommended consultation among the parties to the treaty. The assembly approved the report and advised League members to refrain from action that would hinder China's ability to resist Japan. In September 1938 China again appealed to the League, and when Japan refused temporary membership under Article 17 the council "authorized and urged" the application of individual sanctions against Japan. A similar resolution was passed by the council on May 27, 1939.

In response to a League suggestion, Belgium called a meeting of the signatories to the Nine Power Treaty and other interested parties. The Conference of Brussels met in November 1937 with representatives of eighteen nations in attendance, although Japan and Russia did not participate. While many governments hoped that Roosevelt would provide leadership in devising means to stop Japan, the president declined to consider methods other than negotiation and conciliation, and the initiative was not taken by any other nation. The use of sanctions was not discussed, and the meeting ended with a reaffirmation of the principles of the Nine Power Treaty that Japan insisted had become obsolete in light of changing conditions. The conference failed to reach any agreement on what should be done to save China, and if Roosevelt looked on the meeting as a means of bringing "all possible moral pressure" to bear on Japan it was a dismal failure.[27] The conference demonstrated that collective action to thwart aggression was no more successful outside the League than it was in, even with the cooperation of the United States, whose unwillingness to go beyond words was revealed.

The final dispute to come before the League was brought by Finland which, on December 3, 1939, appealed under Articles 11 and 15 for measures to halt Soviet aggression. A report by a special committee found that Russia had violated pacts with Finland, Article 12 of the covenant, and the Kellogg-Briand treaty. When the council met it decided that Russia was no longer a member of the League in accordance with Article 16, section 4. The League had made its last gesture as an organization for collective security.

Various explanations have been offered for the breakdown of this elaborate organization as an instrument of peace, and one writer has asserted that "Statesmen and peoples alike tried to place the responsibility for the catastrophe on the system rather than on their own failure to use it."[28] Of perhaps greater significance is why it was not used, a question which this account has tried to answer.

## NOTES

1. Quincy Wright, *A Study of War* (Chicago, 1942), vol. 2, p. 1431. For a list of the disputes see p. 1430. Shotwell and Salvin enumerate forty-four "Security Disputes before the Council." James T. Shotwell and M. Salvin, *Lessons on Security and Disarmament from the History of the League of Nations* (New York, 1949), pp. 45–80. See also Hans Aufricht, *Guide to League of Nations Publications* (New York, 1951). Detailed information on the disputes will be found in the League of Nations *Official*

*Journal* and the annual volumes of Arnold J. Toynbee, ed., *Survey of International Affairs* (London, 1924–).

2. F. P. Walters, *A History of the League of Nations*, 2 vols., (London, 1952), vol. 1, p. 161.

3. H. Lauterpacht's sixth edition of Oppenheim, *International Law*, vol. 2, p. 127, quoted in Charles Cheney Hyde, *International Law Chiefly as Interpreted by the United States* (Boston, 1951), vol. 2, p. 1667. See also Quincy Wright, "Opinion of the Commission of Jurists in the Janina-Corfu Affair," *American Journal of International Law* 18(1924):536–544; James Barros, *The Corfu Incident of 1923: Mussolini and the League of Nations* (Princeton, 1965).

4. Ray Stannard Baker and William E. Dodd, ed., *Public Papers of Woodrow Wilson* (New York, 1925–1927), vol. 2, p. 541.

5. Walters, *The League of Nations*, vol. 1, p. 313. Concerning the Greco-Bulgar dispute, one authority has observed that "Greece was a small power, the great powers had for once been united, and there were no political complications; the Council had acted much as the Concert had sometimes acted in the nineteenth century, Greece had been overawed and had submitted. Circumstances such as these were not destined to recur in the later history of the League." J. L. Brierly, "The League of Nations," in David Thomson, ed., *The Era of Violence, 1898–1945* (Cambridge, 1960), p. 486.

6. See Georges V. Sarailieff, *Le conflit gréco-bulgare d'octobre 1925 et son règlement par le Societé des Nations* (Amsterdam, 1927).

7. Henry L. Stimson, *The Far Eastern Crisis* (New York, 1936), p. 34.

8. *Papers Relating to the Foreign Relations of the United States, Japan, 1931–1941* (Washington, 1943), vol. 1, p. 76.

9. Ernest Ralph Perkins, "The Nonapplication of Sanctions Against Japan, 1931–1932," in Dwight E. Lee and George E. McReynolds, eds., *Essays in History and International Relations in Honor of George Hubbard Blakeslee* (Worcester, Mass., 1949), p. 224. In an effort to intimidate Japan, the American fleet maneuvers in the Pacific were extended and the Scouting Force was moved to the west coast. See Charles F. Adams to Admiral Montgomery Meigs Taylor, Washington, May 20, 1932, Taylor Papers, Manuscript Division, Library of Congress; Admiral William D. Leahy, manuscript diary, Manuscript Division, Library of Congress, vol. 2, p. 18, February 29, 1932.

10. See Perkins, "The Nonapplication of Sanctions," pp. 224–225; Richard N. Current, "The Stimson Doctrine and the Hoover Doctrine," *The American Historical Review* 59(1954):513–542. For a good brief account of American policy during the Manchurian crisis, see Robert H. Ferrell, *American Diplomacy in the Great Depression: Hoover-Stimson Foreign Policy, 1929–1933* (New Haven, 1957), pp. 106–158.

11. Walters, *The League of Nations*, p. 499.

12. Stimson, *The Far Eastern Crisis*, p. 56. Regarding economic sanctions under Article 16, a writer in 1932 concluded: "This penalty has never been invoked and it appears likely that it will never be invoked. The reasons for this are two-fold: first, neither the United States nor Russia is a member of the League, and the resources of these two nations are so vast and so varied, that no effective economic boycott could be administered in which they did not participate." John Foster Dulles, "Practicable Sanctions," in Evans Clark, ed., *Boycotts and Peace: A Report by the Committee on Economic Sanctions* (New York, 1932), p. 18.

13. See Royal Institute of International Affairs, *International Sanctions* (London, 1938), p. 127.

14. For additional information on the Manchurian Incident, see Shotwell and Salvin, *Lessons on Security and Disarmament*, pp. 81–91; Sara R. Smith, *The Manchurian Crisis, 1931–1932: A Tragedy in International Relations* (New York, 1938); Westel W. Willoughby, *The Sino-Japanese Controversy and the League of Nations* (Baltimore, 1935); Reginald Bassett, *Democracy and Foreign Policy, A Case History: The Sino-Japanese Dispute, 1931–1933* (New York, 1952); Robert Langer, *Seizure of Territory: The Stimson*

*Doctrine and Related Principles in Legal Theory and Diplomatic Practice* (Princeton, 1947).

15. When Congress approved by joint resolution an embargo on arms to Bolivia and Paraguay in the Chaco War, "It was significant that Congress had given us authority to join in a League action without precedent, for this was the first time the League had ever imposed an embargo against both belligerent nations." *The Memoirs of Cordell Hull* (New York, 1948), vol. 1, p. 346.

16. Royal Institute of International Affairs, *International Sanctions*, p. 30.

17. Ibid., pp. 24–37, for a thoughtful analysis of the arms embargo as a sanction. For the American role, see Elton Atwater, *American Regulation of Arms Exports* (Washington, 1941), pp. 193–202. For the failure of the Paraguayan sanctions, see Kain, "The Chaco Dispute and the Peace System," *Political Science Quarterly* 50(1935):321–335.

18. Ronald B. McCallum, *Public Opinion and the Last Peace* (London, 1944), p. 22.

19. See Henderson B. Braddick, "A New Look at American Policy During the Italo-Ethiopian Crisis, 1935–1936," *Journal of Modern History* 34(1962):64–73, for a recent summation.

20. For the contention that an early oil embargo would have brought Italy to bay, see Royal Institute of International Affairs, *International Sanctions*, p. 108; and Anthony Eden, (Earl of Avon), *Facing the Dictators* (Boston, 1962), pp. 326, 333–334, 365–366.

21. Walters, *The League of Nations*, p. 780.

22. Wright, *A Study of War*, vol. 2, p. 944.

23. Donovan P. Yeuell, Jr., "The German Occupation of the Rhineland," U.S. Naval Institute *Proceedings* 81(1955):1211.

24. Norman J. Padelford. *International Law and Diplomacy in the Spanish Civil War* (New York, 1939), p. 140.

25. Ibid., p. 143.

26. James Ragland, "Franklin D. Roosevelt and the Spanish Civil War," *Year Book of the American Philosophical Society* (1960), p. 421. For additional information see Hugh Thomas, *The Spanish Civil War* (New York, 1961); Dante A. Puzzo, *Spain and the Great Powers, 1936–1941* (New York, 1962); Jay F. Taylor, *The United States and the Spanish Civil War* (New York, 1956).

27. The administration version of the Brussels Conference is found in *The Memoirs of Cordell Hull*, vol. 1, pp. 550–556.

28. Sir Charles Webster, "Sanctions: The Use of Force in an International Organization," in *The Art and Practice of Diplomacy* (New York, 1962), p. 99.

# CHAPTER SIX

# Attempts to Modify or Implement the Sanctioning Provisions of the League Covenant

ONE AUTHORITY HAS CONCLUDED THAT "THE WHOLE HISTORY OF THE League of Nations is a record of attempts to transform it to suit the particular interests of some of its members."[1] Those nations fearing attack, such as France, felt that sanctions were not strong enough and their application was not sufficiently explicit. Those nations confident of avoiding aggression and afraid of being drawn into a conflict to protect another's interests, thought that sanctioning provisions were too extreme. The issue was magnified by the failure of the United States to accept the covenant, which was a severe blow to those who had expected the League to provide security. Psychologically, the defection of the United States lessened the prestige of the new organization and what could be termed its moral force. Moreover, it immediately weakened the sanctioning process, for without American cooperation a boycott would stand little chance of success and a blockade might well be ignored or defied by the American fleet. The fear of being drawn into a punitive action prompted assembly adoption of an amendment in 1921, which, though never ratified, would allow each nation to determine whether it should apply sanctions.

Further complicating the search for security was the question of disarmament. Explicit in the covenant was the belief that armament races helped produce wars, and Article 8 asserted that "The members of the League recognize that the maintenance of peace requires the reduction of national armaments to the lowest point consistent with national safety and enforcement by common action of international obligations." At its first meeting the council established a permanent Military, Naval, and Air Commission as provided by Article 9 to, among other things, advise the council on disarmament matters. The question that early arose in the minds of statesmen concerned the relationship between a reduction or limitation of armaments and the imperatives of national security. Following the Washington naval conference, in September 1922 the third assembly of the League produced "Resolution 14," in which the interdependence of these two problems was recognized. Nations consenting to a reduction of armaments were to be permitted to join in a "defensive agreement which should be open to all countries, binding them to provide immediate and effective assistance in accordance with a pre-arranged plan in the event of one of them being attacked. . . ."[2] The following year the Temporary Mixed Commission brought forth a Draft Treaty of Mutual Assistance designed to implement Resolution 14, in which the reduction of armaments was coupled with guarantees, the process to be accomplished in stages. Though the question of whether security or disarmament should come first was "by-passed . . . in a truly ingenious fashion,"[3] the treaty foundered over objections from members and nonmembers to whom it had been submitted for comment. Opposition stressed the failure to define aggression, "the long delay which is liable to occur before the forces at the disposal of the League of Nations can be brought into effective operation against an aggressor state,"[4] the considerable powers vested in the council, the Russian reply that denied any relationship between disarmament and security, and the assertion by the United States that it could have nothing to do with a treaty associated with the League Covenant.[5]

But out of the controversy over the Draft Treaty there emerged from the League assembly of 1924 the Geneva Protocol for the Pacific Settlement of International Disputes. So called because it was designed to clarify and strengthen the covenant, the Protocol combined the elements of arbitration, security, and disarmament. It plugged the "hole in the covenant" contained in Article 15, section 17, by denying that a state had the right to wage war under any pretext, and an aggressor was defined simply, in effect, as a nation which refused to accept arbitration. Members were pledged to cooperate in any action against a state that resorted to war in defiance of the council or the assembly, and a general disarmament conference was called for 1925. Though the Protocol was unanimously recommended to the governments of member states on October 2, 1924, and enjoyed widespread support in continental Europe and among League members, the agreement was finally rejected by Great Britain. The defeat of the Protocol has often been attributed to the fact that the British Labour government, which was instrumental in formulating its terms, was succeeded by a Conservative government hostile to the concept of further commitments for collective security. Actually, it appears that even the Labour government probably would have rejected the treaty on the grounds that it was too drastic a departure from traditional British policy, that the dominions protested strenuously, and that the United States objected because the proposal seemed to represent "an unfriendly European Concert."[6] Thus what has been called the "highwater mark of the history of the League of Nations as an organization for the maintenance of enduring peace" was defeated in part, at least, by the failure of the United States to join the League. Great Britain was not willing to challenge her Atlantic neighbor over the question of neutral rights, and she was not inclined to risk American displeasure by an ironclad association with international guarantees.

The immediate reaction to the failure of the Geneva Protocol was the conclusion of the Locarno pact in 1925, which provided for territorial assurances and guarantees outside the framework of the League. But the Preparatory Commission for the Disarmament Conference, established by the council in 1924, struggled to resolve the perplexing problem of security which clouded negotiations for the reduction of armaments. Two treaties emerged, the General Act of 1928 and the Draft Treaty to Develop the Means for Preventing War in 1931. The League assembly in 1927 had directed the Preparatory Commission to appoint a subcommittee on arbitration and security under a directive to formulate measures which would provide states with the security necessary to obtain their consent to armament reduction. The British government refused to accept the principle of compulsory arbitration, declaring that "Arbitration duties have no sanction behind them but the force of public opinion in the world at large. Any attempt to provide sanctions of force would involve a burden which no state could accept unless it felt that its vital interests were involved in a particular dispute."[7] Instead, conciliation and regional agreements such as that of Locarno were urged. The Committee on Arbitration and Security found itself divided into two groups: one, led by France, thought that the principles embodied in the abortive Geneva Protocol should be followed; the other group, composed mainly of Great Britain, Italy, and Japan, opposed such a firm and universal approach.

Finally, out of ten draft treaties submitted by the committee, the assembly prepared the General Act for the Pacific Settlement of Disputes. This "final word of the League of Nations in the erection of a correlative system of safeguards of peace alongside the Covenant itself,"[8] was a significant retreat from the provisions of the Geneva Protocol. War was not "outlawed," methods were suggested for the settlement of disputes between nations outside the framework of the League, and ways of avoiding obligations under the covenant were specified. This weakening of the covenant was approved unanimously by the assembly in September 1928, and by 1937 it had been ratified by twenty-three nations. Interestingly enough, the act was adopted by the assembly the month following the signing of the Kellogg-Briand Pact in Paris.[9]

The French bloc, however, which advocated more specific forms of League action in the event of a violation of the covenant or a decision of the council, persisted in its efforts to avoid ambiguities. The British contended that a precise enumeration of powers would weaken the League rather than strengthen it, and on January 23, 1930, the council appointed a committee to reconcile these opposing points of view. There finally emerged the Convention to Improve the Means of Preventing War, which was adopted by the twelfth assembly in September 1931 and offered to nations for ratification. The council, in Articles 2 and 3, was authorized to impose limitations on troop movements and even order the evacuation of troops under certain circumstances. Under Article 5,

> If any violation of the measures defined in Articles 2 and 3 is noted by the Council and continues in spite of its injunctions, the Council shall consider what means of all kinds are necessary to ensure the execution of the present Convention. Should war break out as a consequence of this violation, such violation shall be regarded by the High Contracting Parties as prima facie evidence that the party guilty thereof has resorted to war within the meaning of Article 16 of the Covenant.

And under Article 7 the council's decisions became binding even if an opposing vote was cast by parties to the dispute, thus settling the controversy over the unanimity rule in regard to Article 11 of the covenant. In spite of this tightening of League measures against aggression, France was not satisfied, for she wanted more rigid provisions for the institution of sanctions. Even this compromise accepted by the assembly never took effect, for at this point in time the Mukden incident of 1931 occurred and eventually only about half of the League members ratified the convention. Japan, who had abstained from the assembly vote on the measure, had been, as noted above, in favor of regional pacts for security. If the convention had been in effect Japan would have been unable to veto the council recommendation for the withdrawal of her troops.[10]

The discussion of League reform continued, but "during the years that followed [1931], none among the chief Members of the League were ready to contemplate increasing the powers of a Council whose authority was determined by their own weakness and disunion."[11] A less severe but more perceptive assessment was made at the International Studies Conference on collective security in 1935, where speakers mentioned the paradox of the League system which forbade "nations to resort to war for the defense of their own interests, that is, for the causes which affect them the most deeply, and to make it, on the contrary, their duty to throw themselves into the struggle to ensure the respect of abstract rules which have no roots in their sentiments, their beliefs, or their passions."[12] In 1937, with the League composed of fifty-three members, seventeen thought that sanctions were important and fourteen thought that regional security pacts were desirable.[13] By this time the pendulum had swung completely from the commitments of 1919, and it could be truly said that " 'the League' itself was little more than a name serving to describe the members collectively."[14] It had ceased to be effective as an instrument for security and it was virtually ignored as the world moved toward war. The League's next contribution to peace was in providing experience for those who were to construct the succeeding international organization.

## NOTES

1. Sir Charles Webster, "Sanctions: The Use of Force in an International Organization," in *The Art and Practice of Diplomacy* (New York, 1962), p. 92. According to Anthony Eden, "The terms of the Covenant were variously interpreted, by France and her European allies as upholding the territorial gains of the peace treaties, by Germany and Hungary as affording an opportunity for revision." Anthony Eden, *Facing the Dictators* (Boston, 1962), p. 9.

2. The text of the resolution is printed in James T. Shotwell and Marina Salvin, *Lessons on Security and Disarmament from the History of the League of Nations* (New York, 1949), pp. 111–112.

3. Andrew Martin, *Collective Security: A Progress Report* (Paris, 1952), p. 37.

4. Note of British government, 1924, quoted in Royal Institute of International Affairs, *International Sanctions* (London, 1938), p. 116.

5. Ibid., pp. 116–118; F. P. Walters, *A History of the League of Nations* 2 vols. (London, 1952), vol. 1, pp. 223–227; Shotwell and Salvin, *Lessons on Security and Disarmament*, pp. 20–23.

6. See Henry R. Winkler, "Arthur Henderson," in Gordon A. Craig and Felix Gilbert, ed., *The Diplomats, 1919–1939* (Princeton, 1953), p. 317; Richard W. Lyman, *The First Labour Government, 1924* (London, 1957), pp. 176–177; William R. Tucker, *The Attitude of the British Labour Party towards European and Collective Security Problems, 1920–1939* (Geneva, 1950); David D. Burks, "The United States and the Geneva Protocol of 1924: 'A New Holy Alliance?' " *American Historical Review* 54(1959):891–905.

7. Quoted in Shotwell and Salvin, *Lessons on Security and Disarmament*, p. 34.

8. Ibid., p. 38. At this time one writer observed that "The course the League has taken in its first eight years is more important than the terms of the Covenant." Charles P. Howland, *Survey of American Foreign Relations, 1928* (New Haven, 1928), p. 315.

9. For the background and formulation of the General Act, see Arnold J. Toynbee, *Survey of International Affairs, 1928* (London, 1929), part 1A, sec. 3; Shotwell and Salvin, *Lessons on Security and Disarmament*, pp. 31–39. The text is printed on pp. 125–138.

10. For an account of the origins of the General Convention, see Arnold J. Toynbee, *Survey of International Affairs, 1931* (London, 1932), pp. 254–259; Shotwell and Salvin, *Lessons on Security and Disarmament*, pp. 40–41. The text is printed on pp. 139–149.

11. Walters, *A History of the League of Nations*, vol. 2, p. 381.

12. "Final Report," *Collective Security*, International Studies Conference, p. 444, quoted in Edwin Borchard and William P. Lage, *Neutrality for the United States* (New Haven, 1937), p. 255.

13. For a table of "Opinions of Governments with Respect to Forms of International Organization, 1937," see Wright, *A Study of War*, vol. 2, p. 1446. Much of Wright's information came from S. Engel, "League Reform: An Analysis of Official Proposals and Discussions, 1936–1939," *Geneva Studies*, vol. 11, nos. 3–4 (August, 1940).

14. J. L. Brierly, "The League of Nations," in David Thomson, ed., *The Era of Violence, 1898–1945* (Cambridge, 1960), p. 476.

# CHAPTER SEVEN

# Agreements Embodying Sanctions Outside the League Covenant: Violations and Responses

THE TREATY OF VERSAILLES CONTAINED PROVISION FOR THE IMPOSITION OF sanctions outside the framework of the League Covenant. A new type of judicial sanctions was included in Article 227, which arraigned the former German emperor "for a supreme offense against international morality." Germans accused of atrocities were to be turned over to the Allied and associated powers for trial under Article 228. Neither of these efforts was successful, for the Netherlands government refused to release William II to the authorities and the other war criminals were tried by German courts. But the precedent was not ignored at the end of World War II.

A provision for sanctions was included under Article 414, which authorized the governing body of the International Labor Organization to "recommend" measures of "an economic nature" if a nation violated a Labor convention made under the auspices of the International Labor Conference. "This" as one report put it, "is an interesting instance of the institution by a treaty of a possible sanction to secure fulfillment of an international obligation of a peaceful character."[1]

More important for subsequent developments in Europe were the sanctioning provisions in connection with reparations payments contained in sections 17 and 18 of annex 2 of part 8 of the Versailles treaty, which were:

> In case of default by Germany in the performance of any obligation under this part of the present Treaty, the Commission will forthwith give notice of such default to each of the interested Powers and may make such recommendation as to the action to be taken in consequence of such default as it may think necessary.

The measures which the Allied and Associated Powers shall have the right to take, in case of voluntary default by Germany, and which Germany agrees not to regard as acts of war, may include economic and financial prohibitions and reprisals and, in general, such other measures as the respective governments may determine to be necessary in the circumstances.

The interpretation of these clauses by the various governments and the manner in which they were carried out will be discussed later.

Closely associated with the peace negotiations and of interest to the student of collective security are the treaties that France concluded with Great Britain and the United States at Versailles. During the deliberations France, dissatisfied with the security provisions of the covenant and anxious to guard against a Germany that had twice invaded her territory in less than fifty years, insisted on separating the Rhineland and creating an autonomous republic. Wilson, protesting that this would violate his stated principle of self-determination of peoples, effected a compromise. In exchange for French consent to a demilitarized Rhineland with Allied occupation, the United States and Great Britain signed alliances with France which provided for military assistance in the event of an attack by Germany. When this Treaty of Guarantee was not ratified by the United States, Great Britain, under the terms of the treaty, was released from the agreement. France, then, lost both the plea for an autonomous Rhine republic and the guarantee against agression and was thrown back on the covenant for security. France's search for firmer support against a resurgent Germany dominated French foreign policy throughout the inter-war period.[2]

Allied dissatisfaction with German reparation payments led to the use of sanctions on several occasions, but the most significant attempt at coercion occurred in 1923.[3] The French government had been concerned about the delivery of raw materials as reparations payments, much of which came from the rich Ruhr valley. In December 1922 and January 1923 the Reparations Commission voted, with British dissent, that Germany was in default on timber and coal deliveries. France and Belgium then prepared to send a mission into the Ruhr with military support to administer the production and delivery of materials. The German government promptly took steps to defeat this action, including the discontinuance of reparations payments, strikes, uncontrolled inflation, and other forms of passive resistance. Sporadic fighting took place and economic chaos accompanied the occupation. Finally, a new German government under Gustav Stresemann abandoned the policy of resistance and a settlement was reached in cooperation with a special committee under the chairmanship of Charles G. Dawes.

A number of conclusions may be drawn from this particular experience. It was probably unwise to institute such drastic action in view of the lack of unanimity in the Reparations Commission. British displeasure was evident, and "His Majesty's Government had never concealed their view that the Franco-Belgian action in occupying the Ruhr, quite apart from the question of expediency, was not a sanction authorized by the Treaty [of Versailles] itself."[4] Lacking support from one of the two most powerful enforcers of the treaty, the occupation lost much of its moral strength and Germany was given further encouragement for resistance. This breach of Allied unity marked a decay in Franco-British relations, and in England the occupation "seemed to many an example of the unreasonable rigidity of the victor toward the fallen foe and created a certain sentiment against France."[5] Moreover, the incident set back German economic recovery which in turn adversely affected the entire economy of Western Europe. In this instance it appears that the cure was worse than the disease and not only because of the economic repercussions. The conflict in British and French policies over the treatment of Germany was accentuated with its implications for European security, and anti-French sentiment in Germany reached a new high.

On the credit side of the ledger the occupation was a success in that it finally induced the German government to cease resistance, and it led to a more equitable system of reparations payments under the Dawes Plan. The incident may have been of some psychological benefit to the French, for it demonstrated their ability to coerce their former enemy. On reflection, however, the episode reveals the danger of applying sanctions in the face of a divided front and the necessity for carefully weighing in advance the disadvantages as well as the advantages of a particular course of action.[6]

Dissatisfaction with the security provisions of the League Covenant prompted attempts at revision or clarification, on the one hand, by those nations that wanted firmer commitments for collective action, and on the other hand, by those nations that wished to weaken the security stipulations. The "collective security" group prevailed in 1924 with the Geneva Protocol, but this effort was subsequently defeated by Great Britain. Soon after this frustration, however, and after only two weeks of negotiation, there emerged the Treaty of Mutual Guarantee, signed at Locarno on October 16, 1925. Though the impetus for the pact came from Germany, there is little question that support was forthcoming from other signatories because of the failure at Geneva to provide more adequate security measures. This treaty is of particular significance because (1) it is the most notable of inter-war efforts to provide for collective security outside the framework of the League; (2) it furnishes insight into the motives and aspirations of the various nations; and (3) its subsequent violation by Germany marked the collapse of collective efforts to maintain the status quo and the peace of Europe.

By the terms of the Locarno pact, Germany, Belgium, and France agreed to respect and maintain their respective frontiers and the demilitarized zone as established by the Treaty of Versailles. The three nations renounced war against each other except for defense or in support of League action, and they agreed to conciliation and arbitration procedures. Great Britain and Italy acted as guarantors, pledging military assistance in the event of a flagrant violation of the treaty. One contemporary assessor of the pact called it "the first successful step taken to solve the tremendous problems of European security, after five years of failure."[7] More recently, a historian observed that "The Locarno agreements, signed at the end of 1925, represent the highwater mark of the movement for collective guarantees in the period between the wars."[8] The architects of the pact— Briand, Austen Chamberlain, and Stresemann—were jointly awarded the Nobel Peace Prize for their efforts, and the "spirit of Locarno" caught the public imagination and augured a new era in international affairs.

An observer might ask why Great Britain, which had so recently rejected the entanglements of the Geneva Protocol, suddenly reversed its course and accepted a firm military commitment. There are probably two major reasons for what at first glance seems to be an inconsistency. The Protocol was rejected because the commitment was too broad, i.e., it pledged British assistance under circumstances that could not be foreseen and in support of principles which might not be in the interest of Britain to defend. Secondly, much of the sanctioning activity that could occur under the general terms of the Protocol would involve a conflict with the United States over the trading rights of neutrals, and Great Britain as the major League sea power would have the responsibility of implementing any blockade imposed.

The Locarno pact overcame both of these objections. Great Britain was assuming an obligation to defend a specific agreement, an agreement which it was greatly to her interest to maintain. Moreover, since in all likelihood any violation of the pact would be made by Germany, the use of sanctions would probably not lead to a clash with the United States. In this regard, it is worth noting that while dominion objections helped defeat the Geneva Protocol, the British government approved the Locarno pact without consulting the dominions.

It should also be noted that the Treaty of Mutual Assistance was not merely a military alliance along traditional lines. In its provision for conciliation, arbitration, and League affiliation, it combined the more recent devices for solving disputes without recourse to war. The provision for sanctions, to be imposed under League authority except in the case of a flagrant violation of the treaty, was certainly consistent with the concept of collective security as embodied in the covenant. In effect, the Locarno agreement represented the Geneva Protocol on a smaller scale, directed to a specific problem and embracing parties whose interests were intimately involved. Understandably, this type of regional pact appealed to those who rejected the sweeping generalizations of the covenant but sought to reconcile the imperatives of national interest with the movement for collective security.

An assessment of the pact in its various ramifications is beyond the scope of this study, and its breakdown in 1936 when challenged by Germany will be treated later, but certain observations are pertinent. Some opponents of war regarded the pact as a backward step because, in case of a flagrant attack, military sanctions could be imposed without reference to the League council.[9] Then, too, there was some question as to where the real advantages of the pact lay. France received the military guarantees she had sought since Versailles, and Germany voluntarily accepted the western borders accorded her by the victorious allies. In many respects Germany benefited most from the pact. Her acceptance as an equal in the negotiation and conclusion of the treaty meant an escape from her "conquered nation" status. The western orientation of the pact left Germany free to extend her influence eastward, and a wedge had been driven between those traditional allies for the containment of Germany, namely, France and Russia. The signing of the Russo-German treaty at Berlin on April 24, 1926, revealed the tactics of Stresemann as he sought to restore his nation's position in Europe. It is clear that Briand regarded the pact as a device for maintaining the status quo, whereas Stresemann saw it as a step toward revision of the Versailles settlement. Perhaps most dangerous was the impression which emerged that Locarno represented the answer to the question of how peace could be maintained. The "Locarno spirit" was out of all proportion to the true significance of the agreement, and it proved to be an illusion that created a false sense of security.[10]

In many respects the high-water mark of the tide for peace was reached in the Treaty for the Renunciation of War, signed August 27, 1928, and proclaimed in effect July 24, 1929. Known variously as the Pact of Paris, the Kellogg-Briand Pact, and the Briand-Kellogg Treaty, this agreement pledged the signatories to refrain from using war "as an instrument of national policy" and to settle disputes "by pacific means."[11] The idea for the outlawing of war had its origins among interested private citizens, especially those engaged in the widespread peace movement in the United States. It was given world prominence in April 6, 1927, when the French foreign minister, Aristide Briand, addressed a message to the American people to "outlaw war." Though the administration was cool to the proposal, partly due to an aversion to "alliances" and partly in resentment to Briand's appeal outside official channels, pressure in favor of such a treaty built up among the public, organized peace groups, distinguished citizens, and members of Congress. Senator William E. Borah played a prominent role in promoting an agreement, and he overcame some of the objections by proposing that the treaty be multilateral rather than bilateral. After considering numerous drafts and consulting the governments of other nations, a simple two paragraph statement was agreed upon and signed initially by fifteen nations. Subsequently, sixty-three nations adhered to the pact.

The brevity and simplicity of the agreement were responsible in large part for its acceptance. Many governments insisted on clear-cut interpretations and reservations before signing, and in many ways the pact was emasculated in terms of the intentions of its initial supporters.[12] Secretary of State Frank B. Kellogg, a late convert to the idea of such a pact, early robbed the instrument of much of its meaning and at the same time reassured governments skeptical of its implications. Speaking on the question of self-defense under the treaty, Kellogg emphasized that "Every nation is free at all times and regardless of treaty provisions to defend its territory from attack or invasion, and it alone is competent to decide whether circumstances require recourse to war in self-defense."[13] The American historian, James T. Shotwell, who as a private citizen was instrumental in promoting the pact, has criticized Kellogg for "keeping his treaty free from any attempt to impose a sanction upon the violator and in refusing to limit the obligation to wars of aggression." Shotwell concluded that "History was to show that the American amendment to M. Briand's proposal made the document both meaningless and futile."[14] There seems little question that an attempt to link the pact to League membership or cooperation in collective action would have rendered it unpalatable to the American public and the Congress. The administration was thoroughly in accord with the feeling that entanglements of this sort should be avoided.[15]

Prominent among many of the questions raised by the pact was that of action to be taken in the event of a violation. When President Hoover proclaimed the pact on July 24, 1929, he envisioned it as a device by which he could "lead the United States in full cooperation with world moral forces to preserve peace."[16] Senator Borah made his position clear in 1929. "If a nation violates the treaty," he asked, "are we under any obligation, express or implied, to apply coercive or punitive measures? I answer emphatically, no!" Undoubtedly, most Americans were in agreement with the senator, otherwise there would not have been so much enthusiasm for the pact. Many persons, however, believed that the treaty rested on more than a mere appeal to world opinion for its enforcement and less than a commitment of its signatories to apply sanctions. As one writer expressed it:

> Through the Kellogg Pact, the United States does not assume the juridical obligation to take part in the sanctions of the League of Nations. It only agrees not to consider sanctions of this kind . . . as a violation of the treaty. But America is *morally* obliged by the Kellogg Pact to treat differently a state belonging to the League of Nations which has violated the law, and states resorting to war of sanction according to the Covenant of the League of Nations. There is no doubt about that.[17]

Presumably, this difference of treatment could extend from denunciatory statements to outright collaboration in coercive measures, for one authority has asserted that "The Pact of Paris permitted its parties to engage in physical sanctions against violators of the Pact."[18] The crucial question, of course, was not what international "experts" thought the pact demanded or authorized in the way of sanctions but what responsible statesmen would do when confronted with a specific violation. This matter will be explored after a consideration of efforts to amend and extend the provisions of the pact.

It was immediately apparent that in certain respects the Kellogg-Briand Treaty was at odds with the League Covenant. The former prohibited war "as an instrument of national policy" and the latter permitted it in certain cases. Nor was the covenant so comprehensive in its exhortation to use peaceful methods for settling disputes. The existence of two separate instruments for maintaining peace was confusing to the public, could present a dilemma for statesmen in the event of violations, and promised diverse approaches to peace that might impede collective action. In the League's tenth assembly, Prime Minister Ramsay MacDonald made a strong plea for a revision of Articles 12 and 15 of the covenant, and three days later, on September 6, 1929, British Foreign Secretary Arthur Henderson introduced a resolution asking that a study of revision be made in light of the Pact of Paris. Though proposals for a modification of the covenant were rejected, the assembly did adopt a General Act for the Pacific Settlement of International Disputes which implemented that portion of the Kellogg pact pertaining to the resolution of disputes "by pacific means." It appeared that changes in the covenant to incorporate the remainder of the pact would result in further commitments under the sanctioning provisions of Article 16, and sentiment among many League members at this time was in the other direction.[19]

Subsequently, the provisions of the Pact of Paris were broadened by the conclusion of regional agreements. As the result of a resolution adopted

at the Sixth Pan American Conference in 1928, a special meeting of representatives from the Latin American republics was held in Washington
from December 10, 1928, to January 5, 1929. Agreement was reached on
a document that denounced aggressive war and provided for conciliation
and arbitration in the event of disputes. In Europe, at the instigation of the
Soviet Union, the "Litvinov Protocol" to the Pact of Paris was signed on
February 9, 1929. Adhering to this agreement were Russia, Estonia, Latvia, Poland, Rumania, Turkey, Persia, Lithuania, and Danzig. This marked
the third attempt by the Soviet Union to conclude some type of security
pact with the Baltic states and achieve an "eastern Locarno."[20]

The most obvious shortcoming of the Kellogg-Briand Treaty was its
failure to provide machinery for its implementation. The efforts of the
United States in the Russo-Chinese dispute in 1929 immediately revealed
this defect, and Hoover's desire to provide a partial remedy by amending
the pact to establish consultative procedures indicated an awareness of the
problem. Yet the president had no intention of departing from his es-
pousal of the moral force of world opinion as a means of insuring compliance with the treaty, and consultation was designed to reach a solution
to the dispute as well as serve to mobilize public opinion. Even so, it was
apparent to many that "such action may be insufficient unless it is followed by economic and financial pressure."[21] Hoover's position against
such additional measures was clearly revealed at the time of the Manchurian Incident in 1931. In this connection there was also the question of
whether action of this type would conflict with the obligations of the
United States under the neutrality provisions of the Hague conventions,
though the same objection could be made in regard to those nations who
adhered to the League Covenant. The conflict between the covenant and
the Kellogg pact was a constant source of friction and jealousy and
promised jurisdictional squabbles that would weaken collective action
against threats to peace. Fundamentally, the general terms of the pact
which made it so acceptable to so many nations were in many respects its
greatest weakness. A unilateral approach to situations was encouraged if
not made mandatory, and the pressure exerted by a divided effort was
bound to be less effective.

The first significant challenge to both the covenant and the Pact of
Paris as devices for peace came with the Manchurian Incident of 1931.
Granted that the issues were far from clear (this episode is treated in
chapter 5), the inadequacies of both these instruments were revealed. Japan
succeeded in her conquest with no more than moral condemnation and
the onus of the doctrine of nonrecognition of the territory acquired through
the use of arms. This "nonrecognition" dictum as announced by the
United States was based on the Pact of Paris, although a justification

could have been found in the Nine Power Treaty of 1922 that guaranteed the territorial integrity of China. When Germany announced on March 16, 1935, that she was rearming in violation of the Versailles treaty, the nations responsible for the treaty's enforcement made no concerted effort to halt this action but relied on unilateral diplomatic protests. The American secretary of state affirmed his nation's belief that "the moral influence of the United States and its people must always encourage living up to treaties," but no agreement to which the United States was a party permitted any other course even if it had been practicable.[22] Germany's remilitarization of the Rhineland on March 7, 1936, was a violation of several treaties and drastic action was possible under both regional and international agreements. Yet again there was an unwillingness to take collective measures, not because the machinery did not exist, but because of a complexity of domestic and foreign factors that served to befuddle the issue and raise sufficient doubts as to the wisdom of a course that threatened war.

Meanwhile, the Far East was demanding further attention. The renewal of the Sino-Japanese conflict in July 1937 provoked Franklin Roosevelt to call for a "quarantine" of aggressor nations in the interest of peace. The domestic reaction to this speech of October 5, 1937, was mixed and it probably convinced the president that the nation was not prepared to participate in collective measures to preserve peace. But on October 6, 1937, the League assembly denounced Japan for violating both the Nine Power Treaty and the Paris Pact, and the State Department declared that the government of the United States was in agreement with the resolution. Encouraged by Roosevelt's speech, the League recommended a meeting of the signatories of the Nine Power Treaty, and in November representatives of eighteen nations gathered at Brussels without Japan. The leadership which many expected from the United States was lacking, and it was evident that the president had not contemplated the adoption of any coercive measures. The American delegation refused to discuss sanctions, and the conference ended with no more than a reaffirmation of the principles of the Nine Power Treaty.

Perhaps none of the interests of the powers were sufficiently great to warrant a risk of war with Japan, and probably the European nations were unwilling to become deeply involved in the Far East at a time when the peace of Europe was being jeopardized by Germany and Italy. The conference, however, demonstrated that effective collective action against an aggressor was improbable without the cooperation of the United States and revealed that such cooperation was not forthcoming. Whether Roosevelt himself would have liked to commit the United States to coercive measures is problematical, but there is little question that he was acutely conscious of American public opinion. There is evidence to indicate that the president had hoped the conference would "educate" the people to the point where they would support a firmer American policy, but apparently the president felt that it had not. The failure of the conference, in fact, further solidified the attitude against stronger commitments.

There is no doubt that the international situation weighed heavily on the president's mind. The failure of the League to halt aggression in Manchuria and Ethiopia, the breakdown of the treaties of Versailles and Locarno, and the resumption of hostilities in China provoked him to cast about for some means of halting the trend. When Japanese planes attacked the U.S. gunboat *Panay* in December 1937, it was apparent that the nation could no longer insulate itself from aggression. Though Japan immediately offered apologies and indemnities, a conference of State Department and military authorites revealed that the armed forces were incapable of waging a successful war against Japan in the Far East. Rearmament, military conversations with Great Britain, and an overture to the British prime minister for cooperation (which was rebuffed) constituted the major American responses to the acceleration of treaty violation. Roosevelt had to contend with a domestic opinion that opposed further involvement in world affairs, and in January of 1938 the Ludlow Amendment to the Constitution, which would require a popular referendum before waging war except in the case of an attack, narrowly escaped a House vote to force it out of the committee. War and the probability of war abroad had driven the American people further away from the concept of collective security and from the direction in which the president wanted them to be headed.

The president's dedication to the peaceful solution of disputes was revealed by his congratulatory telegram to Prime Minister Chamberlain before the Munich conference of 1938, though he probably shared the disillusionment that followed Hitler's occupation of the remainder of Czechoslovakia on March 15, 1939. The president continued to seek a revision of existing neutrality legislation to permit, in effect, the institution of economic sanctions against an aggressor nation, but he could not secure public and congressional support. He could and did impose economic sanctions on Japan, first by refusing to renew the Commercial Treaty of 1911, which expired in January of 1940, and secondly, by placing an embargo on certain strategic materials under a congressional act of July 2, 1940. Additional items were placed on the prohibited list in response to Japanese aggressive moves.

This shift from the moral force of verbal indignation to the more tangible impact of economic coercion was justified "on the theory of permissive sanctions under the Pact of Paris."[23] In August 1940, when Japan demanded and received air bases in Indochina, the United States retaliated the following month by granting a loan to China and placing a complete embargo on iron and steel scrap. When Japan occupied southern Indo-china in July 1941, Roosevelt, on July 26, froze Japanese funds, halted oil exports, and closed the Panama Canal to Japanese shipping. Great Britain, her dominions and the Netherlands East Indies joined the United States by stopping trade with Japan. Japan, faced with the loss of her conquests and her position as a great power, chose the alternative of war.

In retrospect, the policy of economic sanctions failed just as diplomatic sanctions had failed. Japan continued to ignore treaties and the impor-tunities of the United States. By the time joint economic measures were taken, which threatened domestic hardship and a slowing of the military machine, it was too late. The Japanese leaders had gone too far and the nation was too committed to the course of action that had begun in 1931. Retreat at this stage of the game was unthinkable, and the sanctions that had been instituted to end the war in China helped provoke a world con-flagration. Concerted action and proper timing probably would have made them effective.

Meantime, the president also had been occupied with the situation in Europe. As German military successes continued, he moved from a pro-fessed neutrality through various stages of intervention to cobelligerency and outright war. While he maintained that his actions, however far re-moved from neutrality, were designed to protect the nation and keep it out of war, the United States exchanged destroyers for bases, patrolled the Atlantic sea-lanes, enacted Lend-Lease, tracked German submarines, escorted vessels, occupied British and neutral territory, formulated joint war plans and coordinated foreign policy with the enemies of aggression. Though all of these activities may be regarded as cooperative sanctions, it would be difficult to relate them directly to the violation of treaties and a response to such violations. They were, however, methods designed to support efforts of other nations to resist those who had violated treaties and deprive them of the fruits of this violation.  ·

One interesting example from the point of view of international law and the sanctity of treaties is the destroyer-bases agreement with Great Britain, concluded on September 2, 1940. With the fall of France and the Low Countries in the spring of 1940, the buffer states that stood between Hitler and the Atlantic were eliminated, and Great Britain was in desperate straits. Yielding to an appeal from Prime Minister Churchill for some "overaged" destroyers to be used as escort vessels, the president exchanged fifty of these ships for leases on naval and air bases under an executive agreement. The constitutionality of this action was defended by an opinion of the attorney general, but in providing these vessels, the United States violated Article 6 of the Hague convention of 1907, which stated that "The supply, in any manner, directly or indirectly by a neutral Power to a belligerent Power, of war-ships, ammunition, or war material of any kind whatever, is forbidden."[24] It has been contended that the agreement was consistent with American treaty obligations since the United States was not a neutral but a "nonbelligerent" in view of Germany and Italy being "aggressor" nations.[25] Such a conclusion would carry with it the assumption that for signatories of the Pact of Paris there was no neutrality in the event of war, and the further assumption that the pact permitted the use of sanctions against a transgressor. The unilateral interpretation of the pact permitted its use under a variety of circumstances and simplified the vexing question of what constituted an aggressor. It also weakened the effectiveness of the pact by virtually ruling out the opportunity for collective action.

In any event, the United States responded to treaty violations during this period of the 1930s with what might be called a graduated application of sanctions, from diplomatic protest to the use of armed force. The degree or type of sanction was not determined by the severity of the treaty infraction or by the amount of coercion deemed sufficient to accomplish the objective. The graduated response was dictated by what the public, the Congress, and the law permitted and the president's version of the powers of his office. These efforts were uniformly unsuccessful so long as they stopped short of all-out war. They might have been successful if applied at the right time, in concert with the right nations, and in the right degree. Under the circumstances it is difficult to see how this could have been done.

## NOTES

1. Royal Institute of International Affairs, *International Sanctions* (London, 1938), p. 12.

2. See Louis A. R. Yates, *The United States and French Security, 1917–1921* (New York, 1957).

3. For other instances see Arnold J. Toynbee, *Survey of International Affairs, 1920–1923* (London, 1925), pp. 131, 139, 144–145, 196; Charles P. Howland, *Survey of American Foreign Relations, 1928* (New Haven, 1928), pp. 95, 340, 345, 348–350, 372, 398.

4. G. M. Gathorne-Hardy, *A Short History of International Affairs, 1920 to 1939*, third ed. (London, 1942), p. 51.

5. Anthony Eden, *Facing the Dictators* (Boston, 1962), p. 103.

6. For the Franco-Belgian occupation of the Ruhr in 1923, see Arnold J. Toynbee, *Survey of International Affairs, 1924* (London, 1928), pp. 268–300; E. J. Schuster, "The Question as to the Legality of the Ruhr Occupation," *American Journal of International Law* 18(June 1924):407–418; A. D. McNair, "The Legality of the Occupation of the Ruhr," *British Year Book of International Law, 1924.*

7. R. B. Mowat, *A History of European Diplomacy, 1914–1925* (London, 1927), p. 311.

8. Dexter Perkins, "The Department of State and American Public Opinion," in Gordon A. Craig and Felix Gilbert, eds., *The Diplomats, 1919–1939* (Princeton, 1953), p. 293.

9. "Since the League of Nations has given Art. 11 of the Covenant precedence over Art. 16, it is to be assumed that the members of the League of Nations will always have to postpone the sanctions until the Council has taken measures in accordance with Art. 11 and has determined the aggressor. Cf. the correct interpretation in *Rapports des Résolutions concernant l'article 16 du Pacte* (Geneva, 1927), p. 83." Hans Wehberg, *The Outlawry of War* (Washington, 1931), p. 38, note 1.

10. For recent treatments see Z. J. Gasiorowski, "Benes and Locarno," *Review of Politics* 20(1958):209–224; George A. Grun, "Locarno: Idea and Reality," *International Affairs* 31(1955):477–485; A. J. P. Taylor, *The Origins of the Second World War* (New York, 1961), pp. 50–58; Piotr S. Wandycz, *France and Her Eastern Allies, 1919–1925: French Czechoslovak-Polish Relations from the Paris Peace Conference to Locarno* (Minneapolis, 1962), emphasizes the efforts to keep France and Russia apart. Stresemann's methods and objectives are treated in Eric Sutton, *Gustav Stresemann, his diaries, letters, and papers* (London, 1935–1940); and Hans W. Gatzke, *Stresemann and the Rearmament of Germany* (Baltimore, 1954).

11. See U.S., Department of State, *Papers Relating to the Foreign Relations of the United States, 1928,* vol. 1, pp. 1–157.

12. The reservations of France, Britain, and Japan, and the interpretations of the United States and the Soviet government, are contained in John W. Wheeler-Bennett, *Documents on International Affairs, 1928* (London, 1929), pp. 2–14. See also, A. N. Mandelstam, *L'Interpretation du Pacte Briand-Kellogg par les gouvernements et les parlements des Etats signataire* (Paris, 1934).

13. Excerpt from an address entitled "The French Draft of the Multi-lateral Treaty for the Renunciation of War," delivered before the American Society of International Law, Washington, April 28, 1928, quoted in *Foreign Relations,* 1929, vol. 1, p. 256, note 71.

14. James T. Shotwell and Marina Salvin, *Lessons on Security and Disarmament* (New York, 1949), p. 33.

15. See Robert H. Ferrell, *Peace in Their Time: The Origins of the Kellogg-Briand Pact* (New Haven, 1952); David Hunter Miller, *The Peace Pacts of Paris* (New York, 1928); James T. Shotwell, *War as an Instrument of National Policy* (New York, 1929); John E. Stoner, *S. O. Levinson and the Pact of Paris* (New York, 1943); John C. Vinson, *William E. Borah and the Outlawry of War* (Athens, Ga., 1957); L. Ethan Ellis, *Frank B. Kellogg and American Foreign Relations, 1925–1929* (New Brunswick, N.J., 1961).

16. Herbert Hoover, *The Memoirs of Herbert Hoover: The Cabinet and the Presidency* (New York, 1952), p. 330.

17. Hans Wehberg, *The Outlawry of War* (Washington, 1931), pp. 86–87. Wehberg's italics.

18. Quincy Wright, *A Study of War* (Chicago, 1942), vol. 2, p. 941. For brief accounts of the various interpretations, see Wehberg, *The Outlawry of War,* pp. 82–88, and Russel M. Cooper, *American Consultation in World Affairs for the Preservation of Peace* (New York, 1934).

19. Wehberg, *The Outlawry of War,* pp. 88–93; Shotwell and Salvin, *Lessons on Security and Disarmament,* pp. 40–41; J. L. Brierly, "The League of Nations," in David Thomason, ed., *The Era of Violence, 1898–1945* (Cambridge, 1960), pp. 487–488.

20. John W. Wheeler-Bennett, *Disarmament and Security Since Locarno, 1925–1931* (London, 1932), p. 254; Arnold J. Toynbee, *Survey of International Affairs, 1929* (London, 1930), pp. 63–69.

21. Evans Clark, ed., *Boycotts and Peace: A Report by the Committee on Economic Sanctions* (New York, 1932), p. 123.

22. Cordell Hull, *The Memoirs of Cordell Hull* (New York, 1948), vol. 1, p. 243.

23. Wright, *A Study of War,* vol. 2, p. 943, note 62.

24. Malloy's *Treaties,* vol. 2, p. 2359.

25. Quincy Wright, "The Transfer of Destroyers to Great Britain," *American Journal of International Law* 34(October 1940):680–689. See this issue for incisive appraisals of the destroyer-bases exchange.

# CHAPTER EIGHT

# United States Responses to Treaty Violations by the Use of Sanctions, 1931–1941

DURING THE DECADE FOLLOWING WORLD WAR I THE UNITED STATES became a party to two multilateral treaties that provided the basis for the institution of sanctions by the American government against violators. The first of these was the Nine Power Treaty, concluded at the Washington conference of 1921–1922. The second was the Treaty for the Renunciation of War, often known as the Pact of Paris or the Kellogg-Briand Pact, signed August 27, 1928, and proclaimed in effect July 24, 1929.

The negotiation of agreements embodying sanctions or guarantees, their violation, and the responses of signatories to violations, must be viewed in the context of the international situation following World War I. The defeat of Germany and the chaos in Russia that accompanied the revolution combined to destroy the balance of power in Europe that had existed since the end of the Napoleonic wars. France, aided by Great Britain and Italy, immediately moved to fill the vacuum, and this attempt was moderately successful until the 1930s. In the Far East, Japan had secured hegemony by the elimination of German and Russian influence and the preoccupation of Great Britain with the war in Europe. Of the Allied powers, Japan was the most disappointed in the Versailles settlement, for she had not received what she believed to be her rightful share of the spoils. Out of these conditions and the various aspirations of the major nations there arose a desire among the satisfied nations for means to preserve the status quo and a somewhat reluctant acquiescence on the part of the frustrated nations, victor and vanquished alike. It is within this perspective that these treaties and their outcome must be viewed.

The Nine Power Treaty emerged from this complexity of changes in world power relationships. British and American concern over Japanese ambitions and a general desire to halt the costly naval arms race that developed after the war prompted President Harding to call a conference in Washington to discuss Far Eastern affairs and strive to reduce armaments. Delegates from Great Britain, Japan, France, Italy, China, the Netherlands, Belgium, and Portugal met in November 1921. Three treaties resulted, each intimately related to the others. The Naval Limitation Treaty established a relative position of power in capital ships and aircraft carriers among Great Britain, the United States, Japan, France, and Italy. The Four Power Treaty recognized the status quo in regard to Pacific possessions and ended the twenty-year-old Anglo-Japanese military alliance, which had posed a threat to the United States. The Nine Power Treaty affirmed the territorial integrity of China and the principle of the Open Door and included nonaggression pledges and a provision for consultation in the event of disputes between the parties, although there was no express provision for imposing sanctions. Thus the United States was formally committed by a duly approved and ratified treaty to what had previously been a unilateral administration policy, and it was further committed to some form of collective action in the event of a violation. The subsequent interpretation of American obligations under this pact was to involve the nation in the application of sanctions.

The Treaty for the Renunciation of War, which was also to serve as justification for coercive action, was negotiated and concluded at a time when American resistance to foreign involvement was at its peak. Shortly before the president was to announce that the pact was in effect, Secretary of State Henry L. Stimson, aware that Russia and China were on the brink of war, addressed appeals to both nations reminding them of their obligations under the treaty. Both governments affirmed their commitment to peace on July 23, 1929. By fall of that year Stimson felt that another appeal was necessary, but on this occasion he addressed his plea only to Russia. The reply was a caustic rebuff that asserted "The Pact of Paris does not give any single state or group of states the function of protector of the Pact."[1] A suggestion by the secretary of state that all signatories having treaty relations with Russia and China urge the disputants to settle their differences by arbitration was ineffectual.

This episode seemed to demonstrate that the pact would be impotent "if states must have recourse in a given case to the cumbersome method of an exchange of views through diplomatic channels."[2] Evidently President Hoover reached this conclusion, for when Prime Minister MacDonald visited the United States in October 1929 the president proposed an amendment to the Treaty for the Renunciation of War. The proposed amendment provided that in a dispute between nations a committee should be appointed consisting of members of the aggrieved nations and some impartial members.[3] MacDonald expressed interest in the proposal but he thought it might conflict with the League Covenant, and it was finally decided that each government should consider further whether such a move would be desirable and how it should be handled. As reported by the prime minister, "It became clear as the discussion proceeded that the President's advisors—and especially Mr. Cotton, the Under Secretary of State—were far from convinced that the people of the United States would be prepared to enter into so far-reaching an engagement at the present time."[4] Further attempts to amend the pact to provide for consultation were unsuccessful due to four factors: the furore raised over the suggestion that the United States enter into a similar agreement during the London Naval Conference of 1930, the conflict with League machinery, the impact of the depression on the administration, and the general tendency in the country to avoid entanglements.

The first application of sanctions under the authority of the Kellogg-Briand Pact occurred during the Japanese invasion of Manchuria, which began in 1931. The Chinese government appealed to the United States as a sponsor of the Kellogg-Briand Pact to restore peace, and to the League under Article 11. Efforts by the council were unavailing, and the American government refrained from exerting pressure because the issues were not clear and it wanted to give the civilian authorities in Japan an opportunity to "get control of the situation."[5] The confusion over American policy was reflected in the press, where there was some feeling that Japan was justified in its actions. When in October 1931 the United States placed a representative at the League discussions and supported the council invocation of the Pact of Paris on October 17, there was an attack on this involvement led by the Hearst papers. Though no representative attended the council meeting that resumed in Paris in November, Ambassador Charles G. Dawes in London was reported as being "available." During November and December the United States in successive notes rejected the Japanese explanation for troops remaining in Manchuria and expressed its concern over the situation as a signatory of the Pact of Paris and the Nine Power Treaty. Then, on January 7, 1932, Stimson sent identical notes to China and Japan asserting that the government "cannot admit the legality of any situation *de facto* nor does it intend to recognize any treaty or agreement which may impair the treaty rights of the United States . . . and that it does not intend to recognize any situation, treaty, or agreement which may be brought about by means contrary to the covenants and obligations of the Pact of Paris."[16] This departure from the previous policy of conciliation was prompted by the failure of Japanese statesmen to halt aggression, a consolidation of press and public opinion against Japan, and the occupation of Chinchow.[17] It was not an abrupt departure, however, but represented more of a graduated response to Japanese aggression as the pattern become clearer and support for stronger measures became more apparent. Watchful waiting, understanding, mild League cooperation, and diplomatic protests had finally culminated in the doctrine of nonrecognition.

"The weapons of this new phase were, however, those of nonrecognition and publicity which in November had been decided upon as the strongest sanctions the American government would use."[8] Evidently Stimson urged then or later that the United States use at least the threat of economic sanctions but Hoover refused to bluff, and he believed that economic sanctions were a first step toward war.[9] Even so, a unilateral application of sanctions would have been of little avail, and no indication of a League stand on the matter was forthcoming. Even if the League had been inclined toward economic sanctions and the president had not been so adamant on the subject, there is little question that press and public reaction would have been hostile to this extent of cooperation.

Though the diplomatic weapons of recognition and nonrecognition had been employed in the past by the United States in an effort to coerce other nations, it is scarcely correct to place the Hoover-Stimson doctrine in the same category.[10] In this instance nonrecognition was based on a multilateral treaty that included most of the nations of the world and that itself contained a self-denying commitment to refrain from using force as an instrument of national policy. The American government, therefore, had a juridical foundation for its action, which the League assembly subsequently endorsed on March 10, 1932. A new dimension of international morality had been invoked, and at least one answer had been provided to the question of how the Pact of Paris would be enforced. Though it did not prevent the conquest of Manchuria and may well have secured increased support within Japan for its government's policies, nonrecognition of the conquest set a precedent for the application of sanctions under the Pact of Paris and helped solidify world opinion.[11]

In a further effort to intimidate Japan, American fleet maneuvers in the Pacific were extended and the Scouting Force was retained on the Pacific Coast. What part Stimson played in this display of the big stick is not clear, but Tokyo expressed concern and the secretary of state thought that the navy's presence was beneficial in restraining the Japanese.[12] Moreover, this action foreshadowed the subsequent use of fleet movements as a means of bringing pressure to bear on Japan.

Stimson felt that signatories to the Kellogg-Briand Pact were authorized, if not obligated, to take whatever measures were necessary to resist aggression. Appearing before the House Committee on Foreign Affairs in 1941 to support the pending Lend-Lease bill, he quoted with approval the interpretation of the pact made at the meeting of the Association of International Law at Budapest in 1934:

> In the event of a violation of the pact by a resort to armed force or war by one signatory state against another, the other state may, without thereby committing a breach of the pact or of any rule of international law do all or any of the following things:
> a. Refuse to admit the exercise by the state violating the pact of belligerent rights such as visit and search, blockade, etc;
> b. Decline to observe toward the state violating the pact the duties prescribed by international law, apart from the pact, for a neutral in relation to a belligerent;
> c. Supply to the state attacked with financial or material assistance, including munitions of war;
> d. Assist with armed forces the state attacked.[13]

Thus the application of graduated sanctions under the authorization of the Pact of Paris was accepted by Stimson, and he evidently believed they could be applied unilaterally or in concert. Such an interpretation is in accord with the contention that there were two meanings to the doctrine of nonrecognition adopted in 1932, Hoover's, which carried no implication of further coercive methods, and Stimson's, which contemplated an escalation of sanctions.[14] The implications of the Stimson position become more significant in light of its adoption by the president-elect, Franklin D. Roosevelt, in January 1933.[15]

The method chosen by the administration to provide for more stringent sanctions was a discretionary embargo on arms exports, to be applied by the president when circumstances warranted. As put by Stimson in a letter supporting legislation for this purpose, "There are times when the hands of the Executive in negotiations for the orderly settlement of international differences would be greatly strengthened if he were in a position in co-operation with other producing nations to control the shipment of arms."[16] Though the desired legislation was voted on favorably by the Senate it never reached the House, being held up by a motion to reconsider. Opposition arose over the provision of the bill that gave the president authority to discriminate in applying the embargo, thereby using it as a sanction against an aggressor nation and deviating from a position of neutrality.[17]

The new president-elect, Franklin Roosevelt, had publicly committed himself to the support of legislation for the regulation of shipments of arms, especially to aggressor nations, and an administration bill was introduced soon after his inauguration. A full-fledged debate occurred over the question of granting discretionary authority to impose embargoes. Some believed that it was putting too much power in the hands of the president; others felt that it would lead the United States away from neutrality and draw the nation into war. Though at one time the bill passed both Houses, its final passage was prevented by the furore that greeted the announcement of Norman Davis at the General Disarmament Conference in May 1934 that the United States would agree not to interfere with collective action taken against an aggressor nation.[18]. While the president may not have employed all of his weapons to secure passage of the bill because of his primary concern with domestic legislation, the episode clearly reveals that he wanted the authority to impose sanctions, unilaterally or collectively, against treaty violators.

As tension developed in Ethiopia in 1935, the Ethiopian government appealed to the United States on July 3 for assistance in securing Italian compliance with the Kellogg-Briand Pact. Desirous of avoiding interference with any action the League might take, Roosevelt declined to do anything. The U.S. government, said the reply, was "loath to believe that either Italy or Ethiopia, as signatories [of the pact] 'would resort to other than pacific means.' "[19] With the situation worsening, England advocated consultations, but France refused and Secretary of State Cordell Hull declined on the grounds that anything less than a full consultation by all the signatories, "for the purpose of mobilizing world opinion," would merely interfere with League functions.[20]

In August 1935 the administration planned to request legislation to permit the president to impose an embargo on arms to either or both Italy and Ethiopia at his discretion, but it was discouraged by the warning that such an attempt to adopt the league system of designating an aggressor would be defeated.[21]

The same month Congress passed the Neutrality Act, which in the event of war not involving the United States made it mandatory on the president to declare an arms embargo on all belligerents and restrict travel on belligerents' vessels. Consequently with the outbreak of hostilities in Ethiopia on October 5 Roosevelt invoked the act, placing an embargo on "the exportation of arms, ammunition, and implements of war" to Italy and Ethiopia, and sought to discourage all trade with both nations.[22] When exports of materials essential in war (oil, copper, trucks, tractors, scrap iron, and scrap steel) but not covered by the terms of the arms embargo increased, Hull in November imposed a "moral embargo," declaring that that "class of trade [was] directly contrary to the policy of this Government . . . and . . . to the general spirit of the recent neutrality act."[23] Three days later the League sanctions went into effect. The two actions, Secretary Hull insisted, were quite independent of each other. The United States was not imposing sanctions but acting instead in conformity with its declared position of neutrality. The embargoes, legal and moral, were not designed to strengthen the action of the League. An attempt to secure legislation adding items to the embargoed list failed. On a moral basis the effect of the embargo was limited. With the end of hostilities the embargo was removed. However, the United States refused to recognize the Italian conquest of Ethiopia. For this extension of the Hoover-Stimson doctrine, Hull tried to gain hemisphere support by basing nonrecognition on the Saavedra Lamas "Anti-War" pact.[24] Hull felt strongly the significance of nonrecognition "as a factor in restoring international law and order." When Britain was contemplating recognition early in 1938 he privately protested, contending that "the nonrecognition policy was still a moral force."[25]

This experience reveals that the president was willing to use the sanctions of nonrecognition and economic embargo in an effort to restrain an aggressor, and he was anxious to secure authorization for more severe measures in support of collective security. He was restrained from doing so because he believed that congressional consent would not be forthcoming and that the cost in securing legislative or public support was too great. Certainly, one of the reasons that Roosevelt was reluctant to become more involved and take more coercive steps was that he did not want to antagonize "isolationist" members of Congress, many of whom had been and were the foremost supporters of his New Deal legislation.[26] The pressure that he did exert on Italy did not affect the outcome of the war, though the early institution of the moral embargo probably encouraged the League to adopt economic sanctions. The failure of the United States to impose a complete embargo of strategic materials or announce a policy of noninterference with League activities doubtless weakened the entire sanctioning process, but such action was out of the question without congressional approval. The administration did, however, make clear its disapproval of Italian aggression and provided a degree of leadership in developing world opinion. These efforts, like those of the League, were too little and too poorly coordinated, but they continued and extended the Hoover-Stimson policy of 1932. Professor Lauterpacht, writing of the economic sanctions applied by the League during the Italo-Ethiopian crisis, says "the nature of the action taken was such as to suggest that the repressive measures were being adopted as a manifestation of moral reprobation rather than as an effective means of coercion."[27] In that event, the United States and the League were following the same pattern.

The resumption of the Sino-Japanese conflict in the summer of 1937 provoked a major presidential effort to promote world peace. In the spring of that year Congress, in enacting new neutrality legislation, had rejected the idea of a discretionary embargo. Nevertheless, in response to the Japanese invasion of China, the president delivered an address on October 5 in which he advocated that peace-loving nations join in a "quarantine" of aggressors. Though "the reaction against the quarantine idea was quick and violent,"[28] the following day the State Department announced that the government regarded Japanese actions as a violation of the Nine Power Treaty and the Kellogg-Briand Pact and was in general agreement with the findings of the League's Far Eastern Committee, which had been adopted by the assembly. In spite of the apparent adverse domestic reaction to the quarantine address, the president continued his efforts for a conference. A League suggestion that signatories of the Nine Power Treaty meet provided the opportunity. In November representatives of eighteen nations gathered at Brussels for what proved, to advocates of collective security, to be a disappointment. The president apparently had in mind nothing more than agreement on certain principles of international conduct which nations should observe, with only nonrecognition of territory acquired through force as a possible sanction. The leadership which some had sought from the United States in the direction of more positive collective action was lacking, and the British foreign minister concluded that "the Americans attached importance to the Conference as an influence for educating their public."[29] The meeting ended with a reaffirmation of the principles of the Nine Power Treaty.[30]

The United States, nevertheless, did not confine its response to renewed hostilities in the Far East to pronouncements and exhortations. Roosevelt refused to invoke the Neutrality Act, ostensibly on the grounds that neither Japan nor China admitted the existence of a state of war. The president's motive evidently included a reluctance to offend Japan and interfere with a lucrative trade, although his action is conventionally interpreted as a desire to continue supplying arms to China, the victim of aggression. The attack on the United States gunboat *Panay* in December 1937 further impressed the president with the dangers inherent in Japan's activities, in spite of the fact that the Japanese government made immediate apologies and offers of indemnities. Though in early 1938 a Gallop poll revealed that seventy percent of the Americans questioned wanted to withdraw completely from China, on June 11 Secretary of State Hull announced that he was asking airplane companies to refrain from selling planes to Japan. This "voluntary" embargo was the first positive application of economic sanctions against Japan, as distinct from the "negative" sanction contained in the refusal to invoke the Neutrality Act. By December the president was asking the Department of State if it could "see any way in which these aircraft, engines and parts and accessories being exported to Japan can be cut down."[31] On December 15, over the opposition of Hull, China was extended credits to the amount of $25,000,000. The lack of enthusiasm in the State Department at this time for more coercive measures has been explained by Hull as follows:

A restrictive attitude comported economic sanctions and possibly military sanctions. Had economic sanctions been imposed against Japan, we should have borne the heaviest burden, because our trade with Japan was almost twice as large as the trade with Japan of all the European countries combined, excluding their Asiatic possessions and India. Had economic sanctions led to war, as might well have been the case, the United States would again have borne the heaviest burden. The first objection did not greatly preoccupy us, but the second was much in our thoughts.[32]

No doubt other vital considerations accounted for the administration's modest efforts. Even though in September 1938 the council had "authorized" members of the League to invoke sanctions against Japan under Article 16 no nation saw fit to apply them, and America accomplished little more than to antagonize Japan and force it to purchase in other markets. Moreover, more stringent economic sanctions would have required congressional approval, and as late as the spring of 1939 legislation introduced to impose an arms embargo on Japan as a violator of the Nine Power Treaty was unsuccessful.[33] Then, too, at this time the situation was not sufficiently serious, for America's vital interests were not threatened and the response was, in part, attuned to this dimension of the situation. For this reason, and because the idea of economic retaliation in this form and for this purpose was a relatively new concept, a gradual approach appeared necessary.

The United States, in its response to the Far Eastern crisis, avoided joint action with other nations though it participated in discussions and occasionally operated along parallel lines. Consultation with Great Britain, of all the Western countries the most vitally concerned over the Japanese move in China, proceeded with increased intensity. The president was afraid that Great Britain, faced with the explosive situation on the Continent, would have to curtail her activities in the Far East, thereby leaving the United States to contain Japan.[34] At the beginning of 1938, Roosevelt offered a rapprochement for "a general world appeasement which would at once make possible the re-establishment of those principles of international conduct to which the Government is so firmly committed and without which it did not believe any permanent peace could be found."[35] Prime Minister Chamberlain rejected this offer and chose unsuccessfully to "appease" Italy and Germany, but conversations dealing with joint naval activity in the Far East were accelerated.

The introduction of the coercive element of armed force was consistent with the Hoover-Stimson use of the fleet in 1932, and correspondence between the former secretary of state and President Roosevelt at this time reveals the attitude of both men toward the situation in the Far East. On

November 15, 1937, Stimson wrote the president that "China is really fighting our battle for freedom and peace in the Orient today," and he advocated more positive action on the part of the United States to resist Japanese penetration. The president, in referring the letter to Hull for reply, wrote "Would you give me a suggestion for a reply to Harry Stimson? You and I will agree with him wholly but we still have not got the answer." The letter that went out to Stimson was noncommittal, but the Roosevelt note is a clear indication of his position.[36] A joint naval demonstration in Asian waters with European powers was suggested by the United States in November 1937. Although consistent with the administration desire for collective action, the overture was rejected by the other nations.[37] In January 1938 the United States began official naval conversations with Britain, cruisers were sent on a visit to the naval base at Singapore to display unity, and the American fleet maneuvers in the Pacific were advanced by a few weeks.[38] On April 1, 1938, both nations announced that the escalation clause of the London Naval Treaty of 1936 was being invoked in response to competitive building by other nations, a joint action obviously aimed at Japan.

Thus the American response to the continuing Japanese aggression in China was a combination of diplomatic, economic, and military pressure, much of which was ostensibly unilateral. Further moves of a more extreme nature were a direct response to specific actions by Japan that modified the status quo in a manner distasteful to the United States. During the spring of 1939 the government resisted British requests for the institution of more severe retaliatory measures. On July 26, however, two days after the conclusion of the Craigie-Arita settlement, by which Britain agreed to refrain from impeding Japanese efforts in China, Hull notified Japan that the 1911 Commercial Treaty due to expire in January 1940 would not be renewed. This action shocked Japan and "cast a dark shadow over the economic future of the empire."[39] The move was also designed to compensate for the expression of British weakness and, in effect, assume additional responsibilities in the Far East as Britain withdrew in order to concentrate on the European threat. Roosevelt had anticipated this development and he was willing to respond to the challenge.

Under the circumstances, however, the president acted only when he believed that the situation compelled him to do so, for he labored under two handicaps. First, he lacked the authority to institute more drastic forms of retaliation. Secondly, as Hull put it, "While advocating international cooperation at all times, we were faced with the extremely delicate task of being careful not to present and urge measures in such numbers as to alarm the people and precipitate isolation as an acute political issue in the nation."[40] When the European war began in September 1939 and the administration sought to repeal the embargo provisions of the Neutrality Act, the argument used was that it would better serve to keep the nation neutral, not the true reason that it would provide greater assistance for the victims of aggression.[41] The expiration of the Commercial Treaty in January 1940 provided the administration with the means to exert greater economic pressure on Japan, and the government increased its restrictions on the export of vital materials.

The startling German military successes in the spring of 1940 left Britain alone in the struggle against Hitler and provided Japan with greater opportunities for expansion in Asia. At this point an act of Congress designed to conserve strategic materials, signed on July 2, "gave us an additional instrument for use in our relations with Japan."[42] When Japan demanded and received from the impotent Vichy government certain air bases in Indochina in August, the United States retaliated by granting a loan to China and placing a complete embargo on iron and steel scrap. Yet the president strove to adjust his sanctions to be commensurate with Japanese moves and the amount of pressure their government would bear. When Secretary of the Interior Harold L. Ickes repeatedly urged an oil embargo, Roosevelt impatiently replied: "I have yours of June 23rd [1941] recommending the immediate stopping of shipments of oil to Japan. Please let me know if this would continue to be your judgment if this were to tip the delicate scales and cause Japan to decide to attack either Russia or the Dutch East Indies."[43] In the following month, however, Japanese troops occupied southern Indochina, and the president froze Japanese funds, halted oil exports, and closed the Panama Canal to Japanese shipping. According to Langer and Gleason, "The freezing order was probably the crucial step in the entire course of Japanese-American relations before Pearl Harbor."[44] When Great Britain, her dominions, and the Netherlands East Indies joined the United States by stopping trade with Japan, an almost complete blockade was in effect. The embargo on oil was of vital importance in bringing Japanese authorities to the decision for war, because it alarmed the Japanese navy and finally brought it into the pro-war camp.[45] Eighty percent of Japan's oil came from the United States and its curtailment promised to immobilize the fleet, if not the rest of the military machine and the civilian economy. The American response to Japanese aggression had finally escalated to the point where it offered Japan's leaders a choice between a humiliating and economically disastrous withdrawal from Asia or a bold attempt to retain Japanese conquests by an expanded war. Faced with certain loss of its empire on one hand and the chance of its preservation on the other, Japan chose to gamble.

To supplement the pressure on Japan exercised by diplomatic and economic sanctions, the president employed the navy, often over the objections of his advisors. When Japan annexed Hainan and the Spratly Islands in the spring of 1939, the fleet visit to the New York World's Fair was canceled and it was ordered back to the Pacific from the Caribbean.[46] Any naval pressure in the Far East was to come from America, because Britain was too involved with the European crisis to make a contribution.[47] Further American naval moves in the Pacific were delayed by the outbreak of war in Europe and the creation of the "safety belt" around the Americas, which was maintained largely by United States warships. But in the spring of 1940 the American fleet, which had conducted its annual maneuvers in the central Pacific, was ordered to remain in Hawaii instead of returning to its normal West Coast bases. When the fleet commander asked, "Why are we here?" the chief of naval operations replied, "You are there because of the deterrent effect which it is thought your presence may have on the Japs going into the East Indies."[48] There was to be a difference of opinion then and later as to the effectiveness of this coercive measure.

On June 17, 1940, the president asked Congress to provide funds for the construction of what amounted to enough ships to maintain major fleets in both the Atlantic and Pacific oceans. There was no indication that this addition was for the purpose of influencing the situations in Asia or Europe. Roosevelt asserted that this rearmament "is, of course, a defensive program, not aimed at intervention in world affairs which do not concern the American hemisphere."[49] It appears, however, that this statement, similar to many made by the president then and later, carried the subtle implication that some affairs throughout the world did concern the Western Hemisphere. In fact, the administration approach throughout this period was global. Early in 1941 the president, writing to Ambassador Grew in Japan, asserted that "we must recognize that the hostilities in Europe, in Africa, and in Asia are all parts of a single world conflict."[50] In May, Hull told the Chinese Ambassador that "I have at all times treated the Far Eastern and the European war situation as one combined movement," and warned that he "could not be certain as to whether a large segment of our Navy still remaining at Hawaii might be sent to the Atlantic."[51]

The type and severity of sanctioning measures that should be applied against Japan was a source of conflict among the president and his advisors. Most vehement of those who believed that Japan would back down if confronted by a firm and militant United States were Stanley K. Hornbeck, political advisor on Far Eastern Affairs, and Secretary of War Henry L. Stimson. Hornbeck insisted that Japan was in no condition to wage war against the United States and that she would agree to a settlement on American terms if convinced of America's willingness to fight.[52] Stimson's position was based on his "belief that Japan had yielded to a firm policy at Shantung in 1919, at the Washington Conference in 1922, and at London in 1930. He remembered also that from 1931 onwards, where it had been impossible to construct firm, consistent policies, the Japanese had not yielded."[53] Yet Stimson went from the extreme of wanting to base the Pacific fleet at Singapore to maintaining with General Marshall (in the spring of 1941) that the fleet should be moved to the Atlantic on the grounds that it was not deterring Japan. Hull resisted, and the president made a mild compromise by shifting certain units to the Atlantic but retaining the majority of the vessels at Pearl Harbor.[54]

There is no question that the presence of the United States fleet at Hawaii did cause the Japanese serious concern and affect their diplomacy. It was early regarded by Japan as an attempt at intimidation and a scarcely veiled threat.[55] Its continued retention at Pearl Harbor, added to the diplomatic and economic pressures, convinced the Japanese that the American government was determined to employ every measure to halt Japan, even war. Just what sort of action would provoke war was as puzzling to the Japanese as it was to Roosevelt and his advisors, but there is no doubt that "the harboring of the Pacific Fleet at Pearl Harbor made a long-lasting impression."[56] Japan's desperate successful attack on December 7 revealed the importance attached to the fleet's presence so far from the West Coast, for it was believed that unless the American navy was immobilized Japan could not venture into Southeast Asia and the Dutch East Indies. Nor is it quite accurate to maintain that instead of acting as a deterrent, the fleet provoked the war. The American resistance which faced Japan was the result of Japan's own actions, and Japan's resort to war in December 1941 stemmed from the conflict between her own aspirations and American intransigence. She weighed the alternatives and made her choice.

In retrospect, the policy of economic, diplomatic, and moderate "military" sanctions failed.[57] Japan continued to ignore treaties and the importunities of the United States. By the time these three forms of coercion had reached the point where they promised domestic hardship and a slowing of the military machine, it was too late. The Japanese leaders had gone too far and the nation was too committed to the course of action that had begun in 1931. Retreat at this stage of the game was unthinkable, and the sanctions which earlier might have halted Japanese aggression helped provoke an attack. Concerted action and proper timing probably would have made the sanctions effective, but the graduated application of sanctions, based not on what was required to ensure compliance with treaties but on what the president could do in terms of his office, Congress, and the public, proved inadequate.

## NOTES

1. John W. Wheeler-Bennett, ed., *Documents on International Affairs, 1929* (London, 1930), p. 278. For the Sino-Soviet conflict of 1929 and United States activities, see U.S., Department of State, *Foreign Relations of the United States, 1929*, vol. 3, p. 30. (Hereafter cited by title only.)

2. Evans Clark, ed., *Boycotts and Peace: A Report by the Committee on Economic Sanctions* (New York, 1932), p. 125.

3. For the United States draft of this proposed amendment, see *Foreign Relations of the United States, 1929*, vol. 3, p. 30.

4. Memorandum by Mr. MacDonald respecting his conversations with President Hoover, *Documents on British Foreign Policy, 1919–1939*, Ernest L. Woodward and Rohan Butler, eds., second series, vol. 1 (London, 1946), p. 116.

5. Henry L. Stimson, *The Far Eastern Crisis* (New York, 1936), p. 34.

6. *Foreign Relations of the United States, Japan, 1931–1941*, vol. 1, p. 76.

7. See George E. McReynolds and E. Tupper, *Japan in American Public Opinion* (New York, 1937), pp. 283–299.

8. Ernest Ralph Perkins, "The Nonapplication of Sanctions Against Japan, 1931–1932," in Dwight E. Lee and George E. McReynolds, eds., *Essays in History and International Relations in Honor of George Hubbard Blakeslee* (Worcester, Mass., 1949), p. 224.

9. Ibid., pp. 224–225; Richard N. Current, "The Stimson Doctrine and the Hoover Doctrine," *American Historical Review* 59(1954):513–542.

10. As does Robert H. Ferrell, *American Diplomacy in the Great Depression: Hoover-Stimson Foreign Policy, 1929–1933* (New Haven, 1957), p. 164.

11. See Paul L. Clyde, "The Diplomacy of 'Playing no Favorites' Secretary Stimson and Manchuria, 1931," *Mississippi Valley Historical Review* 25(1948); James W. Christopher, *Conflict in the Far East: American Diplomacy in China from 1928–1933* (Leiden, 1950); *Foreign Relations of the United States, 1931*, vol. 3, pp. 1–715.

12. Charles F. Adams to Admiral Montgomery Meigs Taylor, May 20, 1932, Taylor Papers, Manuscript Division, Library of Congress; Fleet Admiral William D. Leahy, manuscript diary, (February 29, 1932), vol. 2, p. 18; *Foreign Relations of the United States, 1932*, vol. 3, p. 449, and vol. 4, pp. 197, 302, 325, and 344; Michael D. Reagan, "The Far Eastern Crisis of 1931–1932: Stimson, Hoover and the Armed Forces," in Harold Stein, ed., *American Civil-Military Decisions* (Birmingham, Ala., 1963), pp. 27–40.

13. House of Representatives, 77th Cong., 1st sess., Committee on Foreign Affairs, *Hearings . . . Lend-Lease Bill* (Washington, 1941), p. 104.

14. Current, "The Stimson Doctrine and the Hoover Doctrine," pp. 513–542.

15. See Bernard Sternsher, "The Stimson Doctrine: F.D.R. *versus* Moley and Tugwell," *Pacific Historical Review*, August 1962, pp. 281–289.

16. January 6, 1933, quoted in Elton Atwater, *American Regulation of Arms Exports* (Washington, 1941), p. 183.

17. Ibid., pp. 182–186; Edwin Borchard and William P. Lage, *Neutrality for the United States* (New Haven, 1937), pp. 304–305.

18. Borchard and Lage, *Neutrality*, pp. 305–311; Atwater, *American Regulation of Arms Exports*, pp. 188–192; and Robert A. Divine, "Franklin D. Roosevelt and Collective Security, 1933," *Mississippi Valley Historical Review* 48(1961):42–59.

19. U.S., Department of State, *Peace and War: United States Foreign Policy 1931–1941* (Washington, 1943), pp. 266–271.

20. Cordell Hull, *The Memoirs of Cordell Hull* (New York, 1948), vol. 1, p. 427; *Foreign Relations, 1935*, vol. 1, pp. 724–725.

21. Hull, *The Memoirs of Cordell Hull*, vol. 1, pp. 410–412; Wayne S. Cole, "Senator Key Pittman and American Neutrality Policies, 1933–1940," *Mississippi Valley Historical Review* 46(1960):653–654.

22. U.S., Department of State, *Peace and War*, p. 283.

23. On arms embargoes, "Despite the fact that the Department of State cannot withhold licenses for the export of arms except in accordance with a law or treaty, it has on a few occasions accomplished what amounted in effect to an informal embargo by simply requesting the American manufacturers and exporters not to ship arms to a particular destination. Inasmuch as the American Government is the best potential customer of the armaments industry, the latter is generally willing to follow the government's wishes, and the government is thereby able to exercise an informal degree of control over the export of war material from the United States regardless of any law which Congress may pass." Atwater, *American Regulation of Arms Exports*, p. 214. The "moral embargo" of the Italo-Ethiopian war embraced more than arms and was not especially successful.

24. Hull, *The Memoirs of Cordell Hull*, vol. 1, p. 469.

25. Ibid., p. 581.

26. John C. Donovan, "Congressional Isolationists and the Roosevelt Foreign Policy," *World Politics* 3(1950):307.

27. L. Oppenheim, *International Law*, ed. H. Lauterpacht, sixth ed. (1944), vol. 2, p. 140, as quoted in Hans J. Morgenthau, *Politics Among Nations: The Struggle for Power and Peace* (New York, 1953), p. 236.

28. Hull, *The Memoirs of Cordell Hull*, vol. 1, p. 545. See also Dorothy Borg, "Notes on Roosevelt's Quarantine Speech," *Political Science Quarterly* 72(1957):405–453; and John M. Haight, Jr., "Roosevelt and the Aftermath of the Quarantine Speech," *Review of Politics* 24(1962):233–259.

29. Anthony Eden, *Facing the Dictators* (Boston, 1962), pp. 610.

30. See Hull, *The Memoirs of Cordell Hull*, vol. 1, pp. 550–556; and *Foreign Relations of the United States, 1937*, vol. 4, pp. 1–235.

31. Roosevelt to Undersecretary of State, December 10, 1938, Official File 197—Japan, Roosevelt Papers, Hyde Park.

32. Hull, *The Memoirs of Cordell Hull*, vol. 1, pp. 570–571. See also Seiji Hishida, *Japan Among the Great Powers* (London, 1940), p. 377.

33. Cole, "Senator Key Pittman and American Neutrality Policies," pp. 657–658.

34. See report of conversation between Eden and Norman Davis, November 2, 1937, in Eden, *Facing the Dictators*, pp. 609–610.

35. Welles, Memorandum of conversation with the British ambassador, February 25, 1938, *Foreign Relations of the United States, 1938*, vol. 1, p. 138.

36. Roosevelt to Stimson, November 2, 1937, with Stimson letter and Roosevelt note to Hull dated November 22 attached, in President's Personal File 20, Roosevelt Papers, Hyde Park.

37. See report of conversation between Hull and Admiral Leahy, November 28, 1937, in Fleet Admiral William D. Leahy, manuscript diary, vol. 3, p. 139, Manuscript Division, Library of Congress.

38. Samuel Eliot Morison, *The Rising Sun in the Pacific, 1931—April 1942* (Boston, 1948), p. 49; Eden, *Facing the Dictators*, p. 620.

39. David J. Lu, *From the Marco Polo Bridge to Pearl Harbor: Japan's Entry into World War II* (Washington, 1961), p. 55.

40. Hull, *The Memoirs of Cordell Hull*, vol. 1, p. 155.

41. See Roosevelt's remarks in "Conference of the President with Democratic and Republican Leaders preceding the opening of a special session of the Congress," September 20, 1939. Roosevelt Papers, Hyde Park. The president contended that retention

of existing neutrality legislation was equivalent to giving Germany a fleet, and he commended a member of Congress for saying to the press "something that I couldn't say and that is without question the overwhelming sentiment in this country is in favor of France and England winning the war."

42. Hull, *The Memoirs of Cordell Hull*, vol. 1, p. 901.

43. Roosevelt to Ickes, June 23, 1941, printed in *The Secret Diary of Harold L. Ickes* (New York, 1954), vol. 3, p. 538.

44. William L. Langer and S. Everett Gleason, *The Undeclared War, 1940–1941* (New York, 1953), p. 708.

45. See Lu, *From the Marco Polo Bridge to Pearl Harbor*, pp. 188–189, 238.

46. Morison, *Rising Sun in the Pacific*, p. 38.

47. Leahy diary, vol. 4, section 2, p. 85.

48. Morison, *Rising Sun in the Pacific*, p. 43.

49. Roosevelt acceptance of Secretary of War Woodring's resignation, June 20, 1940. FDR Official File 18, Department of the Navy.

50. Roosevelt to Grew, January 21, 1941, *Foreign Relations of the United States, 1941*, vol. 4, p. 7.

51. Ibid., Memorandum of Conversation with the Chinese Ambassador Hu Shih, May 23, 1941, p. 209. See also record of telephone conversation between Maxwell M. Hamilton and Hull, July 17, 1941, on p. 326.

52. See Ibid., pp. 146, 419, 512; Langer and Gleason, *The Undeclared War*, p. 40.

53. Elting E. Morison, *Turmoil and Tradition: A Study of the Life and Times of Henry L. Stimson* (Boston, 1960), p. 523.

54. Stimson manuscript diary, Yale University Library, entries for April 23, April 24, May 5; *Hearings before the Joint Committee on the Investigation of the Pearl Harbor Attack*, 79th Cong., 1st sess., 39 vols. (Washington, 1946), vol. 19, pp. 3656–3659.

55. *Foreign Relations of the United States, 1931–1941, Japan*, vol. 2, p. 67.

56. Lu, *Marco Polo Bridge to Pearl Harbor*, p. 120. See also Langer and Gleason, *The Challenge to Isolation, 1937–1940* (New York, 1952), pp. 558, 593–594, 604.

57. "The United States justified its departures from neutrality to the disadvantage of the Axis powers prior to its entry into the war in December, 1941, on the theory of permissive sanctions under the Pact of Paris." Quincy Wright, *A Study of War* (Chicago, 1942), vol. 2, p. 943, note 62.

# CHAPTER NINE

# The Sanction of Nonrecognition as Practiced by the United States

SOON AFTER SECRETARY OF STATE HENRY L. STIMSON DECLARED IN JANuary 1932 that the United States government did not "intend to recognize any situation, treaty or agreement which may be brought about by means contrary to the covenants and obligations of the Pact of Paris of August 27, 1928," one authority observed that "state practice of withholding and delaying recognitions of revolutionary or illegitimate governments, of new states and territorial acquisitions, and treaties affecting third parties, as a measure of coercion is not at all new in the history of international relations."[1] Also acknowledged was the fact that "most of the policies of non-recognition constitute a kind of sanction for international law or foreign policy."[2] On May 4, 1932, Acting Secretary of State William R. Castle, Jr., spoke of nonrecognition as "a powerful sanction without the use of force," thus admitting its employment by the administration as a peaceful measure designed to influence the Japanese government.[3] Unquestionably, nonrecognition of territorial acquisitions, new states, and new governments has been applied as a sanction by many nations during the past 150 years.[4] Moreover, one writer has contended that "the United States has gone furthest among the great Powers in practicing and binding itself by treaty to practice nonrecognition as a means of discouraging 'illegal' violence."[5] This essay will consider certain occasions on which the United States has applied the sanction of nonrecognition as a coercive instrument of diplomacy.

Some preliminary observations on the significance of recognition will illustrate the value of its denial as a sanction. According to Lauterpacht "a State is, and becomes, an International Person through recognition only and exclusively," and "identity" is achieved by a nation through recognition accorded by other nations.[6] As to the significance of the act, one writer has stated that "the doctrine of recognition . . . carries with it the clear acceptance of a common system of international rights and duties binding on all members of the family of nations. That is perhaps why the doctrine has been called the 'basis of international law.' "[7] A nation, then, becomes an entity and a recipient of the benefits of the international community only through its formal acceptance by other states.

The results of a failure to secure this international acceptance are summed up as follows:

> The withholding of recognition from a state or government places the government and nationals of the unrecognized state under a serious handicap, especially in the conduct of economic relations. The nonrecognized government is barred access to the courts of the state withholding recognition; it is deprived of judicial protection in other states of its public interests; the ordinary immunities of public property of the non-recognized state or government, of public ships, of diplomatic representatives, in fact of the government itself, according to decisions of the courts, appear to be non-existant. The money markets of the states withholding recognition are normally closed to the unrecognized state.[8]

In addition to the foregoing, failure to extend recognition denies a state many other normal forms of intercourse with other nations, and it invokes the moral and prestigious sanction of disapproval. The efficacy of these measures, about which there is considerable debate, will be discussed later, but their use as coercive acts intended to bring about a modification of an impending or accomplished action is clear. Also, there is general agreement among statesmen and scholars that "once the new government has fulfilled the requirements laid down by general international law, refusal to grant recognition for any reason is an act of intervention."[9] The deleterious effects of nonrecognition, then, are manifest in the material injury sustained, the blow to morale, and the belief that its use constitutes interference in the internal affairs of a state. That it should arouse such resentment is further evidence that the device is not without merit as a coercive instrument.

The American use of nonrecognition as a sanction is comprehensible only if viewed within the context of the origins of the nation and its development of a recognition policy. When the colonies declared themselves independent in 1776 they were ardently seeking assistance from other nations in the struggle against the mother country. France, which had been extending modest but clandestine aid, realized the value of this new nation in curtailing the power of England. The Franco-American Alliance of 1778 was accepted as overt intervention and led to war with Great Britain, for at that time, as Julius Goebel put it, "recognition as a separate concept was a thing unknown not only to the law, but also to the diplomacy of the time."[10] The principle of "legitimacy" of government was so well established that the French action was regarded as virtual heresy and understandable only as a means of regaining the power position which earlier had been lost to Great Britain.[11]

When the United States was faced with its first decision on the recognition of a new government that had been established in violation of the doctrine of "legitimacy," the responsible statesmen bore in mind their own experience. Secretary of State Thomas Jefferson, on November 7, 1792, wrote the American minister in Paris, Gouverneur Morris, "it accords with our principles to acknowledge any Government to be rightful which is formed by the will of the nation, substantially declared." And on March 12, 1793, in a letter authorizing Morris to recognize the new French government if it exercised control, Jefferson stated:

> We surely can not deny to any nation that right whereon our own Government is founded—that every one may govern itself according to whatever form it pleases, and change these forms at its own will; and that it may transact its business with foreign nations through whatever organ it thinks proper, whether king, convention, assembly, committee, president, or anything else it may choose. The will of the nation is the only thing essential to be regarded.[12]

Jefferson thus enunciated his own type of "legitimacy," namely, the will of the nation, and this criterion plus the requirement of *de facto* control formed the original basis of American recognition policy. It is not accurate to maintain, however, that this precedent was "followed by successive governments to the days of Woodrow Wilson."[13] Modifications of the Jeffersonian dicta have been legion, and these modifications have been employed on numerous occasions as sanctions in an effort, occasionally successful, to achieve a diplomatic objective.

The first corollary to the initial recognition policy of the United States was asserted by Secretary of State John Quincy Adams in regard to the newly established Latin American nations. Adams and Monroe had resisted congressional pressure to extend recognition on the grounds that it would have been premature and constituted an unfriendly act toward Spain. By 1821, however, the president and the secretary of state were convinced that the former colonies had established their independence. Furthermore, the treaty with Spain for the cession of Florida had been ratified and there was no need to placate the former mother country. Then, too, privateers operating under letters of marque from the rebelling governments, particularly from Buenos Aires, were interfering with American and other neutral commerce. Adams forthrightly declared that these new nations "cannot claim the rights & prerogatives of independent

States without conforming to the duties by which independent states are bound."[14] Consequently, Adams withheld recognition of the Buenos Aires government until, in the words of Samuel Flagg Bemis, "it could demonstrate its power to stop them [the privateers]. To satisfy the complaints the Buenos Aires authorities revoked all commissions to privateers on October 6, 1821. When this became known in Washington it removed the last impediment to recognition."[15] Thus the first American effort to use nonrecognition as a sanction involved the incorporation of a new criterion for recognition. It was designed to further American commercial interests and incidentally those of other countries; it invoked the principles of international law; and it was eminently successful.[16]

The foregoing incident is of considerable significance in regard to one of the fundamental considerations involved in the granting of recognition. There is a distinction between a government's "ability" to observe international obligations and its "willingness" to do so. According to Lauterpacht:

> Recognition has often been refused on the ground that the new government has been unwilling either to give an undertaking to fulfill international obligations contracted by its predecessor or to desist from its own illegal conduct. This particular test of recognition, which must be distinguished from that of *ability* to fulfill international obligations, is of comparatively recent origin. Apparently it was first given clear expression by the United States in 1877 in connection with the recognition of the Díaz Government in Mexico.[17]

Although this writer is in error historically the point is worthy of note, for American recognition policy has not always applied the standard first enunciated so clearly by John Quincy Adams. When it has done so, the commitment to a particular type of behavior usually has been required in order to secure a concession in exchange for recognition.

Another instance of nonrecognition also occurred during the presidency of Monroe, and while the official explanation stressed the sanction element there is evidence that domestic considerations were prominent if not paramount. When the Republic of Haiti formally applied for recognition by the United States in 1823 the president explained his rejection of the request on the grounds that the Haitian government imposed higher duties on American commerce, it discriminated against whites, and its independence from France was not clearly established. Not mentioned, but a significant factor, was the hostility of Southern congressmen, who opposed the recognition of a nation and a government established as the result of a slave insurrection.[18] The president imposed conditions for recognition that amounted to a rejection of the simple Jeffersonian dicta and were coercive in nature. Although the Haitian government offered to adjust the tariff and end discrimination, it was not accorded recognition until 1862.

The question of the recognition of the Texas Republic did not involve the application of a sanction but it witnessed another corollary to the recognition policy of the United States. President Andrew Jackson on December 21, 1836, quoted with approval resolutions by both houses of Congress "that the independence of Texas ought to be acknowledged by the United States whenever satisfactory information should be received that it had in successful operation a civil government capable of performing the duties and fulfilling the obligations of an independent power."[19] The key word is "capable," and the statement represents a retreat from the position taken by Secretary Adams. Even this qualification was eliminated as subsequent administrations returned to the Jeffersonian criteria. When extending recognition to the French Republic in 1848, Secretary of State James Buchanan wrote, "In its intercourse with foreign nations the Government of the United States has, from its origin, always recognized *de facto* governments. . . . It is sufficient for us to know that a government exists capable of maintaining itself; and then its recognition on our part inevitably follows."[20] President Franklin Pierce, in his message to Congress on May 15, 1856, announced: "It is the established policy of the United States to recognize all governments without question of their source, or organization, or of the means by which the governing persons attain their power, provided there be a government *de facto* accepted by the people of the country."[21] "We do not," he continued, "go behind the fact of a foreign government exercising actual power to investigate questions of legitimacy; we do not inquire into the causes which may have led to a change of government. To us it is indifferent whether a successful revolution has been aided by foreign intervention or not; whether insurrection has overthrown existing government, and another has been established in its place according to preexisting forms or in a manner adopted for the occasion by those whom we may find in the actual possession of power."[22] It appeared that the pendulum had swung past its original position with the elimination from American recognition policy of the requirements of ability or willingness to observe international obligations, the Jeffersonian dictum of the "will of the nation, substantially declared," and the rejection of nonrecognition as a means of promoting American interests. This shift may be accounted for by the fact that a less demanding policy was deemed better suited to the circumstances and of greater benefit to the United States than would have been the more exacting criteria of Jefferson, Adams, and Jackson. As one writer has observed, "The practice of the United States [in the matter of the recognition of new states or governments] appears to have been governed by mixed motives of expediency, sympathy with democratic movements, and supposed legality."23 It also appears that one or more of these motives may have been predominant at specific times, depending on the orientation of the responsible statesmen, the domestic situation, and the anticipated effectiveness of the action.

The most drastic departure from previous American recognition policy was made in connection with secession of the Southern states and the establishment of the Maximilian government in Mexico. The United States, in an effort to thwart the efforts of the Confederacy to secure recognition, reversed the *de facto* basis of recognition and resorted to the old European doctrine of "legitimacy." In a circular to all American ministers dated February 28, 1861, Secretary of State Jeremiah S. Black asserted that "the States have no constitutional power to secede from the Union," and therefore were not eligible for recognition as a separate government or nation.24 Secretary of State William H. Seward reiterated this position in a circular of March 9, 1861, and warned other nations against the implications of a recognition of the Confederacy.25 Seward later reaffirmed the dangers of recognizing the South in an almost threatening letter to England, in which he ponderously asserted that "to recognize the independence of a new state, and so favor, possibly determine, its admission into the family of nations, is the highest possible exercise of sovereign power, because it affects in any case the welfare of two nations, and often the peace of the world."26 The introduction of the standard of "illegality" or "constitutional legitimacy" as an argument for not recognizing the Confederacy was motivated by a desire to restore the Union, and it proved extremely useful in thwarting European intervention in the affairs of the Western Hemisphere.

The occasion for applying the legitimacy policy abroad arose in 1864 when Archduke Maximilian of Austria became emperor of Mexico. The constitutional government under President Benito Juárez had suffered repeated military reverses at the hands of the French army, which with the aid of Mexican monarchists placed Maximilian on the throne. Seward resisted all efforts by France and Maximilian to secure recognition of the new government and continued to maintain diplomatic relations with the Juárez administration. The secretary of state claimed that this policy reflected a position of neutrality, but he repeatedly asserted that the United States regarded "the effort to establish permanently a foreign and imperial government in Mexico as disallowable and impracticable."27 In assuming this attitude Seward was supported by a unanimous resolution of the House of Representatives passed on April 4, 1864.28 With the end of the Civil War sufficient pressure was applied on France to secure a withdrawal of her troops, and the Juárez government was able to overthrow Maximilian within a short time.

Undoubtedly many factors contributed to the downfall of Maximilian's empire. The fact remains, however, that nonrecognition was avowedly employed by the United States as a sanction, and its purpose was to eliminate a foreign power from the Western Hemisphere in support of the Monroe Doctrine and American security. It was also designed to enable the Mexicans to control their own affairs. The Juárez government probably would have disintegrated without the continued recognition by the United States and the aid it furnished—prestige and moral support as well as money and munitions. By refusing to recognize Maximilian the United States proclaimed its disapproval of his government, helped discredit the regime in Mexico and abroad, and contributed to the French emperor's conclusion that his Mexican venture could not succeed. In this instance nonrecognition proved to be a valuable coercive instrument of foreign policy in protecting the interests of the United States and a Latin American neighbor.[29]

It was some time before the "legitimacy" principle was eliminated from the recognition policy of the United States. In 1866 when some rapid changes in the government of Peru took place through revolution, the United States refrained from extending recognition even though many other nations had done so. Seward explained this nonrecognition by writing that "the policy of the United States is settled upon the principle that revolutions in republican states ought not to be accepted until the people have adopted them by organic law with the solemnities which would seem sufficient to guarantee their stability and permanency. This," he said, "is the result of reflecting upon national trials of our own."[30] The change from a long-standing *de facto* policy to one of "constitutionalism" or an insistence on electoral approval was not strictly inconsistent with the Jeffersonian criterion of the "will of the nation substantially declared," though neither Jefferson himself nor numerous other administrations had so interpreted the statement. Nor could it be explained solely by an American predilection for representative institutions, although this motive may well have been present. Seward, by his own admission, was still under the impact of his exhortations against a recognition of the Confederacy. But his attitude resulted in the application of nonrecognition as a sanction designed to coerce revolutionary governments into formalizing their existence by practicing republican methods. Latin American nations might understand the adoption of a "legalistic" recognition practice under the pressure of civil war or European activity in Mexico. But extending it to domestic upheavals in other countries was an unpopular form of intervention.

The next major attempt by the United States to employ nonrecognition as a sanction occurred in 1877 when General Porfirio Díaz overthrew the existing government in Mexico, and formal recognition was withheld for nearly a year after it had been granted by a number of Latin American and European nations. The Washington authorities were reluctant to recognize a regime that had subverted the constitutional government and gained power by armed rebellion, and assurances were sought regarding American citizens, property, and the security of the border. A host of successive instructions finally culminated in a dispatch from the acting secretary of state. F. W. Seward, which stated that the United States would "wait before recognizing General Díaz as President of Mexico until it shall be assured that his election is approved by the Mexican people, and that his administration is possessed of stability to endure and of *disposition* to comply with the rules of international comity and the obligations of treaties."[31] Except for a possible interpretation of "disposition" as meaning "willingness" or "capability," this position represented a virtual synthesis of all the previous criteria that had been used in granting or withholding recognition. The Hayes administration, criticized in Congress and the press for the delay, was accused of trying to provoke war in an effort to divert attention from domestic affairs and to acquire the northern portion of Mexico.[32] Finally the president declared that recognition had been delayed because of a continuance of border disorders, which involved raids into the United States by Indians and bandits from across the Rio Grande.[33] This public admission that non-recognition was serving as a means to induce the Mexican government to meet American demands appeared to mollify Congress. When in March of 1878 Secretary of State William M. Evarts instructed the minister to the former government to extend recognition to the Díaz administration, he explained that "it has been gratifying to the government of the United States to observe on the part of the present authorities of Mexico an increased desire to preserve peace and good order on the frontier and an endeavor to adopt more vigorous and efficient measures to repress border depredations and raids on the territory of the United States."[34] Evidently the deliberate use of nonrecognition as a means of inducing Díaz to observe the amenities of conventional international obligations and the formalities of representative government were successful, for the general not only made a greater effort to police the border but he allowed the Mexican people to elect him president by an overwhelming majority.[35]

The conditions imposed preliminary to the recognition of the Díaz government were reasserted in 1879 when the United States withheld recognition of the revolutionary government of Guzmán Blanco in Venezuela in spite of its being accorded by Brazil, England, France, Germany, Italy, and Spain. Secretary of State Evarts observed that the new administration was "not understood to have gained power by any constitutional process of election or endorsement," and he thought recognition should be deferred until there was assurance that "such a step will not only rest on the popular will of Venezuela, but will also be beneficial to the relations between the United States and that country. Good faith in the observance of international obligations," he continued, "is the first essential to the maintenance of such relations." And, he pointed out, "At present there is no indication that any change for the better has taken place, either as regards the payment of the indemnity installments, now for several months in default, or the security of the rights of citizens of the United States sojourning in Venezuela."[36] Yet recognition was extended a year later when Blanco was elected president by the Venezuelan legislature, even though the other questions had not been settled.[37] In this case the United States maintained its "constitutional legitimacy" principle but retreated on the matter of international obligations. Whether the sanction of non-recognition was partially effective in this instance is not clear, but at least the proprieties were observed. Again this diplomatic device had been employed in an effort to exert pressure on another government.[38]

As the nineteenth century neared its end, the United States tended to reject constitutional legitimacy in favor of the *de facto* principle, and a *capacity* to meet international obligations replaced the requirement of a *willingness* to do so.[39] Yet recognition or its denial as a sanction was not ignored. At the time of the Panamanian revolution in 1903 the United States used recognition as a means of securing concessions from the new government, and Washington withheld recognition from the Cuban government until it accepted the restrictions embodied in the Platt Amendment.[40] A significant development took place in 1907, when the Central American republics signed a convention that provided:

> The Governments of the High Contracting Parties shall not recognize any other government which may come into power in any of the five Republics as a consequence of a *coup d'etat*, or of a revolution against the recognized Government, so long as the freely elected representatives of the people thereof, have not constitutionally reorganized the country.[41]

The United States, although not a signatory, agreed to honor the clause, but it failed to do so when the first significant challenge occurred.[42] President Taft used the power of nonrecognition with some success in Nicaragua, although it was supplemented by other methods of intervention.[43] Taft, it appears, was primarily concerned with the protection of American interests, and he was not averse to extorting concessions from governments prior to granting recognition. While sympathetic to republican institutions, it is noteworthy that he withheld recognition from the Huerta revolutionary government in 1913 pending its "assurances that the outstanding questions between this country and Mexico . . . will be dealt with in a satisfactory manner," a settlement of claims, and an answer to "the question of degree to which the population of Mexico assents to the new regime."[44] The brunt of the responsibility for dealing with this new government, however, was to be placed in the hands of the succeeding administration.

It has been customary to assume that, as Hackworth puts it, "the policy of recognition prior to the beginning of the administration of President Wilson uniformly followed the fundamental principles laid down by Jefferson in his instruction to Mr. Morris in 1792."[45] The authority quoted, while admitting occasional modest aberrations such as Seward's "requirement of an 'organic law,' " maintains that "Jefferson's statements carried the implication that a government, such as he described, would be in possession of the machinery of government, would possess stability, and would be able and willing to meet its international obligations."[46] It seems that a great deal more here is being read into the simple Jeffersonian criteria than the words and the practice of recognition at that time would warrant. The biographer of Woodrow Wilson, Arthur S. Link, asserts that the president was "led to repudiate the historic American practice of extending recognition to all governments in power and to improvise for Mexico a radical new test for recognition. It was a test, as Wilson afterward put it, of 'constitutional legitimacy.' "[47] Yet it should be apparent from even the brief evidence presented in this study that no "radical new test for recognition" was introduced.

The essential points of the Wilson-Huerta episode for this study are, first, that the president did employ nonrecognition as a coercive device in an effort to bring about a change in the government of Mexico; second, that the grounds on which he denied recognition did not represent a drastic departure from the previous recognition policy of the United States, nor was it an original or unique application of nonrecognition in terms of the American experience.[48] One might not completely agree with Lauterpacht that Wilson's policy "went back to Jefferson's insistence on 'the will of the nation substantially declared' as a condition of recognition."[49] And MacCorkle seems to be exaggerating when he concludes, "in his [Wilson's] dealings with the Huerta government he simply applied the traditional test of 'popular approval' and 'ability to fulfill international obligations.' He followed a policy long fixed by precedent."[50] What Wilson did, however, was to use more drastic methods to accomplish his purpose and insist on a more substantial demonstration of popular support than had hitherto been required.[51] A third point to be considered is whether Wilson was successful. At least Huerta did not survive as president of Mexico, and Wilson's policy certainly contributed in some measure to Huerta's downfall. On the other hand, nonrecognition was the initial but by no means the only coercive device resorted to by the president in his effort to oust the general.

Wilson did not always insist on constitutionalism, and on several occasions he recognized revolutionary governments.[52] On other occasions he applied the doctrine of constitutional legitimacy with varying degrees of success, particularly to the Dominican Republic from 1913–1916, Ecuador in 1913, and Cuba in 1917.[53] Most noteworthy, however, was the president's refusal to recognize the Tinoco regime in Costa Rica when it overthrew the existing government in 1917. Wilson based his action on the unconstitutional method which Federico Tinoco used to gain power and his own suspicions that American business interests were involved. Although the dictator strove to satisfy the United States and gain recognition his efforts were unsuccessful, and his government finally ended with his resignation in 1919. There is little doubt that Wilson's nonrecognition policy contributed to Tinoco's downfall, although other factors were also involved.[54]

Breaking new ground was the *post facto* reaction to China's acceptance of Japan's twenty-one demands in 1915. Bryan's dispatch stated that the United States would not "recognize any agreement or understanding which has been entered into or which may be entered into between the governments of Japan and China, impairing the treaty rights of the United States and its citizens in China, the political or territorial integrity of the Republic of China, or the international policy relative to China commonly known as the open door policy."[55] Having no discernible immediate effect, the implications of this statement of nonrecognition were to emerge in subsequent American responses to what were regarded as aggressive actions.

Recognition was denied the Soviet government of Russia from 1917 to 1933. The initial reasons advanced by Wilson for this policy included the unconstitutional method of seizing control and the appearance of instability. These objections were dropped by the Harding administration, which emphasized the "unorthodox economic policies of the Bolsheviks" along with continuing concern about confiscated American property, acceptance of the obligations incurred by previous governments, and an end to Communist subversion in the United States.[56] The coercive aspects of this policy were evident, for, as Triska and Slusser put it, "the Soviet government wanted and needed to be recognized because it had to survive."[57] Recognition was finally granted by President Franklin D. Roosevelt in 1933 in exchange for Soviet agreement to certain demands, an agreement which was not kept or which was interpreted in a way not contemplated by the United States. In any event, the withholding of recognition was to some extent responsible for the Soviet willingness to make concessions.[58]

Mexico again was subjected to the sanction of nonrecognition in 1920, when General Obregón was elected president in a thoroughly constitutional manner. On this occasion recognition was denied because the

Mexican government refused to guarantee American lives and property rights by treaty as a condition precedent. The policy begun by Wilson was continued by the Harding administration, and Secretary of State Charles Evans Hughes declared, "when it appears that there is a government in Mexico willing to bind itself to the discharge of primary international obligations, concurrently with that act its recognition will take place."[59] In 1923, after Mexico had agreed to the creation of two mixed claims commissions for the purpose of handling outstanding claims, recognition was extended. Although the settlement was in the nature of a compromise, use of the sanction had produced some concessions.[60]

During the presidency of Calvin Coolidge the United States delayed recognition of several new governments in Latin America because they had secured power by unconstitutional means. The United States waited three years, from 1925 to 1928, before recognizing the Ayora government in Ecuador. In extending recognition, Secretary of State Frank B. Kellogg wrote:

> Having full confidence that the Government of Dr. Ayora has the support of the majority of the people of Ecuador, and is both capable and desirous of maintaining an orderly internal administration, and of observing with scrupulous care all international obligations, my Government is pleased to extend to it as from this date full recognition as the *de jure* Government of Ecuador.[61]

In 1926 the United States refused to recognize the Chamorro government in Nicaragua or that of Chamorro's successor and insisted that a president be elected in a constitutional manner. When this was done, recognition was immediately granted.[62] Kellogg, referring to the 1923 Central American General Treaty of Peace and Amity, which had incorporated the provision of the 1907 agreement concerning the nonrecognition of revolutionary governments, announced, "The United States has adopted the principles of that treaty as its policy in the future recognition of Central American Governments."[63] Thus the sanction of nonrecognition was consistent with a policy embraced by the Central American nations, and it was deliberately designed to function as a coercive measure to promote stability and constitutional rule. In 1931 Secretary of State Henry L. Stimson noted, "Since the adoption by Secretary Hughes, in 1923, of the policy of nonrecognition agreed upon by the five republics in their convention, not one single revolutionary government has been able to maintain itself in those five republics." Each time a revolutionary leader took control, Stimson observed, "the failure to obtain recognition has resulted in his prompt resignation, on account of his inability to borrow money in the international market." The secretary added, "Several times within the same period a contemplated revolution has been abandoned by its conspirators on the simple reminder by a minister from this country or one of the other republics that, even if they were successful, their government would not be recognized."[64]

In spite of these laudatory remarks of Secretary Stimson on the efficacy of nonrecognition in promoting stable and constitutional government in Central America, it was during his tenure in office that the United States adopted a less rigid policy toward other Latin American nations.[65] When a number of revolutionary regimes were established in 1930 and 1931, recognition was extended without regard to the "legality" of the government, and Stimson publicly renounced the "constitutional legitimacy" doctrine which he attributed to the Wilson administration.[66] Although the official reason for rapid recognition was the worldwide depression and a desire to avoid an interruption of economic intercourse with these nations,[67] the change marked a modification of the practice of using nonrecognition as a sanction to support representative institutions. Moreover, by recognizing virtually every government that exercised power and acknowledged its international obligations, the United States avoided partiality and protected its interests, especially economic, regardless of which group was in control.[68]

Stimson was to achieve a sort of immortality by having his name associated with the doctrine of nonrecognition as a sanction. As Japan continued the invasion of Manchuria which had begun in 1931, the American secretary of state sent identical notes to China and Japan asserting that the government "cannot admit the legality of any situation *de facto* nor does it intend to recognize any treaty or agreement which may impair the treaty rights of the United States . . . and that it does not intend to recognize any situation, treaty, or agreement which may be brought about by means contrary to the covenants and obligations of the Pact of Paris."[69] This departure from a previous policy of conciliation was prompted by the failure of Japanese statesmen to halt aggression, a consolidation of press and public opinion against Japan, and the occupation of Chinchow.[70] It was not an abrupt departure, however, but represented more of a graduated response to Japanese aggression as the pattern became more clear and support for stronger measures became more apparent. Watchful waiting, understanding, mild League cooperation, and diplomatic protests had finally culminated in the doctrine of nonrecognition.

Although the diplomatic weapons of recognition and nonrecognition had been employed in the past by the United States in an effort to coerce other nations, it is scarcely correct to place the Hoover-Stimson doctrine in the same category.[71] In this instance nonrecognition was based on a multilateral treaty which included most of the nations of the world and which contained a self-denying commitment to refrain from using force as an instrument of national policy. The American government, therefore, had a juridical foundation for its action, which the League assembly subsequently endorsed on March 10, 1932. A new dimension of international morality had been invoked, and the question of how the Pact of Paris could be implemented had been given one answer, at least. The American action, while it did not prevent the conquest of Manchuria and may have helped secure increased domestic support for Japan's policies, served to mobilize world opinion and set a precedent for subsequent responses to the aggression which took place during the 1930s.[72]

Under the presidency of Franklin D. Roosevelt the doctrine of nonrecognition was employed as a sanction on numerous occasions. The concessions made by the Soviet government in order to secure recognition have been mentioned. In Cuba, the Grau San Martín regime, which held office in 1933–1934, was not recognized pending the receipt of evidence that it was stable and represented the will of the people. In the meantime the withholding of recognition contributed to the government's downfall, for it encouraged resistance on the grounds that the regime was unacceptable to the United States, and it prevented action on a sugar treaty that was badly needed by the Cuban economy.[73] In 1933 the United States and the other American republics signed the Anti-War Treaty of Non-Aggression and Conciliation, which provided that the signatories "will not recognize any territorial arrangement not obtained by pacific means, nor the occupation or acquisition of territories brought about by force of arms."[74] The administration refused to recognize the Italian conquest of Ethiopia in 1936, and when England contemplated recognition in 1938 Roosevelt and Hull protested. Such abandonment of the principle of nonrecognition of conquered territory, said Hull, would be taken by "the desperado nations . . . as a virtual ratification of their policy of outright treaty wrecking and the seizure of land by force of arms." He considered the nonrecognition policy "of universal importance as a factor in restoring international law and order."[75] On the same principle, when Hitler absorbed all of Czechoslovakia in March 1939, the United States continued to recognize the Czech minister;[76] and this policy was followed when Germany seized Poland in September of that year.[77]

In an address before Congress on January 4, 1939, President Roosevelt spoke of using "methods short of war, but stronger and more effective than mere words, of bringing home to aggressor governments the aggregate sentiments of our own people."[78] According to Cordell Hull, one of these methods was an application of the nonrecognition doctrine.[79] In keeping with this policy the United States refused to recognize the conquest of Albania by Italy in April 1939.[80] It refrained from extending recognition to the Nanking puppet government established by Japan in

March 1940, and Hull declared that "the setting up of a new regime at Nanking has the appearance of a further step in a program of one country by armed force to impose its will upon a neighboring country and to block off a large area of the world from normal political and economic relationships with the rest of the world."[81] When Russia virtually annexed the Baltic republics of Estonia, Latvia, and Lithuania, the United States pursued its nonrecognition policy, and continued to recognize the diplomatic and consular missions of those states. Acting Secretary of State Sumner Welles explained on the grounds that "the people of the United States are opposed to predatory activities no matter whether they are carried on by the use of force or by the threat of force. They are likewise opposed to any form of intervention on the part of one state, however powerful, in the domestic concerns of any other sovereign state, however weak."[82]

With American formal entry into the war against the Axis powers in 1941, a new factor was introduced into the administration's recognition policy, namely, "whether the new government was friendly or unfriendly to our war purposes."[83] The significance of this factor was also acknowledged by other American republics, and in Montevideo in 1943, at the suggestion of the Uruguayan representative, the Emergency Advisory Committee for Political Defense of the Continent recommended that no government that had been established by force be recognized until there had been joint consideration of the situation by the other American governments.[84] The principle was generally accepted and ten governments, including the United States, subsequently acted jointly to delay recognition of the Villaroel regime in Bolivia for six months until positive steps were taken to remove Nazi influence and to support the Allied war effort.[85] Recognition of the Farrell government which seized power in Argentina in February 1944 was withheld because of its sympathy for the Axis and the strong Axis influence both within the government and emanating from Argentina. Farrell, however, did little to correct the situation and refused to declare war on the Axis nations until March 1945, when it became clear that their cause was lost. Earlier in the month, the Conference of Foreign Ministers meeting at Mexico City had made recognition of the Farrell regime conditional upon such a declaration and upon Argentine adherence to the Act of Chapultepec, which had been signed at that conference. Having fulfilled both conditions, the Farrell government was recognized by the United States on April 9, 1945.[86] In each of these cases the sanction proved effective and other Latin American nations cooperated in its application.

Following World War II, President Truman, in his State of the Union address on January 21, 1946, openly espoused the doctrine of nonrecognition as an instrument to promote stability and discourage aggression. "We shall refuse to recognize," he declared, "any government imposed upon any nation by the force of any foreign power. In some cases," he continued, "it may be impossible to prevent forceful imposition of such a government. But the United States will not recognize any such government."[87] In a somewhat different category, the continued refusal of the United States to recognize the Communist government that assumed control of mainland China in 1949 has been the subject of a good deal of controversy. While conventional reasons have been advanced for this policy of nonrecognition, it seems clear that the American position has been dictated largely by a desire to halt the spread of Communism, prevent its success, and encourage democratic institutions.[88] Invoked as a diplomatic weapon in waging the Cold War, nonrecognition has not been an unqualified success.

Nonrecognition has also been employed as a means of discouraging other undemocratic movements. When a military junta took over the government in Peru on July 18, 1962, the Kennedy administration deplored the incident, withheld recognition, and suspended aid operations. After the junta appeared to enjoy a fair amount of popular support and promised an early return to constitutional processes, the United States on August 17 extended recognition. Although the regime was not overthrown, the American action, as a contemporary account put it, "may have helped incline the junta to a moderate and constructive policy and discouraged similar actions elsewhere."[89] Just how many "similar actions" were discouraged is not known, and recent developments in certain Latin American countries indicate that the impact of this American pressure was at best short-lived. The association of economic and technical assistance with diplomatic relations, however, adds another dimension to the efficacy of nonrecognition as a sanction and may be more potent than trade or financial arrangements.

The situation in the Western Hemisphere has, in the past, been somewhat unique, for the consequences of nonrecognition by the United States usually have been more severe than when the doctrine was applied to nations in Europe and Asia. The economy and general well-being of the Latin American countries have been so dependent on the "Colossus of the North" that the denial of the benefits of recognition could prove disastrous to a new regime. It should be emphasized that nonrecognition involves more than merely the onus of moral disapprobation, and much of the criticism directed against the practice as a sanction tends to ignore this fact.[90] The recently emerged nations and their dependence on the United States for economic, cultural, and military assistance make their position somewhat analogous to that of the Latin American countries, and the curtailment of diplomatic relations can have serious implications for any new government. It is the consequences that flow from the denial of recognition that make it most effective as a sanction.

No doubt it is, as one writer observes, "a serious matter when the executive uses recognition as a bludgeon in the contests of diplomacy."[91] Nevertheless, the United States has adopted, in the words of a State Department release, "diplomatic recognition as an instrument of national policy which it is both its right and its duty to use in the enlightened self-interest of the nation."[92] It is a coercive measure that has been applied with varying degrees of success, and its effectiveness depends on the circumstances of the particular case. But in the past nonrecognition has demonstrated its usefulness as a nonmilitary sanction to further the diplomatic objectives of the nation. Being a historian I shall resist the temptation to explain the present and predict the future.

## NOTES

1. Frederick Arnold Middlebush, "Non-Recognition as a Sanction of International Law," *Proceedings, American Society of International Law* 27(1933):40. "In practice non-recognition does not always imply that the existence of the unrecognized state is a matter of doubt. States have discovered that the granting or withholding of recognition can be used to further a national policy." J. L. Brierly, *The Law of Nations*, Sir Humphrey Waldock, ed., sixth ed. (New York, 1963), p. 140.

2. Chesney Hill, "Recent Policies of Non-Recognition," *International Conciliation*, no. 293 (October 1933), p. 359.

3. "Non-Recognition: A Reconsideration," *University of Chicago Law Review* 22(1954):266, note 19.

4. "European governments, at least in the nineteenth century, seem to have been guided in the matter of the recognition of new states or governments almost wholly by considerations of policy or expediency and (perhaps we should add) sympathy with monarchical regimes." Amos S. Hershey, "Notes on the Recognition of de facto Governments by European States," *American Journal of International Law* 14(1920):516.

5. Percy E. Corbett, *Law in Diplomacy* (Princeton, 1959), pp. 79–80.

6. L. Oppenheim, *International Law*, H. Lauterpacht, ed. (London, 1955), vol. 1, p. 125. The editor observes that "Many writers do not agree with this opinion." A brief intelligible discussion of whether recognition is a constitutive or declaratory act may be found in Arthur H. Dean, "Note on Diplomatic Recognition of Governments," The American Assembly, *The United States and the Far East* (New York, 1956), pp. 207–210.

7. John Fischer Williams, "Some Thoughts on the Doctrine of Recognition in International Law," *Harvard Law Review* 17(1934):777.

8. Middlebush, "Non-Recognition as a Sanction of International Law," p. 51. See also Edwin D. Dickinson, "The Unrecognized Government or State in English and American Law," *Michigan Law Review* 22(1923):29–45, 118–134; John C. Hervey, *The Legal Effects of Recognition in International Law as Interpreted by the Courts of the United States* (Philadelphia, 1928); Edwin M. Borchard, "The Unrecognized Government in American Courts," *American Journal of International Law* 26(April 1932):261–271.

9. Ann Van Wynen Thomas and A. J. Thomas, Jr., *Non-Intervention: The Law and Its Import in the Americas* (Dallas, 1956), p. 257; D. A. Graber, *Crisis Diplomacy: A*

*History of United States Intervention Policies and Practices* (Washington, 1959), p. 29; Oppenheim, *International Law*, vol. 1, p. 128.

10. Julius Goebel, Jr., *The Recognition Policy of the United States* (New York, 1915), p. 72.

11. See E. S. Corwin, *French Policy and the American Alliance of 1778* (Princeton, 1916); and Samuel Flagg Bemis, *The Diplomacy of the American Revolution* (New York, 1935).

12. Both quotations are from John Bassett Moore, *International Law Digest* (Washington, 1906), vol. 1, p. 120. For a detailed account see Goebel, *Recognition Policy of the United States*, pp. 97–115.

13. Alexander DeConde, *Entangling Alliance: Politics and Diplomacy Under George Washington* (Durham, N.C., 1958), p. 190.

14. Julius W. Pratt, *A History of United States Foreign Policy* (New York, 1955), p. 174.

15. Samuel Flagg Bemis, *John Quincy Adams and the Foundations of American Foreign Policy* (New York, 1949), p. 355; Arthur P. Whitaker, *The United States and the Independence of Latin America, 1800–1830* (Baltimore, 1941), pp. 373–374.

16. The recognition of the Latin American republics is covered in Moore, *International Law Digest* 1:74–93; Goebel, *The Recognition Policy of the United States*, pp. 116–143; and William Spence Robertson, "The Recognition of the Hispanic American Nations by the United States," *Hispanic American Historical Review* 1(1918):239–269. The latter observes (p. 269): "The policy of the government of the United States toward Brazil and the Spanish-American nations during the age of Adams and Monroe promoted the development of an international policy of recognition—a policy which repudiated the European policy of legitimacy and heralded the principle that, when a new state had established its independence *de facto*, it ought to be admitted into the society of nations." The letter from Adams to the Spanish minister, April 6, 1822, which explains United States recognition policy, is in *American State Papers, Class I, Foreign Relations*, vol. 4, p. 846.

17. H. Lauterpacht, *Recognition in International Law* (Cambridge, 1947), p. 109.

18. Rayford W. Logan, *The Diplomatic Relations of the United States with Haiti, 1776–1891* (Chapel Hill, 1941), pp. 188ff.; L. L. Montague, *Haiti and the United States, 1714–1938* (Durham, N.C., 1940), pp. 47ff.

19. Moore, *International Law Digest*, vol. 1, p. 98.

20. Ibid., p. 124.

21. Ibid., p. 142. The Pierce message continues, "We do not go beyond the fact of a foreign government exercising actual power to investigate questions of legitimacy; we do not inquire into the causes which may have led to a change of government." James D. Richardson, *A Compilation of the Messages and Papers of the Presidents* (Washington, n.d.), vol. 6, pp. 2905–2906.

22. Richardson, *A Compilation*, vol. 6, p. 2906; Moore, *International Law Digest*, vol. 1, p. 146.

23. Hershey, "Notes on the Recognition of de facto Governments by European States," p. 517.

24. Moore, *International Law Digest*, vol. 1, pp. 103–104; Department of State, *List of Papers Relating to Foreign Affairs, 1861* (Washington, 1861), pp. 31–32.

25. *List of Papers Relating to Foreign Affairs, 1861*, pp. 32–33; Moore, *International Law Digest*, vol. 1, pp. 104–105. For a severe criticism of this departure from the *de facto* principle, see Goebel, *The Recognition Policy of the United States*, pp. 172ff.

26. Moore, *International Law Digest*, vol. 1, pp. 105–106.

27. Stuart A. MacCorkle, *American Policy of Recognition Towards Mexico* (Baltimore, 1933), p. 62.

28. Ibid., 61.

29. Detailed accounts of the Maximilian episode are to be found in MacCorkle, *American Policy of Recognition Towards Mexico*, and in Dexter Perkins, *The Monroe Doctrine, 1826–1867* (Baltimore, 1933).

30. Goebel, *The Recognition Policy of the United States*, p. 199.

31. Moore, *International Law Digest*, p. 148. Italics added.

32. James Morton Callahan, *American Policy in Mexican Relations* (New York, 1932), p. 390.

33. MacCorkle, *American Policy of Recognition Towards Mexico*, p. 78.

34. Ibid., p. 80.

35. Callahan, *American Policy in Mexican Relations*, pp. 387, 392, 396, 401; Mac-Corkle, *American Policy of Recognition Towards Mexico*, p. 81.

36. Moore, *International Law Digest*, vol. 1, p. 150.

37. Ibid., p. 152.

38. Another application of the "legitimacy" principle occurred in 1889. As one writer has noted, "Woodrow Wilson's action in Mexico in 1913 is usually believed to have been the first refusal by the United States to recognize a revolutionary president because of the *de jure* principle. But Secretary of State Bayard during Cleveland's first administration applied that principle to two revolutionary claimants to the presidency of Haiti. . . . The close student of both Cleveland and of Bayard would conclude that it was the anti-imperialism of the one and the legalism of the other that led to their hands-off policy." Logan, *Diplomatic Relations*, p. 397.

39. "As a general rule, a government which comes into power by violence is desirous of having as early as possible the moral support of recognition by foreign governments, for although this does not sanction the transitory illegality of revolution it at least gives the appearance of permanency. A government which seeks to withhold, for any reason, an acknowledgement of such a de facto power when other nations have already taken the initiative, lays itself open to the suspicion of unfriendliness which often results to its national disadvantage. This was the case with the United States. After some twenty-five years of experience with Seward's recognition policies, we were virtually compelled to return to the principles for which we had originally stood." Goebel, *The Recognition Policy of the United States*, p. 211.

40. Alfred L. P. Dennis, *Adventures in American Diplomacy, 1896–1906* (New York, 1928), pp. 262ff; E. Taylor Parks, *Colombia and the United States, 1765–1934* (Durham, N.C.), p. 422.

41. John L. McMahon, *Recent Changes in the Recognition Policy of the United States* (Washington, 1933), p. 25.

42. Green Haywood Hackworth, *Digest of International Law*, 8 vols. (Washington, 1940–1944), vol. 1, p. 187.

43. Ibid., pp. 187–188; Charles L. Stansifer, "Application of the Tobar Doctrine to Central America," *The Americas* 23(January 1967):256–257.

44. Letters from Secretary of State Philander Knox to Henry Lane Wilson, February 21, 1913, and February 28, 1913, quoted in MacCorkle, *American Policy of Recognition Towards Mexico*, pp. 85–86. Regarding Taft's attitude, "In 1911, before our recognition of Haiti, we required that Haiti give proper written assurances of her intention to safeguard American interests in that country, including the settlement of claims for damages inflicted during the revolt by which the government had come into power." Green Haywood Hackworth, "The Policy of the United States in Recognizing New Governments During the Past Twenty-five Years," *Proceedings, American Society of International Law* (1931), vol. 25, p. 122.

45. Hackworth, "Policy of the United States in Recognizing New Governments," p. 123.

46. Ibid., pp. 121, 123.

47. Arthur S. Link, *Wilson: The New Freedom* (Princeton, 1956), p. 350.

48. The myth persists. "By adopting this stance, Wilson reversed traditional American policy. Historically, the United States had always recognized *de facto* regimes and such statesmen as John Quincy Adams and James Buchanan had affirmed this doctrine." Kenneth J. Grieb, *The United States and Huerta* (Lincoln, Neb., 1969), p. 43.

49. Lauterpacht, *Recognition in International Law*, p. 128.

50. MacCorkle, *American Policy of Recognition Towards Mexico*, p. 103.

51. Chen refers to this "constitutional" or "republican" legitimism, though his account of its introduction into American recognition practice is sketchy. Ti-Chiang Chen, *The International Law of Recognition* (London, 1951), pp. 107–108.

52. William L. Neumann, Jr., *Recognition of Governments in the Americas* (Washington, 1947), p. 19; Grieb, *The United States and Huerta*, p. 44.

53. See Hackworth, *Digest of International Law*, vol. 1, pp. 182–185, 240–241; W. H. Callcott, *The Caribbean Policy of the United States, 1890–1920* (Baltimore, 1942).

54. Raymond Leslie Buell, "The United States and Central American Stability," *Foreign Policy Reports*, July 8, 1931, vol. 7; Hackworth, *Digest of International Law;* vol. 1, pp. 233–237; George W. Baker, Jr., "Woodrow Wilson's Use of the Non-Recognition Policy in Costa Rica," *The Americas*, 22(July 1965):3–22. The latter concludes (p. 21), "Wilson's non-recognition policy, because of Tinoco's tenacity, proved to be not only largely ineffective in promoting stable and constitutional regimes in the Caribbean, but even harmful."

55. Bryan to Tokyo Embassy, May 11, 1915, U.S. Department of State, *Documents Relating to the Foreign Relations of the United States, 1915*, p. 146; Roy Watson Curry, *Woodrow Wilson and Far Eastern Policy*, 1913–1921 (New York, 1957), pp. 111–129.

56. Robert Paul Browder, *The Origins of Soviet-American Diplomacy* (Princeton, 1953), p. 18. For a series of statements of successive American administrations on the matter of Russian recognition, see *American Journal of International Law* 28(1934):89–94.

57. Jan F. Triska and Robert M. Slusser, *The Theory, Law, and Policy of Soviet Treaties* (Stanford, 1962), p. 183. One aspect was that "the two problems, recognition and trade, presented a dilemma to Soviet foreign policy . . . without the one there was no chance for the other."

58. Browder, *Origins of Soviet-American Diplomacy*, pp. 141–150.

59. MacCorkle, *American Policy of Recognition Towards Mexico*, p. 96.

60. See Callahan, *American Policy in Mexican Relations*, pp. 586–595.

61. Hackworth, *Digest of International Law*, vol. 1, p. 245 (August 13, 1928).

62. Ibid., pp. 266–268; L. H. Woolsey, "The Non-Recognition of the Chamorro Government in Nicaragua," *American Journal of International Law* 20(1926):543:549.

63. Woolsey, *Non-Recognition of the Chamorro Government*, p. 543. "There is not the slightest possibility of the United States extending recognition to any Government in Nicaragua, headed either by Sacasa or by anybody else, which is based upon armed force or insurrection." Frank B. Kellogg to Admiral Latimer, January 27, 1927, in *Foreign Relations of the United States, 1927*, vol. 3, p. 305.

64. Address of February 6, 1931, quoted in C. P. Anderson, "Our Policy of Non-Recognition in Central America," *American Journal of International Law* 25(1931):299.

65. Bryce Wood, *The Making of the Good Neighbor Policy* (New York, 1961), p. 126; Stansifer, "Application of the Tobar Doctrine to Central America," p. 267.

66. Walter Lippmann and William O. Scroggs, *The United States in World Affairs, 1931* (New York, 1932), p. 67.

67. Ibid., p. 64, and text of a Stimson address, pp. 332–334. The proposal of the Mexican foreign minister, Genaro Estrada, may have had some influence. For this "doctrine," see Phillip C. Jessup, "The Estrada Doctrine," *American Journal of International Law* 25(1931):408. In 1930 the foreign minister called for the abolition of a recognition policy "which allows foreign governments to pass upon the legitimacy or illegitimacy of the regime existing in another country" on the grounds that it was "an insulting practice" and an act of intervention. Thomas and Thomas, *Non-Intervention: The Law and its Import*, pp. 50–51.

68. C. Neale Ronning, *Law and Politics in Inter-American Diplomacy* (New York, 1963), pp. 9–10.

69. *Foreign Relations of the United States, Japan, 1931–1941*, vol. 1, p. 76.

70. See Robert Langer, *The Seizure of Territory, the Stimson Doctrine and Related Principles in Legal Theory and Diplomatic Practice* (Princeton, 1947); Armin Rappaport, *Henry L. Stimson and Japan, 1931–1933* (Chicago, 1963); Quincy Wright, ed., *Legal Problems in the Far Eastern Conflict* (New York, 1941).

71. "Non-Recognition: A Reconsideration," p. 267.

72. For this episode and subsequent applications of the "Stimson Doctrine," see Marjorie M. Whiteman, *Digest of International Law* (Washington, 1965), vol. 5, pp. 874–965.

73. Wood, *The Making of the Good Neighbor Policy*, pp. 81–84; E. David Cronon, "Interpreting the New Good Neighbor Policy: The Cuban Crisis of 1933," *Hispanic American Historical Review* 39(1959):538–567.

74. J. Lloyd Mecham, *The United States and Inter-American Security, 1889–1960* (Austin, Texas, 1961), pp. 118–120. This agreement was also known as the Saavedra Lamas treaty.

75. Hull, *The Memoirs of Cordell Hull* (New York, 1948), vol. 1, pp. 579–582.

76. Ibid., p. 615.

77. Ibid., p. 686.

78. U.S., Department of State, *Peace and War: United States Foreign Policy, 1931–1941* (Washington, 1943), p. 449.

79. Hull, *The Memoirs of Cordell Hull*, vol. 1, p. 614.

80. Ibid., p. 619.

81. Ibid., p. 725.

82. Graber, *Crisis Diplomacy*, p. 29.

83. Hull, *The Memoirs of Cordell Hull*, vol. 2, pp. 1401–1402.

84. Carl B. Spaeth and William Sanders, "The Emergency Advisory Committee for Political Defense," *American Journal of International Law* 38(1944):218–241; Neumann, *Recognition of Governments in the Americas*, pp. 33ff; O. Edmund Smith, Jr., *Yankee Diplomacy: U.S. Intervention in Argentina* (Dallas, 1953), pp. 90ff.

85. Neumann, *Recognition of Governments in the Americas*, pp. 34–35; Hull, *Memoirs of Cordell Hull*, vol. 2, pp. 1397–1399.

86. Smith, *Yankee Diplomacy*, pp. 134–136; Hull, *Memoirs of Cordell Hull*, vol. 2, pp. 1401–1408.

87. U.S., *Public Papers of the Presidents of the United States, Harry S. Truman, 1946*, vol. 1, p. 18.

88. Perhaps the clearest expression of nonrecognition as a method of halting the spread of Communism is contained in an address by Secretary of State John Foster Dulles, entitled "Our Policies Toward Communism in China," June 28, 1957. Department of State press release 393 of the same date.

89. Richard P. Stebbins, *The United States in World Affairs, 1962* (New York, 1963), p. 285. For a survey of a topic not adequately covered in this paper, see Donald M. Dozer, "Recognition in Contemporary Inter-American Relations," *Journal of Inter-American Studies* 8(April 1966):318–335.

90. For example, Manfred Lachs, "Recognition and Modern Methods of International Co-operation," *British Yearbook of International Law* 35(1959):252–259; Arnold D. McNair, "The Stimson Doctrine of Non-Recognition," *British Yearbook of International Law* 14(1933):65–74; John F. Williams "Some Thoughts on the Doctrine of Recognition in International Law," *Harvard Law Review* 48(1934):776–794. For a careful exposition of the effect of nonrecognition, see Marjorie M. Whiteman, *Digest of International Law* 2(1963):604–665.

91. Dickinson, "The Unrecognized Government or State in English and American Law," p. 134.

92. U.S. Department of State, Memorandum to Missions Abroad, August 11, 1958, p. 39, Department of State Bulletin 385 (1958).

# CHAPTER TEN

# Roosevelt and Churchill: A Reinterpretation of the Diplomacy of World War II

THE CONVENTIONAL INTERPRETATION OF THE DIPLOMACY OF THE SECOND World War contends that Roosevelt, unlike Churchill, did not understand the correlation between force and diplomacy; that the president was obsessed with the military aspects of the war, ignored the political objectives inherent in the use of armed force, prolonged the conflict, and made it possible for the Soviet Union to shape the peace, dominate Eastern Europe, and threaten the security of the Western World. My own opinion is that the reverse is more nearly correct. Of course after reading some of the masses of literature on the subject of World War II it is possible to conclude that nothing that anyone did was right, and I intend to make my contribution to this assessment.

At the outset I want to indicate briefly what the Allies were fighting for, since it is only in this context that the military-diplomatic measures make sense. France and England declared war against Germany in September 1939 not primarily to save Poland but to prevent Germany from dominating Europe. Roosevelt, in an effort to aid these Allies, took over many of their responsibilities in the Far East so they could concentrate on Germany. The president accelerated economic sanctions as Japan took advantage of German successes to move into French Indochina and threaten British and Dutch interests. After Russia entered the war, Roosevelt sought to prevent Japan from moving south to cut the British lifeline or north to attack Russia, since either move would have an adverse effect on the European conflict. If Germany and Italy were defeated, the combined pressure of the other nations might be sufficient to dissuade Japan from aggression and induce her to relinquish previous gains.

It should be borne in mind, first, that the war was being waged in order to achieve certain political objectives. The armed forces were being used as an instrument—the ultimate instrument—of foreign policy. This was true not only for the United States but for the other nations involved. Consequently, it was imperative that the method of waging the war should be correlated with the political ends desired. Since each of the Allies was seeking its own ends, some of which conflicted with those of the others, the problems of coalition warfare were enormous. And it must be emphasized that differences among the Allies were based on tactical and strategic grounds as well as on conflicting political ambitions. The second point to remember is that if the war were lost or a stalemate reached resulting in a compromise peace, the political objectives would not be achieved. Thus there appeared what might seem a paradoxical situation: in determining how the war was to be fought, should "purely military" considerations prevail or should they be subordinated to political concerns? If the Allies were defeated nothing would be gained. If the Allies thought only in terms of military victory certain fundamental political objectives might be sacrificed. Roosevelt's major problem, which was also that of the other heads of state, was to reconcile his ends and means to the maximum.

So far as war aims are concerned, the United States was fighting to destroy the governments of the aggressor nations, whose actions jeopardized the safety of the United States, the Western Hemisphere, and the rest of the world; to establish a peace that would demonstrate that aggression did not pay and that would eliminate some of the injustices perpetrated by the Treaty of Versailles which provided an excuse if not a justification for aggression; and to create some kind of world order to enforce certain standards of conduct among nations. Russia wanted a settlement that would leave her at least with the gains made as a result of the earlier collaboration with Hitler, and she wanted friendly governments on her borders. British objectives appeared similar to those of the United States, and both Roosevelt and Churchill had agreed on certain principles as proclaimed in the Atlantic Charter in August 1941. The interpretation of these principles and their implementation produced disagreements of serious proportion. Nevertheless, as the prime minister once observed, there was "only one thing worse than fighting with allies, and that is fighting without them." Although the Allies disagreed about what they were fighting for they did know what they were fighting against, and that provided a common bond. Maintaining the coalition's purpose as Axis strength waned and Allied victory became more certain placed greater strains on the alliance.

A potential area of friction was removed when a tentative policy of defeating Germany first was confirmed after official United States entry. Since sufficient men and material were not available to wage a successful war on two fronts, this strategy meant a virtual holding operation in the Pacific while the main thrust was directed toward Europe. Behind this decision were the belief that Germany was the most dangerous foe and the possibility that an Allied victory in Europe would convince Japan that her cause was hopeless. This diversion of effort was opposed by segments of Congress and the American public, but the basic problem was to allocate resources in a way that would most successfully expedite the waging of the war. Too great a delay in relieving the pressure on the Russian front might result in a Nazi victory, and loss of the Soviet ally could be decisive. With the Japanese advance unchecked in the Western Pacific, the desperate plight of the forces in the Philippines, and the deteriorating situation in Southeast Asia and China, the Germany first strategy was viewed by some as an aberration. But the president never wavered, and to satisfy the public, the military advisors, and the Allies was impossible under the best of circumstances. To do this and still win the war against formidable and determined foes was a task so immense that it defies imagination. In fact, reading some of the enormous amount of material relating to the war will lead to the conclusion that it could not be done.

Within the context of the situation outlined above, evidence of Churchill's so-called "perception" in regard to objectives is revealed by his attitude toward Russian territorial demands in the early stages of the war. Prior to America's formal entry, Stalin wanted the British to agree to Soviet retention of all the territory acquired from the deal with Hitler and a bit more. Faced with strong objections from the United States, Churchill merely deferred the issue. Then in early 1942 Churchill, afraid the Russians might accept a negotiated peace with Germany, tried to conclude a military alliance. Stalin insisted on the incorporation of previous territorial demands. Churchill was ready to accede until Roosevelt protested on the grounds that a free hand should be preserved until negotiations could be conducted in a different atmosphere. The implications of the May 1942 German advance into the Crimea probably induced Stalin to accept the alliance without territorial agreements, and the Anglo-Soviet pact was signed on May 26, 1942. Roosevelt thus prevented Churchill from binding England—and indirectly the United States—to boundary concessions without multilateral negotiations, and at a time when the British and American forces were absent from the continent of Europe.

Another issue on which these two leaders differed is that of the second front. Hitler, in the months and years following the conquest of Western Europe and much of Eastern Europe, strove to weld this area into a gigantic fortress. In exploiting these non-German areas for raw materials and forced labor, Germany marshalled the human, natural, and industrial resources of the Continent. So in spite of the enormous drain on the

Eastern front, Hitler's domain became more formidable as time went on. But just as the German defenses of Western Europe were weaker in 1942 and 1943, the Allies were not so well-prepared for a cross-channel invasion in those years as they were in 1944. Therefore American and British forces were employed to occupy North Africa, capture Sicily, and begin the agonizing march up the Italian penninsula. Thus the maximum effort was directed at clearing the Mediterranean—in large part to free it for Britain's communications with Suez and the British empire in the East. Some pressure was being exerted on Germany and a portion of the German resources was being drained from the Eastern front. Meanwhile, the Russians pushed back the German forces and occupied more of Eastern Europe. By the time summit discussions ceased to concentrate on military problems and began to deal with political settlements, Russian troops were in possession of vital territory from which they could be dislodged only by force. The advantage in bargaining power accruing to the Soviet Union was significant.

President Roosevelt and his military advisors wanted a second front in Europe—a cross-channel invasion—in 1942 or 1943 at the latest. The prime minister, after initial consent, changed his mind and persuaded the president to accept a diversion of effort that delayed the second front until June 1944. Basically, the issue involved a dispute over military strategic concepts. The American approach was direct—to engage the major enemy military forces as quickly as possible and bring the war to a conclusion. The British, for historical and other reasons, were committed to an indirect, peripheral strategy that amounted to a war of attrition. If Anglo-American efforts had been directed toward the implementation of a cross-channel invasion a year or so earlier, the troops would have been much further east and would have occupied a great deal more territory when postwar settlements were discussed. Consequently, we would have been in a much stronger position to secure the kind of peace we wanted, and governments that we supported with the free elections we insisted on would have been possible. For example, the subsequent history of Poland probably would have been quite different if we had occupied that territory and administered postwar affairs. Of course a cross-channel invasion in 1943 would have been a bloody operation, but just as we were not so well prepared as we were in 1944, neither were the Germans.

Among the many alleged "mistakes" of World War II attributed to President Roosevelt is the "unconditional surrender" policy. Purportedly, this "doctrine" strengthened enemy morale, prevented resistance movements from overthrowing the Nazis, unnecessarily lengthened the war, and enabled the Soviet Union to emerge with the major fruits of victory. Some confusion over the promulgation of the doctrine was created by an assertion of the prime minister that he first learned of the policy when the president made the announcement at the Casablanca press conference on January 24, 1943. Later, when his memory was refreshed, Churchill admitted that he had known of the policy and had cleared it with the cabinet earlier. What he did not acknowledge, but is revealed by the minutes of the Casablanca conference, is that he was responsible for the public declaration. The minutes record the following conversation on the subject of press releases: "The Prime Minister suggested that at the same time we release a statement to the effect that the United Nations are resolved to pursue the war to the bitter end, neither party relaxing in its efforts until the unconditional surrender of Germany and Japan has been achieved. He said that before issuing such a statement, he would like to consult with his colleagues in London." It should be added that his colleagues in London, i.e., the British cabinet, not only concurred but recommended that Italy be included. The president agreed, and he declared to the press that "The elimination of German, Japanese, and Italian war power means the unconditional surrender by Germany, Italy, and Japan." Then and later denying that the policy implied punitive measures against the nations or the peoples involved, neither the president nor the prime minister was able to prevent its exploitation by propagandists.

Yet the unconditional surrender policy served both tactical and strategic purposes. In the short run, it provided a partial response to Russian recriminations over the further postponement of a cross-channel invasion. Also, it served notice on all combatants that there would be no compromises or deals with the Axis governments, although formal adherence by the Soviets was not forthcoming until October 1943. Longer term advantages included a reinforcement of the ban on a discussion of postwar territorial issues. This served a double purpose in preventing quarrels over issues that might wreck the harmony necessary to prosecute the war, and in postponing commitments on specific political questions until the American and British armies should have a significant presence in Western Europe. Further, the unconditional surrender doctrine unified American public opinion on the need for winning the war, it laid the basis for postwar cooperation between the Allies by preserving American freedom of action with regard to the future of Germany, and it helped dispel the suspicion that secret treaties would emerge to complicate the peace as they had in the first world war.

As to the charge that the unconditional surrender declaration prevented resistance movements from overthrowing the Nazis and ending the war, it should be noted that the predominant resistance leaders wanted Allied assurance that Germany be restored to its prewar size and position in

Europe. Such a concession would have subverted the purpose of the war. Also, many of the resistance leaders were military officers in the old Prussian tradition bent on preserving German military capability. This element, the president insisted, must be eliminated. It should be recalled that efforts to conclude a separate peace were made by both Germany and Russia, though on each occasion the peace feelers were rejected by the other party because *at the time* the minimum demands were not commensurate with the existing military situation. Furthermore, the "unconditional surrender" formula in its total implication was applied solely to Germany. Italy and Japan capitulated "unconditionally" only in regard to their armed forces, and the Soviet Union ignored the phrase when ending the war with Finland, Romania, Bulgaria, and Hungary.

Winston Churchill's complicity in the so-called "rape" of Poland is clearly revealed by the documents. At Teheran in November 1943 during a conversation with Premier Stalin and President Roosevelt, Churchill confessed that "he personally had no attachment to any specific frontier between Poland and the Soviet Union; that he felt that the consideration of Soviet security on their [sic] Western frontiers was a governing factor," and "remarked that it would be very valuable if here in Teheran the representatives of the three governments could work out some agreed understanding on the question of the Polish frontiers which could then be taken up with the Polish government in London."[1] He added that "as far as he was concerned, he would like to see Poland moved westward in the same manner as soldiers at drill execute the drill 'left close.' ... " At a subsequent meeting of the three leaders the prime minister introduced a rationale for imperialistic land-grabbing that, if publicized, would have brought anguished cries from the victims of Axis aggression. As recorded in the minutes of the conversation kept by Charles Bohlen, "The Prime Minister then said that it was important that the nations who would govern the world after the war, and who would be entrusted with the direction of the world after the war, should be satisfied and have no territorial or other ambitions. If that question could be settled in a manner agreeable to the great powers, he felt then that the world might indeed remain at peace. He said that hungry nations and ambitious nations are dangerous, and he would like to see the leading nations of the world in the position of rich, happy men."[2] Such an open invitation to territorial acquisition rendered doubly difficult later attempts to induce the Soviet authorities to accept border and other proposals based on the declaration of the United Nations and the Atlantic Charter.

The conference at Teheran was convened to plan future military operations, and Churchill's introduction of political questions visibly disturbed the president. With the Anglo-American forces barely on the periphery of the German stronghold and the Russians making the major contribution to the Allied cause, the occasion seemed scarcely propitious for a consideration of political matters. But tentative agreement was reached on a number of items, agreement later formalized at Yalta. Again, one is reminded that these conversations took place more than six months prior to the cross-channel invasion that began the Western penetration of the Nazi domain.

In regard to the Balkans, Churchill had wanted to work out with the Russians what he called "divisions of responsibility," but was dissuaded by the Americans. Then, when Churchill went to Moscow in October 1944, he reported that he said to Stalin, "Let us settle about our affairs in the Balkans," and he wrote out on a slip of paper the percentage of influence that each nation should have in each of the countries. Stalin quickly approved. Churchill then suggested that the paper be burned, saying "Might it not be thought rather cynical if it seemed we had disposed of these issues, so fateful to millions of people, in such an offhand manner?" But Stalin said no, you keep it. Churchill adds that they "were only dealing with immediate wartime arrangements. All larger questions were reserved on both sides for what we then hoped would be a peace table when the war was won."[3] Whether the prime minister's interpretation was correct is not known, but he does not claim that the duration of the agreement was specified or even discussed, and these allocations of predominance created many postwar altercations. Significantly, Roosevelt had cabled Churchill that the United States would not consider itself bound by any arrangements made with Stalin at Moscow, and Ambassador Averill Harriman was present only as an observer.

The matter of the areas in Germany that each ally should occupy after victory was another thorny problem. Early in May 1942 the president wrote Stalin that "There is always the possibility that the historic Russian defense, followed by taking the offensive, may cause a crack-up in Germany next winter. In such a case we must be prepared for the many next steps. We are none of us prepared today." Later, in January 1942 en route to Cairo, Roosevelt voiced two objections to Churchill's suggestion that Great Britain occupy the northwestern portion of Germany and the United States occupy the southern portion south of the Moselle River: first, that France was Britain's "baby" and the United States did not want the task of reconstruction in that country; second, that American ships could best use the northern German ports and the United States should occupy Germany as far as Berlin, with the Soviet Union having the territory to the east. "There will definitely be a race for Berlin," the president wrote, adding that "we may have to put the United States divisions into Berlin as soon as possible." If the president had not acceded later to Churchill's insistence on occupation zones, which the prime minister cleared with the

Kremlin before securing American approval, the entire course of subsequent relationships with the Soviets might have been different.

Within the framework of these comments on occupation zones, attention must be given to the criticism of the decision to halt American troops at the Elbe River rather than have them push on with the possibility of capturing Berlin before the Russians. In the first place, this was a purely military decision made by General Eisenhower in his capacity as Supreme Allied Commander. It was estimated that this effort would cost over 100,000 casualties and would not be militarily justified. In the second place, the capture of Berlin by American troops would have had no effect on the occupation. The zones already had been established and a withdrawal of forces after German surrender had been agreed to. The decision was made before the Anglo-American landings in France and was based on Churchill's proposals which, contrary to Roosevelt's position, placed Berlin well within the Soviet zone.

To summarize, the following points seem clear:

*First*, Churchill's peripheral strategy—the indirect approach—was not sound, either militarily or politically. Millitarily, this strategy lengthened the war, demanded the commitment of more resources, and increased casualties on all sides. Politically, it created dissension among the Allies, provoked distrust, and placed Russia in a more advantageous bargaining position.

*Second*, Winston Churchill was willing—in fact anxious—to grant Russia greater territorial concessions in Eastern Europe than was Roosevelt, thereby hindering the president's efforts to restrain Stalin's ambitions.

*Third*, Winston Churchill allocated spheres of influence in the Balkans that permitted Soviet dominance in that area.

*Fourth*, Winston Churchill's allocation of occupation zones in Germany gave Russia a stronger position in Central Europe and created sources of subsequent friction.

I have focused on some of the more controversial dimensions of World War II diplomacy. Obviously, there are many others. But as they say, the best way to make sure of your place in history is to write it yourself. Churchill did, Roosevelt never had the opportunity. As more material becomes available the historian has an obligation to determine whether the accepted versions are compatible with the evidence.

## NOTES

1. U.S. Department of State, *Foreign Relations of the United States, Conferences at Cairo and Tehran, 1943*, p. 512.

2. Ibid., 568.

3. This remarkable episode is reported in Winston Churchill, *Triumph and Tragedy* (Boston, 1953), pp. 227–228.

# CHAPTER ELEVEN

# President Truman's Control of National Security Policy

THE PRESIDENT OF THE UNITED STATES, HERMAN FINER HAS ASSERTED, possesses "the highest temporal power on earth."[1] The validity of this claim rests largely on the extension of executive control in the realm of security policy that took place during the administration of Harry S. Truman. While exercising the powers of his office in virtually every way established by precedent, Truman added new dimensions to the role and authority of the chief executive in military and international affairs. These new dimensions of power and responsibility have become an accepted part of the governmental apparatus. At the time of their inception, however, many of these innovations were strenuously resisted by members of Congress and segments of the public. Regardless of their merits, the adoption and incorporation of these "new dimensions" in the office of the presidency was, to a considerable degree, due to the skill and persistence of Mr. Truman.

"The President," Truman believed, "must use whatever power the Constitution does not expressly deny him."[2] Truman's concept of the office derived from his own personality, his experience as an elected official, his great admiration for Franklin D. Roosevelt, and his interpretation of history. Though he indulged in periods of self-depreciation, Truman had a streak of stubbornness that overcame what some considered his excessive humility. So long as he bore the responsibility he intended to exercise commensurate authority.

Truman was greatly impressed by his predecessor's conduct of the office, especially his extensive use of presidential power. Struck by what he considered Roosevelt's success in foreign affairs, Truman embraced the doctrine and the practice of director and leader in the formation and execution of foreign policy. Believing that "Every great President in our history had a policy of his own, which eventually won the people's support," Truman intended to act as chief educator.[3]

Truman was also aware of instances where presidents had not been successful in securing support for their policies. Like Roosevelt, he had been impressed by Wilson's failure to win Senate approval of the Treaty of Versailles, and he attached considerable importance to the lessons of the past. Truman was fond of Justice Holmes' observation that "a page of history is worth a volume of logic."[4] His own reading of American history revealed that "a successful administration is one of strong Presidential leadership," for "weak leadership—produces failure, often chaos and something else."[5] Each of his presidential heroes had dominated his administration, established precedents, taken unpopular positions, and usually had his views prevail. Significantly, each of these presidents had faced crises where leadership determined the outcome. Truman, deeply conscious of the responsibilities of his office, was ever mindful of the role that his predecessors had played—or failed to play—when the nation's future was at stake. Determined to err on the side of action rather than inaction, he wanted his administration to be remembered for its accomplishments instead of its derelictions.

His own experience and his reading of history had also convinced him that "a President has to be a politician in order to get the majority to go along with him on his program."[6] Politics, to Truman, was a noble profession. The methods of politics—persuasion and manipulation—were not to be derided but respected and fostered, and the practice was an art at which the president should be a master. Truman no doubt realized that the means by which support for a policy is gained often has little relevance to the merits of the proposal.

In this regard, Richard Neustadt has pointed out that a president's "bargaining advantages in seeking what he wants are heightened or diminished by what others think of him."[7] The image projected by Truman is somewhat paradoxical. As a presidential figure he did not possess the dignity normally associated with the office, and in this respect he lacked popular appeal. Yet the public could easily identify with him for he was, unlike Roosevelt, just commonplace Harry.

On the other hand, Truman's reputation as a statesman was usually higher in the Washington community than it was with the general public. "Ideally," concludes Douglass Cater, "a President must earn the favor of both these publics if he is not to suffer an erosion of his powers."[8] But the very characteristics that made Truman attractive as a *person* in high office tended to detract from his image as a president and weakened his appeal as a national leader.

An experienced Washington reporter has observed that "since power is fragmented in the American system, public opinion is called on more regularly than elsewhere to act as arbiter among the competing policies and politicians."9 If this be so, then the problem for plain Harry Truman was compounded, for he felt that he knew what had to be done but his stature made him less effective in this type of leadership. He had, however, a key factor acting in his favor. His administration spanned a period of challenges to national security, and traditionally appeals for unity at moments of danger had been successful. Truman was able to secure Congressional and public support for proposed changes in policy by exploiting what was treated as a crisis situation. Thus much of his success in directing the course of American foreign relations stemmed from his effective dramatization of the threat to the nation's safety and his grim depiction of the alternatives facing the country.

The remainder of this study will be devoted to an account of the development of the new dimensions of the presidency under Truman and the way in which he exercised conventional and other powers in meeting his added responsibilities and wielding his new authority.

The first of these new dimensions was control over nuclear weapons. In his role as commander in chief, he was to be the first president to direct that atomic bombs be used, to be faced with the problem of dealing with the international regulation of this most destructive weapon, to assimilate it into the national defense structure, to possess it as an instrument of diplomacy, and to order the development of its hydrogen successor. His action in each of these cases was determined by considerations of foreign policy, and his control over this weapon added a new dimension to the power of the president in international affairs.

His first opportunity to use the bomb as an instrument of diplomacy occurred at the summit Potsdam Conference. The use of the bomb as a coercive device for securing concessions from the Russians had been considered by the American delegation and rejected. Throughout his administration, Truman refused to employ nuclear weapons overtly as a "big stick" in order to achieve his diplomatic objectives. It was well within his power to employ such a tactic, both in his capacity as commander in chief and as director of foreign relations. He was the only person who could speak authoritatively for the government and the nation on these questions, and the decision was exclusively his.

No doubt there were a number of reasons for Truman's resisting the temptation to use the threat of what Secretary of War Stimson called "the most terrible weapon ever known in human history." The Russians, he realized, knew that the United States would employ the device in the event of an all-out war, for it had done so against Japan. The Russians were also aware that the state of the American armed forces would not permit the waging of a "conventional" conflict against a major power, so a warning that the bomb might be dropped would be a superfluous provocation. Moreover, Truman was just not willing to use the bomb to resolve any of the issues that appeared during his administration. His determination to preserve peace, his awareness of the horrors of nuclear war, and, probably most important, his conviction that such drastic means would be out of all proportion to the desired end, prevented him from brandishing the atomic arsenal.

During the crucial period of America's exclusive possession of nuclear weapons and the breaking of this monopoly by the Soviet Union in 1949, Truman secured congressional consent for his approach to the development of atomic energy and general domestic approval of his program for international control. His latter policy was supported by the Western nations, and he steadfastly refused to accept the Soviet proposal for unilateral nuclear disarmament.

Another vital area in which the president exercised a major influence was in the effect this new weapon was to have on America's postwar military structure. Ideally, the armed forces, as an instrument of foreign policy, should have been designed to conform with American commitments throughout the world. Yet the extent of these commitments was not clear and an immense confrontation with Russia was not anticipated. What may have been apparent to some, but was accepted by few, was the fact that the Second World War had added two vital dimensions to America's defense imperatives. First, improvements in weapons systems made possible sudden large-scale attacks on the United States, which ruled out the luxury of leisurely mobilization. Second, the nation was committed to involvement in European and Far Eastern affairs to a much greater extent than ever before. Then, to further compound the dilemma, the question arose as to how the "ultimate weapon" should be incorporated into the American defense structure.

Truman found himself the focal point of the dispute between the various services over the composition of the armed forces, the share of the budget that each should receive, and the future role of the atomic bomb. He not only had to determine the merits of the individual service claims in regard to fighting efficiency, but he also had to establish American military responsibilities in order to decide what American defense needs should be. Using the joint criteria of economy and preparation for all-out war, Truman's defense policy proved inadequate to support American foreign policy objectives. The shortcomings of this approach were dramatically revealed when the first act of Communist military aggression took place in Korea.

Certainly one of the most vital powers of the president in international affairs is his role as Commander in Chief, and Truman, as Samuel Huntington has observed, "determined the overall level of military effort and the strategy by which it was shaped."[10] The added responsibilities assumed by the United States after World War II markedly increased the peacetime role of force in diplomacy, and the advent of intercontinental aircraft armed with nuclear weapons provided the president with new dimensions of responsibility and power. Truman, by failing to coordinate American capabilities with American commitments, endangered security and world peace. Still, after Japan's surrender, he never authorized the bomb's use in war or overtly employed it as a tool of diplomacy. The final decision in these matters was his alone, and his tight control over this ultimate weapon was never relaxed.

A second dimension of presidential control of security policy was added when the United States assumed responsibility for the unilateral protection of the "Free World." This commitment developed gradually in response to Russian violation of wartime agreements, Soviet intransigence at postwar conferences, Communist aggression, and the inability of the United Nations to preserve the independence of small nations.

The most dramatic and far-reaching step taken by the president in regard to the unilateral protection of the Free World was his announcement of the Truman Doctrine. Truman himself considers it "the turning point in American foreign policy, which now declared that wherever aggression, direct or indirect, threatened the peace, the security of the United States was involved."[11] In this case the decision to furnish assistance to Greece and Turkey was not so difficult as was the problem of convincing Congress and the American people of the necessity for this action.

To secure support for his proposal, the president called congressional leaders to the White House for a briefing by himself and Secretary of State Marshall. At a second meeting the group was presented with the detailed plans for American aid. Senator Vandenberg, aware of the drastic nature of the move, observed that the best method of obtaining the desired legislation would be to go before the nation and scare the hell out of the people. Following this advice, the president on March 12, 1947, before a joint session of Congress, reviewed the situation, outlined the alternatives, and placed the program in the broad framework of American resistance to a new form of totalitarian aggression.

Over two months elapsed before the bill was sent to the president, who thereby secured authorization for a project that marked a drastic departure in American foreign policy. A Republican dominated Congress had responded to the presidential request because it had been handled adroitly and was based on an ultimate threat to national security. Truman's approach, with its emphasis on the crisis proportions of the situation, had won the support of the communications media and the public, both of whom made their influence felt on Congress. The latter had responded to executive initiative largely because of the leadership the United States had gradually assumed in resisting Communist aggression, a leadership that developed from the direction in which the president had led American diplomacy. This instance of bipartisan support for presidential policies in foreign affairs was a direct result of the new role accorded the United States in the world, a role fostered by Truman that added significant powers to his office.

American determination was tested by the Berlin blockade in the summer of 1948, which witnessed the first confrontation with Soviet forces. The president, in making his choice of responses from the alternatives available, received little help from his advisors. Actually, the president's task was not to convince Congress and the public that the United States should resist the blockade—prior developments and the absence of any need for legislation minimized those considerations—but to persuade his assistants that the job could be done.

"Probably no powers granted to the President by Congress," declared Robert A. Dahl, "were quite so significant to the nation's future in the summer of 1948 as the President's inherent discretionary power over our conduct in the Berlin crisis."[12] The Cold War had placed enormous strains on the office, and Truman had called on his constitutional and accrued authority as the struggle intensified. Hard won congressional approval for one step was interpreted, apparently, as consent for presidential action in subsequent similar situations. The crises occasioned by Communist moves enabled the president to adopt more extreme measures on his own initiative to counter Soviet threats. The Berlin emergency evoked no appeal to the legislative branch or a consultation with congressional leaders. Public opinion and the attitude of other nations evidently played little part in the president's decision. The American response to the Berlin blockade was as near complete an exercise of executive prerogative as the nation had seen since the end of World War II. It marked the culmination of presidential efforts to commit the nation to the unilateral protection of the Free World, and it revealed that the future of resistance to Communism would be determined in the White House.

A third dimension of presidential control was provided by the creation of new machinery for the formulation and execution of defense and foreign policy. The National Security Act of 1947 created the most significant new machinery to emerge during the Truman years for the planning and conduct of American diplomacy. The impetus for this legislation came largely from the president, though Congress was not willing to accept all of his recommendations. This new machinery to aid the president in his task of controlling security policy did increase his powers in this field. The centralization of effort enabled him to secure more rapid, concise, and accurate information on American capabilities and foreign intentions. It furnished him with the combined judgments of senior officials, who were compelled to broaden their perspectives by exposure to the positions of their colleagues. Streamlining the national security apparatus tightened the lines of communication that separated decisions from implementation, and thereby expedited the transmission of orders into execution. Moreover, these new agencies constituted power resources on which the president could draw for support. An endorsement of his policies by the Defense Department or the National Security Council weighed heavily with Congress and the public. The National Security Act of 1947 sharpened the weapons at the president's disposal and added a new dimension to his command of American defense policy.

In large measure, the operational efficiency of this new machinery depended on the way it was used by the president. Truman, for example, prudently did not employ the Central Intelligence Agency as an instrument for executing policy. He did rely heavily on the Joint Chiefs of Staff where military operations were involved, as in the Berlin blockade. The National Security Council was especially valuable for complex, long-term policy questions when circumstances did not demand an immediate solution. Under Truman, the degree of urgency and the nature of the crisis often determined the type of consultation that took place. In turn, the type of consultation often determined the nature of the action taken. The president, in selecting the team to which a matter should be referred, usually ensured the kind of advice he wanted.

For Truman, the decision as to *what* should be done was often easy. *How* it should be done troubled him greatly, and in this area of implementation the president relied heavily on his advisors. The new machinery, under his manipulation, augmented the powers of the president in international affairs, and the precedents established by Truman in the utilization of this machinery were not ignored by his successors.

A fourth dimension of presidential control of security policy was added when the nation assumed the task of promoting world prosperity. The experience of securing acceptance of the Anglo-American Financial Agreement alerted Truman to the difficulties of leading the nation into uncharted areas of international obligation. The war had convinced the nation that it should assume limited responsibilities for the preservation of peace through collective security, and the humane feelings of an affluent people condoned temporary relief measures to avoid starvation. Demands for other economic assistance, whose need was not so obvious and whose significance was not so easily understood, were bound to meet resistance. The presidential art of persuasion would be taxed to its utmost if America was to be led further in the direction of promoting world prosperity through unconventional financial outlays.

While the administration followed the painstaking, time-consuming routine of securing congressional approval of the Truman Doctrine, Secretary of State George Marshall returned from abroad with alarming news. Negotiations with the Soviets were at a standstill as they pursued a ruthless campaign to dominate the West. Moreover, the economies of western Europe were nearing collapse. The expected postwar recovery had not materialized, and widespread poverty furnished rich soil for Communist agitation. Unless something were done to restore prosperity, the western European nations might well succumb to the promises of Moscow-inspired leaders.

Determined that communism should not succeed through American default, Truman pushed studies to assess the economic situation and suggest methods for its alleviation. By late spring of 1947 the groundwork had been prepared for a European aid program. Acheson's Cleveland, Mississippi, speech of May 8 had revealed the tentative official line and prepared the way for a major statement of policy by a leading member of the administration.

This momentous task was performed by Secretary of State George Marshall. Combining the prestige of his office with an exalted reputation, Marshall was an ideal choice to advocate a plan requiring both national and international approval. The veneration accorded a military hero was abetted by diplomatic experience, and he was not vulnerable to charges of political partisanship. In these respects, Marshall's promulgation of a drastic foreign policy experiment was more influential than if it had been made by the president. No other person could have so impressed the nation and the world with the urgency and merits of the proposal.

Nevertheless, without the total and unremitting efforts of the president, the Marshall Plan, in its projected form, probably would not have received congressional endorsement. Truman backed his associates fully and consistently from the outset. In speeches, press conferences, informal meetings, and correspondence he fought for the venture. An initial adverse reaction by certain congressional leaders, especially Senator Vandenberg, was overcome by thorough private briefings at the White House and the State Department. Representatives of the news media were given background information by high officials, and the press made a distinct contribution by presenting a thorough, comprehensive account of the proposal, its objectives, and its progress. Negotiations with representatives of other nations were conducted with the full and obvious support of the president, which facilitated the formulation of detailed plans and expedited final agreement.

What Churchill has termed "the most unsordid act in history" was due to a combination of the activities of dedicated individuals and the presence of unusual circumstances. The spectre of communism, the prestige of Marshall, the magnificent performance of Senator Vandenberg, the superb staff work of State Department officials, and the enthusiastic cooperation of the press were among the factors "without which" there probably would have been no implementation of the Marshall Plan. The one absolutely essential figure in the promotion and adoption of the proposal was the president himself. Facing a hostile Republican Congress in the midst of a major economy move, the president manipulated his power resources masterfully in securing a major departure in American foreign policy. Though he realized that the aid might come too late, Truman knew that it had to be done in a constitutional and regular manner. That it was provided in accordance with traditional American practices was a tribute to the function of his office. That it was provided at all is a commentary on the vision and character of the man who occupied that office.

A fifth dimension of presidential control of foreign policy was added by the conclusion of a series of military or quasi-military alliances, culminating with the North Atlantic Treaty of 1949. Like so many diplomatic innovations of the postwar years, this treaty emerged as an evolutionary stage in the efforts to halt communism, when it became evident that all previous efforts to resist Communist subversion and guerilla activity would be wasted if the Red army should march into the militarily weak European democracies. Again, the basic problem was not so much the decision to pursue this objective but the method by which it could be accomplished in the face of a deeply ingrained American aversion to peacetime military pacts.

The opportunity appeared with the failure of the Council of Foreign Ministers meeting in December, 1947. Alarmed by Soviet behavior, Great Britain suggested that France and the Benelux countries join her in a defense pact. The Brussels Treaty of 1948 was finally concluded after its strong endorsement in the formative stage by the United States, and under the impetus of the Communist overthrow of the Czech government. The administration, aware that the Brussels Pact nations needed more political support and were militarily incapable of resisting the Soviet forces, began careful preparations to bring about American participation. Moving slowly to avoid thrusting the issue into the campaign of 1948, the president made a series of speeches citing examples of Communist aggression and emphasizing the cardinal importance of the Brussels agreement in thwarting Soviet ambitions. Ever bearing in mind Woodrow Wilson's sad experience, Truman "meant to have legislative co-operation."[13] The step contemplated was so momentous that he wanted the European nations to know in advance that negotiations for a defense pact were supported by the Senate as well as the president.

The final approval of the North Atlantic Treaty by the Senate on July 21, 1949, was the result of a year and a half of patient, painstaking effort on the part of the executive branch. Encouragement of the Brussels pact, unflagging cooperation with the Senate, laborious negotiations with representatives of eleven European nations, and the task of securing agreement among the various government agencies, make the adoption of the treaty one of the more remarkable accomplishments in modern American political history.

Perhaps in no other way could such a drastic departure from national principles have been accomplished. Any other approach would have created such dissension that the administration's containment policy would have been jeopardized or, possibly, destroyed. The presidential strategy anticipated virtually every aspect of treaty vulnerability. Truman's choice of method, personnel, and procedure ensured the acceptance of what he considered one of the foundations of American foreign policy.

During the Senate hearings and debates on the agreement, one of the crucial questions that emerged dealt with the authority to dispatch troops to Europe in fulfilling the terms of the alliance. Though presidents had often sent troops abroad in their capacity as Commander in Chief, no clear-cut precedent was established for doing so in compliance with a military pact. The administration had thwarted Senate efforts to include a stipulation on the subject, so it remained an open question. It was further complicated by a provision of the treaty which specified that in the event of armed aggression, the type of aid furnished the victim should be determined by each member in accordance with its regular constitutional processes.

When the Korean War began it was feared that Russia might take advantage of the conflict to launch an attack on western Europe, and the president decided to send four American divisions to bolster the NATO defense structure. Truman stoutly denied the need for congressional permission and he carried out the move in spite of opposition from a small but vocal group of senators. In so doing, he expanded the presidential authority as Commander in Chief to encompass the peacetime disposal of forces in meeting the obligations of a military alliance. That he did so without consulting the legislative branch again revealed his concept of the office and his assessment of the strategic demands of the Free World defense perimeter. Still dependent on Congress for the size and composition of the armed forces, the Korean crisis had enabled him to secure legislation for a rapid expansion of the American military establishment. The employment of the men and equipment remained at the discretion of the president.

A sixth dimension of presidential control of security policy was added by membership in the United Nations. American participation in an international organization for the preservation of peace had numerous repercussions on the powers of the president in international affairs. Membership pledged the United States to the concept of collective security, with a commitment to joint action in matters that might only remotely affect the interests of the nation. It demanded full cooperation between the chief executive and Congress in order to secure approval of the charter and the enabling legislation to provide the authority and the funds to meet the prescribed obligations. Finally, participation in a world organization both restricted and enlarged the powers of the president in foreign affairs. On the one hand, a unilateral approach to many problems was impracticable, for policies had to be cleared or coordinated with representatives of other nations. On the other hand, the president could, by effective leadership, secure the assistance of other nations and the machinery of the United Nations for the implementation of American policies. The extent to which American diplomacy was to be furthered or hindered by this new involvement was to depend in large measure on the conduct of the president.

Truman's full cooperation with Congress in the formulation of the UN charter resulted in its quick approval by the Senate and helped him gain an important concession in the legislation that implemented America's membership in the organization. Known as the United Nations Participation Act, this legislation placed the American representative under presidential rather than congressional control. The act did specify, however, that Congress must approve any agreement that promised armed forces "would be made available to the Security Council on its call for the purpose of maintaining international peace and security in accordance with article 43 of said Charter." Truman was to interpret that clause in such a way that he, as director of American United Nations' policy and Commander in Chief, could commit troops without congressional authorization. This interpretation added greatly to his presidential powers.

Throughout his administration, Truman stressed the need for working with the United Nations. Convinced that the League of Nations had failed because none of the major powers had provided direction or lived up to their obligations, the president believed that it was his and America's responsibility to furnish both leadership and an example to ensure that the United Nations did not collapse by default.

Truman's most noteworthy action to strengthen the embryonic organization was his commitment of American forces to the defense of South

Korea. It is important to recall that American military planning had not anticipated this form of aggression. Though elaborate machinery had been erected to deal with security and foreign policy matters, the urgent and unprecedented nature of the threat left no time for normal deliberations. Only the president, under his constitutional and assumed powers, could deal with the situation.

In meeting his responsibility, Truman had to assess the nature of the aggression and its significance in terms of the Communist scheme. If it were merely the first step in a worldwide military offensive, the American response would have to be tempered by demands on defense resources at other vulnerable spots. The limitations imposed on choices by the state of America's armed forces were considerable, for a commitment of troops to Korea would virtually strip other areas. Europe was still considered the most vital Communist target and NATO could not be weakened. In addition to American *capabilities*, there was the question of the amount of support that Truman might expect from Congress and the public. The bipartisan approach to foreign policy had been seriously impaired by the Communist victory in China, and the administration announcement that military assistance would not be extended to Formosa brought opposition to the Korean Aid bill in early 1950. Domestically, the president was not in a strong position to carry through a policy of heavy involvement on the Asian continent that depended on congressional and public backing.

When Truman returned to Washington after hearing the news of the North Korean attack he met with Secretary of State Dean Acheson, his advisors, and key defense chiefs. There seems little doubt that the president had already made up his mind to resist the aggression by whatever means necessary. His previous remarks on the role of the United Nations and the failure of the League of Nations, his telephone conversation with Acheson, and finally his selection of participants in the Blair House conference, all revealed that he approached the meeting "in decision" rather than "in indecision." By not including all members of the National Security Council, political leaders, or members of Congress, he virtually eliminated anyone who might urge caution.

In the succeeding days as the crisis deepened, the president directed an escalation of American military assistance and secured a second resolution from the UN Security Council endorsing his actions. The speed with which these decisions were made and implemented was due to the existing governmental organization, the coordinating efforts of the secretary of state, and the administrative abilities of the president. Basically, the efficient manner in which the operation was carried out reflected the decisive conduct of the president and his unhesitating acceptance of responsibility and exercise of authority. He was determined to leave nothing undone in his efforts to resist communism, prevent a world holocaust, and preserve the United Nations. Future historians were not to be given the satisfaction of repeating the old refrain, "too little and too late."

By presenting the Congress and the nation with a *fait accompli* the president had successfully executed a drastic departure in American security policy. His choice of consultants, forthright assumption of responsibility, decisive manner, and method of procedure enabled him completely to control the nature of the American response. Opposition and devisive or delaying tactics were eliminated by his not allowing the question to become a matter for private or public debate.

Also, for good or ill, Truman perceived the predominantly political aspects of the conflict and conducted affairs accordingly. Though he may have succumbed to the "victory disease" in striving for political unification of Korea, he did secure approval for the step from the General Assembly and the major NATO allies. The president's efforts to confine the war to Korea and avoid a unilateral approach were successful. As Morton Halperin has observed, "The development of the limiting process in the Korean War seems to have been the work, on the whole, of the civilian decision-makers, at least on the American side, in rejecting or approving requests by the military to engage in military operations which would have the effect of expanding the war."[14] On the American side the final decisions were made by Truman.

The Korean experience amplified the role of the president in the conduct of security affairs. The armed forces had always functioned as an arm of foreign policy, but heretofore the president had not directed their activities in wartime with such a careful regard for political consequences. This placed an unprecedented strain on relations between the military and civil authorities, and the Truman-MacArthur dispute was an understandable if regrettable consequence. The peculiar nature of the Cold War, the need for multilateral diplomacy, and the horrifying implications of a nuclear conflict placed a greater premium on statecraft than ever before. The further overlapping of military and political activities raised the controversy to the level of a challenge to the civilian supremacy in government and the constitutional authority of the president. By dismissing MacArthur the chief executive emerged with his image tarnished but with the location of ultimate power clearly established.

Truman's actions during the Korean incident made a better impression abroad than they did at home. Winston Churchill remarked that Truman's courage during the crisis "made him worthy in my estimation to be numbered among the greatest of American Presidents." The incisive relief of MacArthur also contributed to his international stature, for with his control of nuclear weapons, as McGeorge Bundy has pointed out, "nothing adds more to a President's reputation abroad than recognition that he is Commander in Chief in fact as well as in name."[15] The significance of this recognition in implementing the president's role as world leader in difficult to exaggerate. Truman had demonstrated America's determination to resist aggression by whatever means necessary and live up to the collective security obligations of the United Nations. His generally prudent conduct of military operations gratified worried allies and reassured skeptical neutrals. His ability to make his policies prevail in the face of formidable domestic opposition established the president as the dependable leader of resistance to communism, a leader who placed the national interest in the broad framework of world responsibilities. This new dimension of presidential power in security affairs emerged in response to the Communist challenge, but its characteristics were determined by the man who held the office at that time.

Many of the important decisions made by Truman in the field of security affairs represented a change in the course of American policy. If they had not, if they had been in the tradition of earlier practice, their import would not have been so great and the decisions would not have been so remarkable. Nor would they have been so difficult, for it is breaking outside the mold of the past that tests a stateman's courage and draws on all his skill as a leader.

The international responsibilities assumed by the United States during the Truman administration were not "forced" on the nation or the president. Public and congressional opinion in the postwar years was in a state of flux as America attempted to make the transition from the isolationism of the thirties to some form of greater cooperation in world affairs. The extent and form of involvement were uncertain, except for participation in the United Nations. Nor did membership in this organization determine the *degree* of commitment or the manner in which obligations would be fulfilled. Under the circumstances presidential leadership was decisive.

Truman probably would have found it easier to refrain from interference in European affairs, avoid responsibility for the defense of other countries, adopt a passive role in the United Nations, and ignore importunities for economic aid. In short, confinement to the mainstream of American foreign policy most likely would have encountered less resistance than the departures he advocated. Under another president—a Buchanan or a Harding, for example—the story might well have been different. Truman combined a vision of America's role in the world with a firm notion of the president's role in office.

Truman was disdainful of polls, and he perceived the difference between public opinion and published opinion. Yet he was not above dramatizing a crisis in order to secure support for a revolutionary proposal, and he knew that the presidential podium was an unequaled source of power. During Truman's presidency the power spectrum of this podium broadened to encompass the world. Diplomacy by oratory became a potent weapon as America extended her influence over the lives of other peoples.

Few presidents have enjoyed thoroughly satisfactory relations with Congress, and Truman was no exception to the rule. Fortunately, on legislative matters a distinction was drawn between domestic and foreign programs. The president's position on foreign affairs was usually shared by the Democratic leaders, and Republicans such as Senator Vandenberg promoted a bipartisan approach that strengthened the president's hand. During his administration, Truman won and pretty well maintained the initiative in security policy legislation, and each time he secured unprecedented Cold War legislation through an adroit use of his powers he added new dimensions of authority to his office. The bipartisanship that lightened his burden could have resulted in a dilution of his programs in order to make them acceptable, a dilution that might have robbed them of their purpose. That it did not do so is a tribute to the men involved and the skill and perseverance of the president. Willing to compromise on details, Truman persisted on essentials, believing, as he often demonstrated, that in executing the laws he could interpret the letter and spirit as he saw fit.

The presidency is the focal point for decision in the government. The extent to which it performs this function depends on the person holding the office, and his behavior sets the tone for the government, the nation, and beginning with Truman, the world. Regardless of the merits of Truman's policies—a subject with which this study is not concerned—the chief executive who served from 1945 to 1953 seldom left anyone in doubt as to who controlled American security policy or the direction in which it was headed. During the period the scope of action demanded of the president in foreign and military affairs expanded enormously. Under Truman, presidential power increased in proportion to these demands. In adapting the presidency to the nuclear age, Truman added new dimensions of power commensurate with America's strength and her preeminent position in international affairs. Generically different, the office was now prepared to provide the leadership and meet the responsibilities assumed by the nation.

## NOTES

1. Herman Finer, *The Presidency: Crisis and Regeneration* (Chicago, 1960), p. 119.
2. Harry S. Truman, *Memoirs, II, Years of Trial and Hope* (Garden City, 1956), p. 473.
3. Ibid., p. 196.
4. Harry S. Truman, *Mr. Citizen* (New York, 1960), p. 221.

5. Ibid., p. 223.

6. Truman, *Memoirs*, vol. 2, p. 192.

7. Richard E. Neustadt, *Presidential Power: The Politics of Leadership* (New 1962), p. 63.

8. Douglass Cater, *Power in Washington* (New York, 1964), p. 106.

9. Ibid., p. 225.

10. Samuel P. Huntington, *The Common Defense: Strategic Programs in National Politics* (New York, 1961), p. 128.

11. Truman, *Memoirs*, vol. 2, p. 106.

12. Robert A. Dahl, *Congress and Foreign Policy* (New York, 1965), p. 102.

13. Truman, *Memoirs*, vol. 2, p. 243.

14. Morton H. Halperin, "The Limiting Process in the Korean War," *Political Science Quarterly* 78(March 1963):36–37.

15. McGeorge Bundy, "The Presidency and the Peace," *Foreign Affairs* 42(April 1946):357.

# CHAPTER TWELVE

# Victory in Modern War

## THE MEANINGS OF "VICTORY"

IN 1951, GENERAL MACARTHUR EXPRESSED A SENTIMENT SHARED BY MANY Americans dissatisfied with the limitations placed on military activities in Korea when he proclaimed: "War's very objective is victory—not prolonged indecision. In war, indeed, there can be no substitute for victory."[1] Yet the term "victory" as applied to war has meant different things to different people, and it merits classification with other general, abstract, and often absolute words that have influenced the thoughts and actions of individuals. Equating victory with the defeat and surrender of the enemy may have been and may still be consistent with conventional usage, but the modern world experience reveals that such a decisive conclusion to armed conflict is the exception rather than the rule.

Since war functions as a final arbiter in disputes between men and nations, the victory does not consist solely of overcoming the enemy forces; it must include the attainment of the objective for which the conflict was waged. The oft-quoted axiom of Clausewitz that "war is regarded as nothing but *the continuation of state policy with other means*" is amplified by his assertion that the final element in victory is the enemy's "renunciation of his intention."[2] The basic correlation between military and political strategy was developed at great length in the writings of Hans Delbruck. "Politics is the ruling and limiting factor," he observed, "military operations is only one of its means."[3] In stressing the subordination of military to political ends, the theorists, reacting against what they regarded as a tendency for war to become ultimate or absolute, were laying the foundation for a reappraisal of victory by applying the criterion of statecraft rather than hostilities. Activities on the battlefield were viewed as merely one dimension, though usually an essential dimension, of a broader and transcendent undertaking, and this relationship between war and politics has been accepted by the majority of recent strategic theorists.[4] Therefore, as a working definition, in this essay "victory" will mean the cessation of armed conflict under conditions satisfactory to at least one of the combatants in terms of stated objectives. The inapplicability of any single definition to all situations will become apparent.[5]

Mao Tse-tung has rephrased the Clausewitz dictum by declaring that "politics is war without bloodshed, and war is politics with bloodshed."[6] This observation is especially relevant since the advent of nuclear weapons, the surge of nationalistic fervor in former colonies, the conflict between Communism and the Western world, and the appearance of aggression in ambiguous forms have combined to create an environment conducive to limited wars. Usually conceived of as wars restricted in aims, hostilities, and the commitment of resources by at least one side, the rationale is to correlate the means with the end to ensure that the cost is commensurate with the gain.[7] Under these circumstances it becomes imperative, as Sun Tzu put it, "to control victory."[8] The nature of the settlement is crucial, for, as a contemporary analyst has noted, "there are ways of conquering that quickly transform victory into defeat."[9]

An investigation of the meaning of victory includes a consideration of the methods by which war is ended and the factors that lead to its termination. Ordinarily, hostilities stop by agreement between or among the antagonists, the terms of which may vary from the extreme of unconditional surrender by one or more of the participants to a restoration of the situation prevailing when the conflict began. A simple cease-fire arrangement, an armistice with or without conditions, or a formal treaty are the more common devices employed for halting the violence.[10] The circumstances under which war is terminated vary considerably, although it seems obvious that the antagonists must be convinced that a cessation of the fighting will be more advantageous than its continuation. Whatever the initial aims, wars seldom turn out exactly the way either side had anticipated. No nation can be certain that a conflict will improve an existing situation, and at times a government will be induced to accept peace on terms that fail to reflect the actual military position.

## VICTORY IN SELECTED WARS

### The American Revolution

The American Revolution is an example of the complexity of modern war and the unforeseen factors which can alter the nature of the conflict, modify its purpose, and affect the outcome. Beginning in 1775 as a limited war with limited objectives, namely, to secure a redress of "wrongs," it was transformed during the course of hostilities into a world struggle. Each of the allies pursued a different goal, although the common foe was Great Britain. Also, from the American point of view, there occurred an escalation in hostilities and aims as the conflict became a war of national liberation for the thirteen colonies and external aid became crucial. At a time when the fortunes of the new nation seemed at their lowest ebb, a dramatic victory at Yorktown gave opponents of the war in England the opportunity to change the government and spur negotiations for peace. As delegates of the contending powers argued over terms with an emphasis on "necessary" rather than "desirable" treaty provisions, the British forces still occupied key areas in the states, the French allies departed, and the British fleet regained control of the seas. The war, it could be claimed, was lost in London, not on the battlefield. As for the Americans, victory meant independence, not the surrender of the enemy forces; and when the British government was willing to concede the political objective, the fighting stopped.11

## Coalition Warfare and the Napoleonic Wars

In the American Revolution the areas of incompatibility of American, French, and Spanish goals appeared when negotiations became imminent, but the New World diplomats simply ignored their allies in concluding a a treaty. The problems of coalition warfare and diplomacy reached an almost absolute form during the Napoleonic era among those nations drawn together in an effort to thwart French domination of Europe. The conflicting ambitions of the allies were subdued so long as the military danger was paramount; when the enemy weakened perceptibly, the concept of victory embraced by each member of the alliance either changed or became more distinctive.12 At this point, apprehension over a possible collapse of the coalition tended to prompt less demanding members to increase their claims to meet those of the most assertive member.13 A quarrel over the spoils need not await the end of hostilities, and the form of victory envisioned by the participants may vary accordingly. The wars of the French Revolution and the Empire also witnessed the advent of "people's wars," when not merely a government and regular armies were engaged but an entire nation became involved. Both violence and purpose were shorn of many conventional controls, and the primary aim became, as Clausewitz said, "the overthrow of the foe."14 Not for another hundred years would Europe experience such a perversion of an instrument of coercion or what had been dubbed "the sport of kings."

## The War of 1812

The War of 1812 is a classic example of a conflict ending in a return to

the *status quo antebellum*, where none of the American declared aims were
realized. It is also a remarkable instance of negotiations being conducted
by the principals while a war was in progress, and the demands of the
adversaries fluctuated with the course of hostilities, the progress of the
struggle against Napoleon, and pressures from the home front. Although
in a political sense the United States did not "win" the war, militarily it
did not "lose," for there were enough battle successes in this contest with
the mightiest nation on earth to salvage the national honor. Perhaps the
president and his emissaries at Ghent had been reading Machiavelli, who
observed:

> Princes that are attacked cannot then commit a greater error, especially
> when their assailant greatly exceeds them in power, than to refuse all
> accommodation, and more particularly when it has been offered; for no
> terms will ever be so hard but what they will afford some advantage to
> him who accepts them so that he really obtains thereby a share of the
> victory.[15]

Great Britain, as in the case of the Crimean War some forty years later,
settled when the enemy renounced its intention of trying to change an
existing situation.

## Mexico, the Civil War, and Spain

A formal treaty also brought to a close the war with Mexico, although
the military effort vastly exceeded what President Polk had contemplated
initially. The amount of Mexican resistance determined the cost of the
venture, and not until General Scott "conquered a peace" by capturing
the capital (what Clausewitz called "the center of gravity") did the Mexican government accept the American terms, which included a financial
award. The American Civil War was concluded by the surrender of the
Confederate armies in the field with no arrangement with the Southern
government, which was in the process of disintegration. The "splendid little
war" with Spain was ended by an armistice agreement that contained
territorial demands which reflected the American military successes, although the transfer of the Philippine Islands was effected during the negotiations for the final treaty. Vigorously protesting what they considered
a violation of the armistice protocol, the Spanish authorities finally relinquished the islands to avoid a resumption of hostilities and in exchange
for a cash sum.

## The Boer War

What could be considered a partial victory for both sides emerged
from the South African war which began in 1899 when the Boer settlers
revolted against their colonial master, Great Britain. Demanding greater
autonomy, the Boers were soon beaten in the conventional campaigns and

reverted to highly successful ˉguerrilla tactics. The British countered by erecting a series of concrete blockhouses linked by barbed wire, destroying the Boer farms, locating Boer families in concentration camps, and enlisting the aid of the Kaffir native tribesmen. Although the Boers enjoyed a considerable amount of public sympathy throughout the civilized world for their plucky resistance, the British tactics finally prevailed. Among the factors that induced the Boers to sue for peace were the suffering of the women and children, the shortage of food and horses, the task of fighting both the British soldiers and the natives, and the ravaging of their land. Their long and determined resistance becomes even more remarkable in light of the fact that they received no significant aid from any outside source. Relying solely on their own resources, the Boer "commandos" held out for nearly two years after the main forces had been defeated and many of their government officials had fled into exile. Perhaps the valiant effort was not completely in vain, for the British peace terms were generous and granted some of the Boer demands.

## World War I

Whatever merit war might have had as a social institution, the frightful carnage of the First World War led to greater questioning of whether anyone could profit from armed conflict. This was, as Walter Millis observed, "the hypertrophy of war."[16] Apparently, none of the governments initially involved had sought the war, and aims were defined during the course of hostilities, usually to appease allies or in response to the sacrifices demanded of the people as the conflict continued.[17] Perhaps no political advantage could be commensurate with the casualities and human suffering, and President Wilson's efforts to halt the slaughter found him urging a "peace without victory" shortly before the United States entered the war. "Victory" he claimed, "would mean peace forced upon the loser, a victor's terms imposed upon the vanquished. It would be accepted in humiliation, under duress, at an intolerable sacrifice, and would leave a sting, a resentment, a bitter memory upon which terms of a peace would rest, not permanently, but only as upon quicksand."[18] This admonition was not completely forgotten by the president when the nation became involved, and the armistice terms he formulated were accepted under protest by France and Great Britain and vehemently opposed by a number of U.S. political leaders, who advocated, as did General Pershing, nothing less than "unconditional surrender." The subsequent peace conference, from which the Central Powers were excluded, helped create the situation against which the president had warned and to which, in his own way, he had contributed.[19] Some authorities have claimed that the Allied and associated powers were "surprised into peace" before adequate preparation had been made, and others insist that stated war aims should be regarded only as propaganda for domestic consumption. Stressing high moral principles rather than narrow national interest as the issue at stake in the conflict placed the venture in the category of a crusade or "holy war," and gave the illusion of goals that were clearly inconsistent with reality.[20] The subsequent disillusionment over the United States' first and disappointing overt attempt to interfere in the affairs of Europe was shared by all the nations of the civilized world.

## World War II

Prior to the Second World War, all of the conflicts between the United States and foreign nations had been limited in that they did not result in the total military destruction, annihilation, or surrender of the enemy forces. Success was achieved and hostilities were terminated when the adversary indicated a willingness to accede to U.S. political demands, whether for independence, territorial accessions, or the like. The great departure from this tradition allegedly occurred when President Roosevelt declared on January 24, 1943, that the only basis for an end to hostilities would be "the unconditional surrender by Germany, Japan, and Italy." Designed in part to give the allies a free hand in establishing a satisfactory settlement, to prevent a weakening of the coalition by a squabble over the spoils, and to compensate for the Anglo-American failure to establish a second front in Europe, this doctrinaire assertion "became part of the American popular *mystique* of military victory."[21] Then and subsequently the source of much controversy, the declaration was cited as evidence by Roosevelt's critics that he, unlike Winston Churchill, conceived of the war in an exclusively military sense. In any event, the Casablanca statement and the remarkable military successes of the war created an image that does not correspond with the actualities of the past. Moreover, the "evil" nature of the Axis governments, as emphasized by British and U.S. leaders and other publicists, added a moral aspect to the struggle that discouraged compromise and further contributed to a total war and total victory approach. But it should be noted that while the Italian representatives were compelled to sign a document acknowledging "unconditional surrender," a great many conditions were attached; that Finland, Romania, Bulgaria, and Hungary were not required to accept the formula in their armistice agreements; and that the Japanese document of surrender incorporated the phrase only in regard to the armed forces.

## Wars of liberation and American policy after World War II

This global conflict furnished a rationale and a setting for wars of national liberation. The ideological basis was provided by the Atlantic

Charter and the Declaration of the United Nations, and the opportunity was presented when former colonial rulers were ousted or existing governments were eliminated. In spite of Winston Churchill's contention that he did not become prime minister to preside over the dissolution of the British Empire, one of the most far-reaching consequences of the war was the emergence of former European colonies as independent nations composed of nonwhite peoples. A pattern of rebellion begun under occupation by new oppressors was resumed when the old returned, and experience gained in guerrilla operations against a trained and disciplined foe was applied in resisting the "liberators." Victory was conceived of as the attainment of sovereignty, not winning battles or exchanging one set of masters for another.

The position of the U.S. government under these circumstances was somewhat anomalous, for though it had adopted an avowed anticolonial policy it was not anxious to see the establishment of new nations dominated by communism. As the Cold War intensified, the United States, seeking to thwart Communist movements, began to support reactionary, autocratic, and colonial regimes. Ideological issues became blurred as resistance to alleged Soviet and Red Chinese imperialism came to dominate U.S. policy.

The formal American commitment to aid governments threatened by Communist military and subversive action was expressed in the so-called Truman Doctrine, when the president declared, "I believe that it must be the policy of the United States to support free peoples who are resisting attempted subjugation by armed minorities or by outside pressure." Carrying the implication of an open-ended pledge, the doctrine was announced in 1947 to protect Turkey from Russia, and the government of Greece from a Communist-inspired revolt. Victory in the latter instance consisted of the suppression of the domestic uprising, and was secured largely because of the assistance provided by the United States and the loss of Yugoslavia as a base of operations because of her split with the Soviet Union. The success or failure of this attempt to overthrow an existing government depended in large part on the amount and kind of external aid that either side could secure.[22]

*Korea*

The term "limited war" became a part of the common vocabulary as a result of the Korean conflict, when the U.S. government refused to make a maximum military commitment, failed to subdue the enemy, and negotiated a compromise cease-fire agreement. The fighting continued as the conferees debated, until finally both sides made compromises over the repatriation of prisoners. Whether the Communist concession was provoked by a hint that the United States might use nuclear weapons or by a relaxation of Moscow's hard line following the death of Stalin is not known. It seems clear, however, that neither side was willing to pay the price necessary to unify the country, and each was determined to prevent the other from doing so.

Many of the problems inherent in limited wars and wars of national liberation were present and were faced during the Korean conflict. The initial question of armed intervention in a "domestic struggle" was overcome through the legal sanction of United Nations resolutions, whereby the onus of unilateral action was avoided. In this context the reality of overt aggression seemed obvious, and ostensibly the United Nations had fought a long war in order to discourage the use of force as an instrument of policy. A formal declaration of war by the Congress was not requested, one reason being that the United States as a sovereign nation was not engaged in a conflict with another power but was merely acting as an agent of an international organization in aiding a duly recognized government. The president strove to exercise strict control over military operations in an effort to avoid provoking intervention by powers sympathetic to the North Korean cause, and he had to allocate his forces to avoid upsetting the balance of world strategy. The fact that the antagonists were Communists added ideological to anti-imperialist or strategic motives for resistance, which gained support for the president's initial stand but also made him vulnerable to the charge that he was temporizing by not eliminating the threat or striking at its source. The limitations placed on the means and the end seemed alien to a generation nurtured in a total war that had mobilized the resources of the nation for a fight to attain final goals. Restrictions imposed by allies and associates were not so apparent, although they were ever present in the calculations of the president. Word that Truman had even considered the use of atomic weapons brought a hurried visit from the British prime minister, and President Syngman Rhee frequently urged stronger measures for a political unification of the country and the elimination of the Communists.

During the controversy over Korean war policy that led to the removal of General MacArthur from command and its vitriolic aftermath, Lester Pearson, Canadian Minister of Foreign Affairs, appealed for a new approach to victory. "Victory in this type of limited United Nations war," he declared, "may not have to be the kind of complete capitulation of the enemy with which we have been made familiar. Victory is the achievement of our objectives, and those objectives remain the defeat of aggression against the Republic of Korea."[23] General Omar Bradley, chairman of the Joint Chiefs of Staff, asserted that "we would consider it a victory with something less than" a free and United Korea.[24] Later, Truman was to contend that "there is a right kind and a wrong kind of victory, just as there are wars for the right thing and wars that are wrong from every standpoint."[25] The correlation between the degree of military commitment and the magnitude of the goal was responsible for the concept of victory shared by Western leaders in this pursuit of collective security.

## Indochina

The "new look" in defense policy instituted by the United States government in 1953 emphasized the threat of massive retaliation, which prompted the corollary, "there is no alternative to peace." Despite urging a roll back of communism and the "liberation" of satellite nations, in no case did the Eisenhower administration provide military assistance when an uprising took place against Communist authorities. Economic and material aid was forthcoming, however, to help stifle Communist-inspired revolts designed to overthrow existing governments. In Indochina a practice begun by Truman of supporting the French against the Viet Minh was accelerated, and when the French military position deteriorated, the administration seriously contemplated air strikes by U.S. planes. Victory, for France and the United States, meant the subjugation of the rebels and the pacification of the country under the French-sponsored government of Bao Dai.

The situation in Indochina was quite different from that in Korea. The Rhee government suffered less from the stigma of colonialism, and apparently there was little question as to the allegiance of the people in South Korea. Militarily the strategy and tactics of the conflict were dissimilar, for in Indochina conventional methods of warfare were largely replaced by Communist guerrilla operations. While the French sought to transform the irregular nature of the fighting, the conclusive military success was achieved at Dien Bien Phu with a well-planned, vigorous, and incessant attack. A war of insurgency, attrition, and maneuver was brought to an end by the psychological and political impact of a traditional battle. The fall of Dien Bien Phu helped convince the French government that further hostilities were futile and contributed significantly to the settlement at Geneva in 1954.

This final military reverse was only the culmination of a series of frustrations experienced by the French forces, without which Dien Bien Phu would not have been so crucial and without which it would not have occurred. The military genius of the Communist General Giap and the doctrinaire approach of the French leaders were vital factors. Apparently neither was seeking to destroy the enemy forces. Each hoped for a stalemate in which the antagonist, realizing that a conclusive military solution was impracticable, would agree to a satisfactory settlement. As the fighting continued, the process of erosion anticipated by each side took place among the French and the pro-French Vietnamese, who were plagued by inability to find allies, dissension at home, criticism from abroad, and the absence of battle successes. The disintegration of morale at many levels was apparent as the soldiers became more confused over what they were fighting for, and neither political nor military leaders could formulate objectives that warranted the sacrifice.

The Viet Minh, on the other hand, had a number of factors operating in their favor, including a clear and overriding concept of victory, which was defined unequivocally as liberty. Inspired by the belief that their death would contribute to the attainment of this ultimate goal, the insurgents approached their task with a dedication that amazed and bewildered their Western foes. They also coupled their military efforts with constant political, economic, and ideological activities on the part of soldiers and civilians alike. The Viet Minh were waging total war in their own fashion with all the resources at their disposal, and these resources were employed to gain the goal of independence under the government of Ho Chi Minh. The strategy envisaged a maximum effort in the North to achieve a total political end, and a limited effort in the South to secure a long-range solution for that area. The settlement provided for a nonmilitary method of attaining the final goal.

Another factor present in the struggle for Indochina was the calling of conferences for negotiations, first to meet in Berlin and then in Geneva. Although the impact of such a gathering while fighting is in progress is difficult to assess, talks usually signify a willingness to compromise. This in turn might imply to the troops that political leaders are willing to engage in a "sellout" to the enemy, depending on which side is prevailing on the battlefield. In this case, the effect on the French Vietnamese army was catastrophic, for it began to break up and mobilization orders were no longer enforced. Also, two developments took place during the conference that affected the outcome. First, the garrison at Dien Bien Phu surrendered.[26] Second, the French government fell, and the new premier publicly committed himself to ending the conflict within a month. A truly remarkable juxtaposition of events.

The propriety or desirability of direct contacts between adversaries engaged in combat has been questioned, although such an attitude implies that violence and peace bear no relation to each other. Actually, the distinction often drawn between a military and a negotiated settlement is usually artificial because the two are not incompatible. Perhaps what is meant is a "dictated" rather than a negotiated solution, with the latter implying a compromise. The twilight nature of limited war, wherein at least one of the adversaries has not made a total military commitment, places a premium on early if not constant discussion. The role of inter-mediaries, especially those who have a direct interest in the results and who may be providing economic and material aid, can be extremely important. Proxy allies at the conference table who lend their prestige and latent power to the proceedings might be crucial. At Geneva the knowledge that France had lost heart and that neither Great Britain nor the United States would intervene militarily was a significant factor in determining the outcome, as was the presence of Soviet and Red Chinese representatives.

The extent of the French commitment in Indochina was directly related to the terms the government was willing to accept. At stake were territory, prestige, honor, economic advantage, military alliances, ideological concerns, and protection for colonials and those segments of the indigenous population identified with the French. In spite of these many considerations, an international conference enabled the French government to withdraw from what had become an untenable position with a degree of dignity which bilateral conversations would not have permitted. The multilateral approach may have helped induce the Viet Minh to accept a temporary division of the country pending elections, thereby allowing each side to emerge with enough of a victory to warrant the sacrifices entailed. Perhaps the French honor was satisfied by the absence of a complete military defeat, and it is unlikely that a surrender of the French forces would have been acceptable. A modicum of face-saving was indispensable, as in the case of the ancient Britons who allegedly painted their bodies blue so even if they were overcome in battle and stripped of their clothing they would still retain their respectability. Nevertheless, in terms of cost and original objectives, the French suffered a glaring defeat, for the end result was scarcely commensurate with the means or consonant with the preservation of the colonial empire.

The 1954 conference in Geneva also revealed how a multilateral approach to international problems can contribute to victory or defeat at the armistice table. The Communist nations were united in their position on Southeast Asia, whereas the Western nations were divided. The immediate aims of the former were cast in the framework of long-range, clearly conceived objectives. The Western powers were not only apart in their thinking, but individually they had no overall strategic goals that could be used as criteria for immediate solutions. France, which had borne the brunt of the fighting and whose interests were most directly involved, was willing to concede more than some of her sideline associates, who, caring little about the merits of the claims, were primarily concerned with containing communism or protecting possessions. The hazards of coalition diplomacy were evident, and the shock effects of the French submission were shared by her associates and felt throughout the world. The United States suffered a "proxy defeat," and immediately undertook a salvage operation by offering aid to the South Vietnamese government. The full implications of this attempt at retrieval are not yet clear.

## Malaya and Suez

The influence of allies or outside agencies is illustrated by the case of Malaya and the Suez crisis. In the former, the British, acting unilaterally and unhampered by external pressures, overcame their colonial image and secured the support of the populace by identifying victory with freedom and independence. This appeal was especially effective since most of the Communist insurgents were of Chinese origin, so the British were partners in a war of national liberation against foreign interlopers. The results of the Geneva Conference of 1954 further disheartened the revolutionaries, and the granting of independence in 1957 formalized the political victory. Deprived of outside aid and telling propaganda, the Communist resistance gradually collapsed.[27]

In contrast with Malaya, the Suez crisis of 1956 was confused by the differing objectives of the powers directly or indirectly involved. Even the three allies who attacked Egypt had different goals in mind, and the absence of common political objectives was reflected in the shortcoming of the military operations. The British also came to realize that a military victory would deprive them of the kind of political victory they sought. For Great Britain, the means would destroy the end, whereas the French and Israeli political objectives could be achieved only by a military operation inconsistent with the British aims. U.S. opposition to the venture significantly influenced the outcome, for the invasion jeopardized the NATO Alliance, the pound sterling, and the security function of the United Nations. Still, the action by the General Assembly probably enabled the three "aggressors" to accept defeat with less reluctance, for bowing to the will of an international organization carries less of a stigma than submission to an armed adversary.[28]

## Hungary

The effect that the support of a powerful ally can have on a war of liberation is further demonstrated by the Hungarian Revolution of 1956. Seen in the context of the Polish revolt, with its modest goal of securing a greater degree of autonomy, the uprising in Hungary seemed on its way to success. Then the rebels succumbed to the "victory disease" and broadened their demands until they became intolerable to the Soviet leaders. Whatever the reason for the change in Kremlin policy, as the professed aims of the revolutionaries increased, the military activities of the Soviet forces changed from withdrawal to heavy involvement. A tentative acceptance of one Communist regime was withdrawn and replaced by oppressive measures in favor of a more tractable Communist government.

The revolt probably would have succeeded had it not been for the Soviet action. After this intervention, only a massive military effort by the United States could have saved the revolution. When this aid was not forthcoming, some regarded the outcome as a defeat for the West, especially in light of the much-heralded "liberation" policy for satellite nations. So in this instance the intervention of one great power and the failure of another to intervene proved decisive. A direct or indirect military confrontation was avoided as each nation weighed the issues against the cost of success and acted accordingly. The Soviet victory was complete in a military and political sense, while the West gained a moral or limited propaganda victory because of widespread horror at the ruthless methods employed to crush what was viewed as a popular uprising.

*The Bay of Pigs*

The impact of moral, legal, and propaganda considerations on the concept of victory is revealed by the abortive Bay of Pigs invasion in Cuba in 1961. When it became clear that the operation would fail without overt U.S. military participation, President Kennedy decided that a tactical and strategic defeat was preferable to the commitment of armed forces. Influencing the decision were the prospect of an escalation of hostilities and vulnerability to the charge that the United States, which repeatedly had advocated high standards of international behavior, was now adopting the very methods it had condemned. The entire operation, designed to liberate Cuba from the Castro regime, although badly conceived, failed in large part because the president was not willing to place the national image in jeopardy to secure the desired objective. In this respect the United States gained a measure of goodwill in certain quarters. On the other hand, the nation's reputation suffered in two somewhat contrary respects: first, by the government's obvious complicity in the action; and second, by not following the operation through to the final goal. The incompatability of professed ideals with what was conceived to be the national interest severely hampered the president in his conduct of the affair and helped dissuade him from unleashing U.S. forces. The result was a military, political, and propaganda victory for the Castro government, for the attack had failed and the Communist accusations of U.S. aggressive intentions had been confirmed.

## FACTORS INFLUENCING THE OUTCOME OF
## MODERN WARFARE

Although numerous miscalculations contributed to the Bay of Pigs fiasco, it seems clear that barring a massive military effort by an external power, success in these wars of liberation depends largely on the support or at least the tacit consent of the population.[29] The question of who is liberating whom from what is often crucial, and an accurate appraisal of the aspirations of the people can prove decisive. National independence, social justice, and a higher standard of living constitute the more popular appeals that enable revolutionary leaders to mobilize the entire resources of a country regardless of the state of economic and technological development. "Among permanent operating factors which determine victory or defeat in war," says one Soviet source, "the most basic are the stability of the rear and the morale of the army."[30] Within the context of internal wars these two factors are largely contingent on the attitude and activities of the indigenous population. The extent to which this population helps or hinders military operations has proved decisive.

Insurgent operations embrace the entire spectrum of human activity. This places a premium on the exercise of total control of all the elements leading to victory. The troops are an integral part of an all-out offensive that is based on and functions with an intensive political and psychological campaign. The first battle is to win the minds and hearts of the people and secure their commitment to the cause. When this has been accomplished, victory is virtually assured, for defeat can come only through the annihilation of the resistance. Such a strategy is especially effective when engaging an enemy who lacks a clear-cut purpose for fighting or does not understand or share the aspirations of the local populace. Under these circumstances a dedicated minority, spurred by an attractive ideology, can almost ensure that its predictions of victory will come true.[31]

One writer has pointed out that there is a "force 'demagnification' factor that favors the side whose objective is stalemate over the side whose objective is victory."[32] To employ this statement in a way not intended by the author, the victory sought in wars of liberation may be achieved by demonstrating to the opponent that a satisfactory outcome will demand a greater effort than he is willing to make. The Chinese strategist Tu Yu long ago observed that "There are circumstances in war when many cannot attack few, and others when the weak can master the strong. One able to manipulate such circumstances will be victorious."[33] An internal conflict with one side dependent on foreign assistance, and where guerrilla tactics are utilized, is an ideal setting for manipulation by the weak. Psychological factors assume greater significance, both for the troops and for the civilian population. A state of mind that will induce the stronger side to accept defeat can be brought about through war-weariness, despair of success, the promise of escape from the ravages of war, and the creation of a scapegoat.[34] Blame can be placed most conveniently on the political leaders for a variety of reasons, among which are responsibility for involvement in the conflict or a refusal to give the military a free hand.

The saturation point beyond which a populace will not tolerate a continuation of hostilities is probably reached when the feeling becomes sufficiently widespread that the cost outweighs the possible gain, and the government must share or be responsive to these sentiments if the conflict is to be halted.[35] Such a rational approach to war would be consistent with a quantifiable version of limited war as "one for a specific objective which by its very existence will establish a certain commensurability between the force employed and the goal to be attained."[36] But even systems analysis with its sophisticated computer techniques is unable to calculate the worth of an objective in lives, money, and effort. Announcing in advance how much of an investment would be made would reveal one's intentions and could be fatal. Also, the amount of force necessary to achieve a particular goal is determined by the antagonist, who may believe that the stakes warrant an unlimited effort on his part which is inconsistent with his adversary's computation.[37] The extent and nature of the force required are seldom clear at the outset, and wars are rarely stable. The costs of the conflict and the dangers inherent in a continuance of the struggle may expand out of all proportion to the desired end and produce attendant difficulties in its prosecution. A government will then be faced with the two distasteful alternatives of an escalation of military activity or a diminution of objectives.[38] The initial aims may be small, but the failure to achieve these aims, especially by a third party whose prestige and position are at stake, can have enormous repercussions. When the will of a great power is being tested the ceiling of resistance may be unlimited.

Nevertheless, in spite of the difficulties, major nations have accepted "proxy" defeats. The armistice in Korea and the Geneva accords of 1954 are noteworthy examples. The former would fit the category of "total victory" so far as resistance to armed aggression is concerned, and the latter could qualify as a "limited victory" or a "limited defeat" for either side even though the gains were disproportionate. No destruction or surrender of the enemy forces was involved, nor were the national boundaries of any great power affected. Concessions were made, in the one case by those who had attempted to change the status quo and in the other case by those who had resisted a change, when the price of total victory became exorbitant. The exertion and determination of one antagonist were sufficient to convince the other that the desired end would not compensate for the cost.

Avoidance of a humiliating settlement appears desirable if not imperative, especially when the prestige of a great power is involved. One writer has stated categorically: "In no contest should a victory be conceded to the opponent that is not perceptible to him as Pyrrhic. In no contest should a victory be enforced upon the opponent to the point of his military or political desperation."[39] If each antagonist were guided by these precepts the result could be an interminable conflict unless their premises were different, i.e., if a solution could be interpreted by each side as a victory. Assuming that both sides cannot win in an absolute sense, a victor's restraint can minimize the sum of "losses" sustained.[40] Knowing when the optimum point has been reached demands a clear perception of the opponent's capability, intentions, and will. But regardless of the intricacy of the process, which involves an acute exercise of judgment, this awareness can be vital in providing the essential ingredient for a settlement.[41] A trapped adversary, perceiving no honorable escape, may be driven to extreme measures unrelated to the original aim and catastrophic in result. The risks are compounded under the circumstances of proxy warfare, where the implications of defeat transcend local considerations.

Granting that the avoidance of extremes in effecting a settlement may be understandable and even desirable, a compromise that avoids humiliating the opponent is often difficult for a government responsible to an electorate. The unlimited rhetoric of political oratory and the temptation to phrase an issue in absolute terms to secure popular support for a policy allow the authorities little room for maneuvering. Restrictions can be greater when a nation's *interests* are at stake rather than its *rights*, for the former may be less tangible and more susceptible to appeals on principle. Flexibility in action is also sacrificed on the altar of public diplomacy, where every move is exposed and must be vindicated. The least rumor of concession provokes the accusation of "appeasement," with derogatory implications. A totalitarian dictatorship, while it may not be completely impervious to the wishes of the people, need not fear public outbursts, partisan denunciations, or reprisals at the polls.

One of the problems complicating compromise solutions to "brush fire" engagements is that of creating an enemy.[42] Within an ideological framework that makes no clear distinction between war and peace the need is not so great, for the adversary is ever present and the battle is waged continually, with or without violence, in every dimension of activity. The practice of sharply distinguishing between hostilities and peaceful intercourse, with each in a black and white relationship, places a premium on identifying the enemy in an absolute sense so long as the fighting is in progress.[43] The label is especially important for military and domestic morale, and the fact that the circumstances may not warrant the categorization makes it difficult but no less desirable to portray the opponent in an evil light. Temporizing under these conditions places the government in an awkward position, for victory is synonymous with overcoming the enemy.

This yearning for quick, clear-cut solutions to complex problems is widespread, especially in the West, although scarcely compatible with the nature of the many conflicts that have raged throughout the world in the past twenty years, much less those of previous centuries. The implication that a limited war is intended to achieve limited ends occasionally carries the assumption that it can be accomplished with limited domestic support. A clandestine or indirect military involvement is often designed to bring about a solution with a minimum of fanfare and on terms acceptable to both sides. Yet the management of news and official statements later contradicted by overwhelming evidence creates dissension, provokes distrust, affects morale, and puts the government in an untenable position. The mounting pressure can induce a modification of the original goal, either upward to justify a greater military effort or downward to a renunciation of aims and possible withdrawal.

Wars usually end through negotiations on the basis of military activity, and the assertion that a government should only "negotiate from strength" implies that it must demonstrate superiority on the battlefield before considering a settlement. Some degree of military success seems necessary, even though it consists of frustrating the adversary's intentions, if a satisfactory conclusion is to be reached.[44] This "condition precedent" may invalidate latent or potential power unless it directly affects the local situation. Since hostilities ordinarily begin in an effort to change an existing condition, the initiator will resist a conclusion unless he obtains some advantage not previously enjoyed. And while he may not capture territory or win impressive engagements, his activities can be sufficiently irritating to give him a relative degree of strength at the conference table.[45] Perhaps only in this manner can each side gather some of the fruits of victory and escape the "either or" type of peace that may prove unacceptable or sow the seeds for future altercation.

If all the initiator's ambitions are denied he will have suffered a categorical defeat, modest though it may be in relation to his original objective and disproportionate though it may be to the expenditure of resources.[46] The resistor, then, is placed in a position where any concession will represent defeat. Whether it consists of recognizing a rebel group, granting it representation in the existing government, or tacitly accepting a *de facto* border, any alteration of the status quo will constitute a plus and a minus.

The question of a "plus" for anyone after a thermonuclear exchange has occasioned extended controversy. Theorists have differed over the nature of such a conflict, for no nuclear war has ever been waged. Some "defense intellectuals" have envisioned hostilities lasting several days, probably ending by negotiation.[47] Soviet strategists consistently have foreseen an initial phase in which the nuclear weapons would be exhausted, to be followed by a decisive period of conventional warfare. The nation that recovered and reacted most effectively would prevail. Today a good deal of attention is being devoted to what is called "post-nuclear strike planning," or devising a strategy to contest what is left. At this stage the objectives may be obscured and victory may demand more cooperation than competition, but, as Montaigne once observed, "there is no idea so absurd that men will not die for it."

Hostilities are terminated when the antagonists are convinced that a continuation of combat would not serve a useful purpose. Many of the factors involved in reaching that point have been mentioned here. So far no formula has been discovered that will predict the outcome of war, nor does a yardstick exist that equates the price of a military operation with the value of the goal. Human beings do not always react the same way to the same or similar pressures, and circumstances can alter cases in war as in law. Yet the emotional appeal of victory and the repugnance of defeat are endemic. Unless more careful attention is given to the subject of victory it may well become an area of research for the archeologist rather than the historian.

## NOTES

1. U.S., Congress, *Congressional Record*, 82nd Cong., 1st sess., 97, p. 4125.

2. Karl von Clausewitz, *On War*, translated from the German by O. J. Mattius Jolles (New York, 1942), pp. xxix, 182. Author's italics.

3. Gordon A. Craig, "Delbruck: the Military Historian," in Edward Mead Earle, ed., *Makers of Modern Strategy: Military Thought from Machiavelli to Hitler* (Princeton, 1942), p. 261.

4. See Raymond G. O'Connor, "Current Concepts and Philosophies of Warfare," *Naval War College Review* 20(January 1968):3–15.

5. If a definition is to include the term "peace," it must be taken to mean an absence of armed conflict. The victory may or may not result in a "lasting" or "durable" peace, or minimize areas of friction. "What period of suspension of war is necessary to justify the presumption of the restoration of peace has never yet been settled, and must in every case be determined with reference to collateral facts and circumstances." Secretary of State William H. Seward, 1868, quoted in Coleman Phillipson, *Termination of War and Treaties of Peace* (London, 1916), p. 5.

6. Alfred Thayer Mahan wrote that ". . . for a military establishment the distinction between a state of war and a state of peace is one of words, not of fact." Letter to Theodore Roosevelt, 1911, quoted in O'Connor, "Current Concepts and Philosophies of Warfare," p. 5.

7. One writer distinguishes seven categories of limited war: Robert McClintock, *The Meaning of Limited War* (Boston, 1967), p. 10. For some definitions of war see

Quincy Wright, *A Study of War*, (second ed., with a commentary on war since 1942, Chicago, 1965), pp. 8–13. The criteria which Wright used to select wars for his first edition are contained in pp. 636–637, he says, however, "These criteria are not adaptable to hostilities since 1945." His list embracing those from 1945 to 1964, contained in a table following p. 1544, enumerates thirty and includes "all hostilities in which more than 317 persons were killed." Here he follows the method established by Lewis F. Richardson, *Statistics of Deadly Quarrels*, edited by Quincy Wright and C. C. Lienau, (Pittsburgh, 1960). For the legal distinction between "material war" and "formal war," see Lothar Kotzsch, *The Concept of War in Contemporary History and International Law* (Geneva, 1956), pp. 55–62. The literature on types, numbers, and categories of war is voluminous.

8. Sun Tzu, *The Art of War*, translated and edited by Samuel B. Griffith (Oxford, 1963), p. 54.

9. Raymond Aron, *The Century of Total War* (New York, 1954), p. 158. For an incisive study of one such episode, see Arnold J. Toynbee, *The Hannibalic War's Effects on Roman Life*, 2 vols., (New York, 1966).

10. Phillipson, *Termination of War*, p. 3; and Herman Kahn, "Some Comments on Controlled War," in Klaus Knorr and Thornton Read, eds., *Limited Strategic War* (New York, 1962), p. 59.

11. The most recent study of the diplomacy of the American Revolution is Richard B. Morris, *The Peacemakers: The Great Powers and American Independence* (New York, 1965).

12. Gordon A. Craig, "Problems of Coalition Warfare: The Military Alliance Against Napoleon, 1913–14," in Gordon A. Craig, *War, Politics, and Diplomacy: Selected Essays* (New York, 1966), p. 23.

13. Henry A. Kissinger, *A World Restored*, new ed. (New York, 1964), p. 109.

14. Clausewitz, *On War*, p. 583.

15. Niccolo Machiavelli, "Wise Princes and Republics should Content Themselves with Victory: For when they Aim at More, They Generally Lose," *The Prince and the Discourses* (New York, 1940), p. 377.

16. Walter Millis, *Arms and Men* (New York, 1956), p. 307. ". . . there was, until 1914, fairly general agreement that the tasks of the soldier and the statesman (or diplomat) were complementary. Perhaps the most fateful change effected by the First World War was the destruction of this relationship." Gordon A. Craig, "The Revolution in War and Diplomacy, 1914–39," in Craig, *War, Politics, and Diplomacy*, p. 197.

17. A. J. P. Taylor, "The War Aims of the Allies in the First World War," in A. J. P. Taylor, *Politics in Wartime and Other Essays* (New York, 1965), p. 93. For a recent study stressing German aggressive intentions, see Fritz Fischer, *Germany's Aims in the First World War* (London, 1967).

18. "Essential Terms of Peace in Europe," address to the United States Senate, January 22, 1917. Ray Stannard Baker and William E. Dodd, eds., *Selected Literary and Political Papers and Addresses of Woodrow Wilson*, 3 vols. (New York, n.d.), vol. 2, p. 222.

19. Not only were the victorious powers divided over the terms of the treaty, but the British Foreign Office and the India Office were at odds as well. Arnold J. Toynbee, *Acquaintances* (New York, 1967), p. 183.

20. For a brief castigation of the "liberal" approach to war, see David Rees, *Korea: The Limited War* (New York, 1964), pp. x–xvi.

21. Telford Taylor, review, *New York Times* Book Review Section, January 7, 1962.

22. According to Mao Tse-tung, "It is impossible for a genuine people's revolution to win victory in any country without various forms of help from the international revolutionary forces, and even if victory were won, it could not be consolidated." Mao Tse-tung, "On the People's Democratic Dictatorship" (June 30, 1949), in Mao Tse-tung, *Selected Works* (New York, 1956), vol. 5, p. 416. For the "legality" of intervention in civil wars, see Richard A. Falk, ed., *The Vietnam War and International Law*, sponsored by the American Society of International Law (Princeton, 1968).

23. Lester B. Pearson, "The Price of Peace," United Nations *Bulletin* 10 (June 15, 1951):573, 691.

24. Trumbull Higgins, *Korea and the Fall of MacArthur* (New York, 1960), p. 174.

25. Harry S. Truman, *Memoirs* (New York, 1955), vol. 2, p. 446.

26. Actually the conference was called to discuss both Korea and Indochina in that order, and Dien Bien Phu fell two days before the first formal session on Indochina.

27. For a superb analysis of the factors responsible for the government success, see Robert O. Tilman, "The Non-Lessons of the Malayan Emergency," *Asian Survey*, 6(1966):407–419. A popular account is Richard Clutterbuck, *The Long Long War: The Emergency in Malaya, 1948–1960* (London, 1967). The latter concludes (p. 178) that "The way in which a war is won decides how long the peace will last. Ultimately, it is the people who decide; and shortcuts may do more harm than good." The problem of generalizing from one example is obvious.

28. The operation was not an unqualified failure for Israel and Egypt. "Egypt got the Canal and a victory over 'imperialism'; Israel freed the Gulf of Akaba, destroyed the *fedayun* bases in Gaza and ruined Egyptian military prestige." Hugh Thomas, *Suez* (New York, 1967), p. 156.

29. "We know that the *sine qua non* of victory in *modern warfare* is the unconditional support of a population." Roger Trinquier, *Modern Warfare: A French View of Modern Insurgency* (Longon, 1964), p. 8. "Support by the population is much more than an asset; it is the *sine qua non* of victory." Bryce F. Denno, "On Waging Counter-insurgency Warfare," *Orbis* 8(1964):686 (a review of David Galula, *Counter insurgency Warfare: Theory and Practice* [New York, 1964]).

30. Slavko N. Bjelajac, "Unconventional Warfare in the Nuclear Era," *Orbis* 4(1960):332.

31. In the Philippines, the Huk rebels were on the road to success until Ramon Magsaysay revised the government's military tactics and introduced drastic domestic reforms to rob the guerrilla program of its appeal.

32. Thomas E. Phipps, Jr., "Strategy of War Limitation," *Journal of Conflict Resolution* 7(1963):311.

33. Sun Tzu, *The Art of War*, p. 83. A great power suffering under the illusion of invincibility may be especially susceptible to manipulation by the weak, for political realities can be more persuasive than weapons.

34. The Algerian war, with France on the verge of military victory, was officially terminated by granting independence and many other rebel demands.

35. Richardson contends that in wars from the Middle Ages through the nineteenth century "One side admitted defeat when it could not bear any more suffering. The chief form of suffering was casualties." *Statistics of Deadly Quarrels*, p. 161. The proportion of deaths to population is treated on pp. 298 ff. I feel that too many variables are ignored in this approach, as is apparent in this essay.

36. Henry A. Kissinger, "Force and Diplomacy in the Nuclear Age," *Foreign Affairs* 34(1956):356.

37. One writer concludes "that rational criteria exist for the choice of power to be applied and that a nexus exists between this power and the objective to be achieved." Robert W. Selton, "Rational Victory," U.S. Naval Institute, *Proceedings* 94(February 1968):32. The nature of the "criteria" is not indicated.

38. Dwight D. Eisenhower stated, "I do not believe in 'gradualism' in fighting a war. I believe in putting in the kind of military strength we need to win, and getting it over with as soon as possible." "Eisenhower Speaks His Mind," *U.S. News and World Reports*, November 7, 1966, p. 42. Bernard Brodie has noted "a bias endemic in all the armed services which works against any use of restraint upon one's strength during war time." Bernard Brodie, "More About Limited War," *World Politics* 10(1957):115.

39. Phipps, "Strategy of War Limitation," p. 219. Author's italics.

40. One writer contends "war is pressed by the victor, but peace is made by the vanquished." H. A. Calahan, *What Makes a War End?* (New York, 1944), p. 18. Obviously, I do not agree.

41. For a discussion of the "symbols of defeat and victory," see Lewis A. Coser, "The Termination of Conflict," *Journal of Conflict Resolution* 5(1961):347–353.

42. See Arthur Gladstone, "The Conception of the Enemy," *Journal of Conflict Resolution*, 3(June, 1959):132–137.

43. For circumstances where status of the enemy is "temporary," see Hans Speier, "War Aims in Political Warfare," in Hans Speier, *Social Order and the Risks of War* (New York, 1952), p. 382.

44. "It is clearer still that the experience of the recent past does not bear out the extreme argument that military power has lost its former utility." Robert E. Osgood and Robert W. Tucker, *Force, Order, and Justice* (Baltimore, Md., 1967), p. 357.

45. The Arab-Israeli War of 1967 is a remarkable example of the military victor being completely frustrated insofar as negotiations for a political settlement are concerned. The role of "third parties" on the concept of victory is again revealed.

46. The tendency persists to identify "winning" with the end while ignoring the cost of the means. The "gain-loss" calculation is usually missing. For example, see Leilyn M. Young, "'Win': Its Meaning in Crisis Resolution," *Military Review* 46 (January, 1966):30–39; and William I. Gordon, "What Do We Mean by 'Win'?" *Military Review* 46(June, 1966):3–11.

47. Herman Kahn, *On Thermonuclear War* (Princeton, 1960), p. 107.

# Index

Acheson, Dean, 137
Act of Chapultepec, 111
Adams, John, 2
Adams, John Quincy, 99, 100
Albania: freedom of under League of Nations, 47–48
American League to Enforce Peace, 42
Anglo-American Financial Agreement, 132
Anglo-French Naval Compromise (1928), 27
Anglo-Japanese Alliance (1902), 14
Anti-War Treaty of Non-Aggression and Conciliation (1933), 10
Argentina: recognition of Farrell government by U.S., 111
Atlantic Charter, 119, 123, 147

Bay of Pigs invasion, 154, 155
Berlin blockade, 131, 132
Bismarck, Otto von, 4
Black, Jeremiah S., 102
Blanco, Guzmán, 104, 105
Blum, Leon, 58
Boer War, 145
Bolivia: recognition of Villaroel regime by U.S., 111
Borah, William E., 73
Bradley, Omar, 149
Briand, Aristide, 49, 71, 72
Brussels Treaty (1948), 134
Bryan, William Jennings, 40, 41
Buchanan, James, 101

Bulgaria: dispute with Greece (1925), 49

Casablanca conference, 122
Castle, William R., Jr., 97
Castro, Fidel: government of, 154
Cecil, Robert, 43
Central American General Treaty of Peace and Amity (1923), 108
Central Intelligence Agency, 132
Chaco War, 31, 52–53
Chamberlain, Arthur Neville, 77, 89
Chamberlain, Austen, 71
China: invasion by Japan, 7, 31, 50, 59, 83, 109; Open Door policy, 23, 24, 25, 82; recognition of Communist government by U.S., 112
Churchill, Winston, 78; diplomacy of during World War II, 118–125; and Marshall Plan, 134
Civil War (American), 4, 102, 145
Clausewitz, Karl von, 2, 142, 144
Cleveland, Grover, 4
Commercial Treaty (1911), 77, 90, 91
Committee of Neutrals, 52
Concert of Europe, 38, 39, 50
Conference for the Reduction and Limitation of Armaments. See World Disarmament Conference
Conference of Foreign Ministers (1945), 111
Convention to Improve the Means of Preventing War (1931), 66
Coolidge, Calvin, 26, 108

Corfu incident (1923), 48, 49
Costa Rica: Tinoco regime in, 107
Council of Foreign Ministers (1947), 134
Craigie-Arita settlement, 90
Crimean War, 145
Cuba, 10, 105, 107; Bay of Pigs invasion, 154, 155; Castro regime, 154; recognition of Grau San Martín regime, 110

Davis, Norman, 31, 32, 86
Dawes, Charles G., 69, 83
Dewey, George: victory at Manila Bay, 5
Díaz, Porfirio, 103, 104
Dien Bien Phu, 19, 150, 151
Dominican Republic: recognition by U.S., 107; U.S. troops in, 6
Draft Treaty of Mutual Assistance (1923), 64
Draft Treaty to Develop the Means for Preventing War (1931), 65

Ecuador: Ayora government in, 108; recognition by U.S., 107, 108
Eisenhower, Dwight D: and post World War II diplomacy, 8–9, 150
Embargo: as a form of sanction, 52, 53, 78, 85, 87
Emergency Advisory Committee for Political Defense of the Continent (1943), 111
Evarts, William M., 104

Four Power Treaty, 24, 25, 82
Fourteen Points, 22, 42
France: and the Anglo-French Naval Compromise of 1928, 27; and the Brussels Treaty of 1948, 134; fall of, 78; and the Haitian government, 100–101; in Indochina, 150–153; and League of Nations, 52; and London Naval Conference of 1930, 29, 33; and Revolutionary War, 2, 144; and Treaty of Versailles, 31; troops in Mexico during Civil War, 4
Franco-American Alliance (1778), 98

French Revolution, 37

General Act for the Pacific Settlement of Disputes (1928), 65
General Disarmament Conference (1934), 86
Geneva Conference (1954), 150, 152, 153, 156
Geneva Naval Conference (1927), 26
Geneva Protocol for the Pacific Settlement of International Disputes (1924), 64–65, 70, 71, 72
George, Lloyd, 48
Germany: occupation of Czechoslovakia (1939), 77, 110; as a power in the Pacific, 4; remilitarization of the Rhineland (1936), 54, 76; reparation payments after World War I, 69; and the World Disarmament Conference, 31. *See also* Hitler, Adolf
Gibson, Hugh, 28
Great Britain: and Anglo-French Naval Compromise (1928), 27; and Anglo-Japanese Alliance (1902), 4; and border dispute with Venezuela, 4; and Geneva Naval Conference (1927), 26; Malaya crisis, 153; naval power, 14–19 passim; Revolutionary War, 2, 144; and Suez crisis, 153. *See also* Churchill, Winston
Greece: dispute with Bulgaria (1925), 49
Gunboat diplomacy, 5

Hague Court, 40
Haiti: recognition by U.S., 100; U.S. troops in, 6
Harding, Warren G., 82, 108
Harriman, Averill, 124
Hay, John, 40
Hayes, Rutherford B: administration of, 104
Henderson, Arthur, 74
Hitler, Adolf, 53, 57, 91
Hoare-Laval compromise plan (1935), 54
Ho Chi Minh, 151

Hoover, Herbert, 29, 30, 31; and the Kellogg-Briand Pact, 73, 82
Hoover-Stimson doctrine, 51, 84, 87, 89, 109
Hornbeck, Stanley K., 92
Hughes, Charles Evans, 108
Hull, Cordell, 55, 86, 88, 89, 110
Hungarian Revolution (1956), 153–154

Ickes, Harold L., 91
Indochina, 9–10, 150–153
Inter-American Commission of Investigation and Conciliation, 52
International Labor Organization, 68
Italo-Ethiopian War, 7, 53, 86, 87, 110

Jackson, Andrew, 3, 101
Japan: annexation of Hainan and the Spratly Islands (1939), 92; attack on Shanghai, 51; invasion of Manchuria, 31, 50–51, 59, 75, 83; resumption of conflict with China in 1937, 76, 87, 109. See also Manchurian Incident
Jay Treaty (1795), 40
Jefferson, Thomas, 3, 99
Juárez, Benito, 102
Jutland, Battle of, 15

Kellogg-Briand Pact, 6, 27–30 passim, 50–66 passim; applications of sanctions, 82–85, 110; as high point in postwar tide for peace, 72–75
Kellogg, Frank B., 73, 108
Kennedy, John F., 112, 154
Korean War, 9, 19, 135–138; meaning of victory in terms of, 148–150

Laval, Pierre, 53
League Covenant, 22, 26; application of or threat of sanctions under, 47–60; modification of sanctions, 63–67; specific sanctions in, 44. See also League of Nations
League of Nations, 6, 22; Conference of Ambassadors of, 47, 48, 49; demise of, 54; disputes brought before, 47–60

League Preparatory Commission for a Disarmament Conference. See World Disarmament Conference
Lend-Lease bill, 7, 78, 84
Litvinov, Maxim, 56
"Litvinov Protocol," 75
Locarno pact, 26, 57, 58, 65; assessment of, 72; significance of, 70–71
London Conference. See London Naval Conference (1930)
London Naval Conference (1930), 6, 16, 29–30
London Naval Treaty (1930), 30, 33, 51
London Naval Treaty (1936), 90
Ludlow Amendment, 77
Lytton Report, 51

MacArthur, Douglas, 19, 138, 142, 149
MacDonald, Ramsay, 28, 29, 33, 74, 82
Mackinder, Halford, 11
Mahan, Alfred Thayer, 3, 5, 12, 18; influence of, 13; naval strategy of, 3, 12–13
Manchurian Incident (1931), 50–51, 66, 75
Mao Tse-tung, 143
Marshall, George, 130, 133
Marshall Plan, 9, 133–134
Maximilian, Archduke, 102
Mexico: Diaz government and recognition of, 103–104; Huerta government and recognition of, 6, 106; Maximilian government in, 102; Obregon government in, 107, 108; war with, 3–4, 145
Monroe Doctrine, 4–5, 10, 23, 103
Monroe, James, 99, 100
Morison, Samuel Eliot, 18
Mukden incident. See Manchurian Incident
Munich conference (1938), 7, 77, 89
Mussolini, Benito, 53, 54

Napoleon, Louis, 4
Napoleonic Wars, 144

National Security Act (1947), 131, 132
NATO, 9, 134–138 passim, 153
Naval Construction Bill (1916), 16
Naval Limitation Treaty (1922), 16, 24, 25, 26, 33, 82
Naval Strategy. *See* Strategy, naval
Navy, U.S.: conditions for growth of, 12; during World Wars, 14–19; and rise of technology, 14–15; Seventh Fleet, 20; Sixth Fleet, 20. *See also* Strategy, naval
Neutrality Act (1935), 86, 88, 91
Nicaragua: nonrecognition used as sanction, 105, 108
Nimitz, Chester W., 11, 14
Nine Power Treaty (1922), 24, 60, 76; historical background, 81–82, 83, 88, 89
Nonrecognition, as a sanction, 97–113
North Atlantic Coast Fisheries Arbitration (1910), 41

Olney, Richard, 4
Open Door policy, 23, 24, 25, 82
Oregon Territory, 3

Pact of Paris. *See* Kellogg-Briand Pact
Panama: Canal, 91; revolution in (1903), 5, 105
*Panay*, 7, 77, 88
Pearl Harbor, 17
Pershing, George, 146
Peru, 112
Platt Amendment, 105
Point Four Program, 9
Poland: discussed at Teheran, 123; invasion of, 7
Polk, James K., 3
Pope Benedict XV, 42
Potsdam Conference, 128

Quadruple Alliance (1815), 37
"Quarantine" speech of Roosevelt (1937), 59, 76

Radford, Arthur, 19

Reparations Commission, 69, 70
Revolutionary War, American, 98, 143–144
Rhee, Syngman, 149
Rio Pact, 9
Roosevelt, Franklin D., 32, 85, 88, 110; diplomacy of during World War II, 118–126
Roosevelt, Theodore, 5, 13, 40
Root, Elihu, 25, 40, 41
Ruhr, invasion of by France and Belgium, 49
Russo-German treaty (1926), 72

Seward, F. W., 104
Seward, William H., 4, 102
Sheridan, Philip, 4
Shotwell, James T., 73
Sino-Japanese conflict: in Manchuria, 31, 50–51, 59, 75, 83; resumption of in 1937, 76, 87, 109. *See also* Manchurian Incident
Sixth Pan American Conference (1928), 75
Smuts, Jan, 43
Soviet Union: and Hungarian Revolution, 153–154; naval power of, 19, 20; recognition of by U.S., 107; after World War II, 9. *See also* Stalin, Joseph
Spain: and Spanish Florida, 3
Spanish-American War, 5, 145
Spanish Civil War, 58–59
Spanish Embargo Act, 59
Stalin, Joseph, 123, 124
Stimson, Henry L., 82, 92, 108–110 passim; and Hoover-Stimson doctrine, 84; and League of Nations, 50; and London Naval Conference of 1930, 28, 29; and nonrecognition, 97
Strategy, naval, 11–22; and aircraft, 15–16; "Blue Water" school, 14; "Bolt from the Blue" school, 14; French school of, 12; influence of technology on, 14–16; and Mahan, 3, 12–13; in World War II, 18–19
Stresemann, Gustav, 69, 71, 72
Suez crisis (1956), 153

Taft, William H., 105
"Tardieu Plan," 31
Teheran conference, 123
Texas Republic, recognition of by U.S., 101
Tinoco, Federico, 107
Treaties, notable prior to 1900, 36–38
Treaty for the Renunciation of War. *See* Kellogg-Briand Pact
Treaty of London (1915), 47
Treaty of Mutual Guarantee. *See* Locarno pact
Truman Doctrine (1947), 9, 130, 133, 148
Truman, Harry S: and national policy, 126–140; and nonrecognition as policy, 112; sends *Missouri* to Istanbul, 20. *See also* Truman Doctrine

United Nations, 10, 122, 123, 126; and Korean War, 137–138, 149; and Suez crisis (1956), 153

Vandenberg, Arthur H., 130, 134
Vattel, Emer de, 36

Venezuela, 104–105
Versailles, Treaty of, 31, 53, 54, 58, 68, 119
Viet Minh, 150, 151, 152
Villa, Francisco, 6

War of 1812, 3, 144–145
Washington Conference on the Limitation of Armaments (1921–1922): 6, 16, 23; results of, 24–25, 81–82. *See also* Nine Power Treaty, Four Power Treaty, Naval Limitation Treaty
Welles, Sumner, 111
Wilson, Woodrow, 6, 40, 43, 49, 69; and the Fourteen Points, 22, 42; and the Huerta government of Mexico, 6, 106
World Disarmament Conference (1932), 31–32
World War I: and internationalism 6; meaning of victory in terms of, 146–147; and naval strategy, 14
World War II: diplomacy during, 8–9, 118–125; meaning of victory in terms of, 147; and naval strategy, 18–19